CHINESE BUDDHISM

CHINESE BUDDHISM

A Thematic History

Chün-fang Yü

University of Hawai'i Press
Honolulu

25 24 23 22 21 20   6 5 4 3 2 1

Library of Congress Cataloging-in-Publication Data

Names: Yü, Chün-fang, author.
Title: Chinese Buddhism : a thematic history / Chün-fang Yü.
Description: Honolulu : University of Hawai'i Press, 2020. | Includes
bibliographical references and index.
Identifiers: LCCN 2020007860 | ISBN 9780824881580 (cloth) | ISBN
9780824883478 (paperback) | ISBN 9780824883508 (epub) | ISBN
9780824883492 (kindle edition) | ISBN 9780824883485 (pdf)
Subjects: LCSH: Buddhism—China.
Classification: LCC BQ44 .Y8 2020 | DDC 294.30951—dc23
LC record available at https://lccn.loc.gov/2020007860

Cover art: Guanyin. Northern Song Dynasty, ca. 1025.
Honolulu Museum of Art.

For my students

Contents

Preface

For more than forty years, I taught undergraduate courses such as Introduction to Buddhism and Chinese Religions. During all those years, I had difficulty finding suitable materials to cover Chinese Buddhism. There are of course a number of good textbooks on both Buddhism and Chinese religions. However, in most surveys of Buddhism, Chinese Buddhism is given only a small part. Similarly, textbooks about Chinese religions allot limited space to the discussion of Chinese Buddhism. Moreover, the chapters that are devoted to Chinese Buddhism in these texts tend to focus mainly on its philosophical and doctrinal aspects. This preference leads naturally to a discussion of only some Chinese Buddhist traditions, of which Chan takes up the lion's share. This is for two reasons. The first has to do with popular culture. Many Americans have become familiar with Zen, the Japanese counterpart of Chan, since the 1950s. The second is the comparatively abundant secondary literature. Chan studies dominated the academic field for several decades in the twentieth century, and as a result many books have been published on this subject.

In order to have a comprehensive understanding of Chinese Buddhism, it is necessary to know about other aspects of the religion. For instance, what are the Buddhist scriptures that teach the Chinese people about the religion? What are the Buddhist divinities that people worship? What are the festivals and the rituals? It would be helpful to know the story of some of the monks, both foreign and Chinese, who played essential roles in the creation and development of Buddhism during its long history of some two thousand years. How did Buddhism, an originally foreign religion, interact with the native Chinese philosophical and religious traditions? What was its relationship with the imperial authority? How did it influence family structure and gender roles? These are some questions that recent scholarship has addressed, and they are also the ones that interest me and inspired me to write this book.

In saying that I was unable to find a textbook on Chinese Buddhism, I do not mean that there was no book on this subject. In fact, two books have served as the standard references for scholars over the last half century: Eric Zürcher's *The Buddhist Conquest of China: The Spread and Adaptation of Buddhism in Early Medieval China* (1959) and Kenneth Ch'en's *Buddhism in China: A Historical Survey* (1964). But Zürcher's book concentrates on the first five centuries only, ending before the real florescence of the new faith during the Sui (581–618) and Tang (618–907) dynasties. Although Ch'en covers the history of Buddhism chronologically from its introduction to the twentieth century, the coverage is uneven, with Buddhism in the period after the Song (960–1279) receiving less attention. A more serious shortcoming is that he, like other scholars of his generation, regarded post-Tang Buddhism as being in a state of decline, a view that is no longer valid. For these reasons, there is a need for a new textbook on Chinese Buddhism. Furthermore, both of these books were published decades ago. It is time to have a book suitable for college students and general readers that incorporates material on more recent developments.

This book does not attempt to provide a chronological history of Chinese Buddhism following the dynastic order. Instead, it focuses on the highlights of and key points about the religion in Chinese society. Textbooks cannot be comprehensive because they reflect each author's own choice of what to include. I use both synchronic and diachronic approaches. Some chapters, such as those on the introduction of Buddhism into China and Buddhism in modern China, discuss their subjects synchronically. But other chapters, such as those on the major scriptures, worship of buddhas and bodhisattvas, and festivals and rituals, do not refer to any specific historical time and thus discuss their subjects diachronically. This is a thematic history. Each chapter deals with one theme and its related issues.

The introduction presents the basic tenets of Buddhism and the indigenous religious beliefs during the Han, the time when Buddhism entered China; it sets the stage for the chapters to follow. How the Chinese tried to understand Buddhism and what challenges they faced in this effort were perhaps most striking in the first five centuries, but these issues would continue in subsequent periods as well. Since the Chinese came to know Buddhism through the Chinese translations of Buddhist scriptures and the teaching of missionary monks, it is necessary to know something about how the translations were carried out. This chapter also discusses some famous foreign monks, their methods of translation, and their Chinese disciples who contributed to the long process of making Buddhism into a Chinese religion.

Chapter 1 discusses the major ideas found in some of the most famous Mahayana sutras that became foundational in Chinese Buddhism. It also discusses the seminal teaching of Buddha nature and inherent enlightenment. This idea was central to the creation of independent Buddhist schools in the sixth century and later. It was a sign of the maturity of the Chinese Buddhism, for it was not found in India.

The cults of buddhas and bodhisattvas are explored in chapter 2. It discusses the worship of the historical Buddha, the future Buddha Maitreya, the Medicine Buddha, and Amitābha, the Buddha of the Western Paradise, as well as Guanyin, the most important bodhisattva. It discusses the casting of Buddhist images and the iconography of these holy figures. The chapter also describes the construction of monumental Buddhist caves decorated with wall paintings and sculptures as well as the building of temples in which the icons are installed. Both visual and material cultures are integral to Chinese Buddhism.

Buddhist annual festivals and major rituals are the chief ways by which the common people come to know Buddhism in China. Traditional China was an agrarian society, and the yearly festivals followed the agrarian cycle. Buddhist festivals meshed well with the existing seasonal celebrations. By offering succor to dead loved ones, Buddhist rituals have transformed the pre-Buddhist cult of ancestor worship, while strengthing it. They are discussed in chapter 3.

Chapter 4 is on the monastic order. It discusses the layout of monasteries and the different types of monasteries. The requirements for becoming monks and nuns, and the social and economic functions of monasteries and monastics are also topics covered in this chapter.

Tiantai and Huayan, the two doctrinal schools that are the unique Chinese contribution to Buddhism, are discussed in chapter 5. The two schools for religious practice, Chan and Pure Land, have been followed by many Chinese Buddhists and have also received more scholarly attention in the West. I treat them separately in two chapters: chapter 6 on Chan and chapter 7 on Pure Land.

Chapter 8, on Buddhism and gender, traces the different Buddhist attitudes toward women found in India and China. Buddhism is a world religion, offering universal salvation to all people regardless of gender. However, like Christianity and Islam, it reflects the social and historical conditions in which it exists. Just as Buddhism is not a monolithic tradition, its views on women are also multifaceted.

New developments of Chinese Buddhism in the modern period are discussed in chapter 9, concentrating on its engagement with science and nationalism. The chapter describes some current trends in Buddhism since its resurgence in China in the 1980s and concludes with a case study of Taiwanese nuns. The order of nuns was established in China as early as the fifth century and is undergoing a new revival in Taiwan.

At the end of each chapter I provide a list of discussion questions and suggestions for further reading. The discussion questions focus on some important points raised in the chapter. The suggestions for further reading facilitate a deeper understanding of the subject matter.

I titled this book *Chinese Buddhism* because it focuses on the Buddhism practiced by the Han Chinese. I do not discuss Tibetan Buddhism, esoteric Buddhism, or the various Buddhist traditions of the many ethnic minorities of China. There are two reasons for this. Although it was the case that under some rulers, the courts of the Yuan, Ming, and Qing patronized Tibetan Buddhism, and although esoteric Buddhist elements are found in some of the most popular Chinese Buddhist rituals discussed in chapter 3, neither is a part of the mainstream Chinese Buddhist tradition. I will, however, point out how the esoteric Buddhist scriptures influenced image making and mortuary rites. I will also note the newfound popularity Tibetan Buddhism enjoys in both China and Taiwan.

I wish to thank all the teachers under whom I studied, all the scholars whose writings I consulted, and above all, all the students I have taught, for it was they who, by their frequent questions, compelled me to read more broadly and think more deeply. This book is my effort to return the kindness I have received from all the people above. The writing of the book was supported by a grant from the Sheng Yen Education Foundation. I also wish to thank two anonymous readers of the manuscript for their very helpful comments and suggestions. I hope this book will provide readers an introduction to some fundamental aspects of Chinese Buddhism, something I wish I had when I started teaching many years ago.

A Note on the Transcription of Sanskrit Terms and Names

Since this is a book for students and general readers, I do not use diacritical marks for terms that appear in Merriam-Webster's Collegiate Dictionary, such as sutra, samsara, nirvana, Hinayana, or Mahayana. I retain diacritical marks for Sanskrit terms not found in the dictionary, such as *upāya* or *śūnyatā*, as well as proper names, such as Kumārajīva or Vimalakīrti.

Introduction

When Buddhism appeared in China around the first century of the Common Era, during the second half of the Han dynasty (206 BCE–220 CE), China already had a history of over a thousand years, and Buddhism had undergone many changes during the four hundred years since the time of the Buddha. The Buddha was Indian and lived in a Hindu society; therefore, Buddhism shared many beliefs with Hinduism. The meeting and interaction between these two ancient civilizations, Chinese and Indian, is one of the most fascinating stories of humankind. In order to understand how Buddhism, a foreign religion, became Chinese, it is necessary to provide some background information about Buddhism as well as Han religious beliefs and philosophical ideas.

The Buddha

Buddha means "the awakened one." It is a title given to someone who is enlightened. The personal name of the Buddha was Siddhārtha, and his clan name was Gautama. He was most commonly called Śākyamuni or "the sage of the Śākyas," because he came from the people known as Śākyas.

Hindu society consisted of four major castes and many subcastes, still extant today. The Śākyas belonged to the warrior caste, which was below the priest caste but above the artisan and servant castes. We do not know the exact date Siddhārtha was born, and scholars have suggested different dates. The traditional view was that he lived either from 566 to 486 BCE or from 563 to 483 BCE. But recent scholarship puts his time nearly a century later, from 490 to 410 BCE or 480 to 400 BCE. Siddhārtha was born at a place called Lumbinī in a small republic at the foot of the Himalayas in what is now Nepal. Just as Jesus was born a Jew, Buddha was born a Hindu. He received the traditional training of a Hindu prince and enjoyed a life of luxury and sensual pleasure. He was married at the age of sixteen and had a son. Because a fortune-teller predicted that when Siddhārtha grew up, he would become either a world conqueror or a great religious leader, his father made sure that he was shielded from the real conditions of everyday life. However, a climactic change took place when he was twenty-nine. During his outings in that year, he encountered an old man, a sick person, and a corpse. His charioteer explained that everyone, even he, the prince, was destined to become old, get sick, and die. This realization made Siddhārtha deeply depressed. But a final encounter with a wandering mendicant who exuded serenity inspired him to make the decision to pursue a religious life. He experimented with various forms of meditation and ascetic practices. Finally, at the age of thirty-five, while meditating under the Bodhi tree during a long night, he defeated Mara, the Tempter, and achieved enlightenment at dawn. Siddhārtha became the Buddha.

Buddhist sources describe the enlightenment as gaining the "threefold knowledge." During the first watch of the night, he remembered all his previous lives; during the second watch of the night, he saw the rebirth of all beings according to their karma. Finally, at dawn, the end of the third watch, he achieved insight into the cause of human suffering and the way to end it. His search for the answer to why we grow old, become sick, and die—the question that had propelled him to embark on his long journey—finally ended. He found the way to change the human condition. While the first two knowledges provided experiential proof of the workings of karma and rebirth (samsara), two central tenets shared with all mainstream Indian religions, the third knowledge, which later traditions identified as the Law of Dependent Origination, was unique to Buddhism. This is the Buddhist law of causality, which says that when there is a cause, there must be an effect, and with the elimination of the cause, the effect will also disappear. This Law of Dependent Origination was expounded in the Buddha's first sermon on the Four Noble Truths. For the next forty-five years the Buddha taught the Dharma, or the truths that he had discovered. By the time he died, or entered nirvana, at the age of eighty, there were monks and nuns who followed his teachings and laymen and laywomen who supported them. Monks and nuns were people who left their homes and led celibate lives in a community. They were members of the monastic order or sangha, a historically unique institution that had no precedent either in India or in the rest of the world.

Hindu males of the higher castes are supposed to go through four stages of life: student, householder, forest dweller, and wandering ascetic. Being a member of the warrior caste, the Buddha himself underwent the first three stages by studying the Vedas (the holy scriptures of Hinduism) and other arts, getting married, and leaving his family in search of enlightenment. One should be celibate as a student and as a forest dweller. However, although there was already an ascetic tradition prior to the establishment of the sangha, the path was limited to men of the higher castes. Neither women nor lower-caste men were given this option. They were also not allowed to study the Vedas. The sangha, however, admitted both men and women from all walks of life. For this reason, we must consider the founding of Buddhism a revolutionary event.

Early Buddhism

According to Buddhist cosmology, human beings live in the World of Desire, a world below those of Form and Formlessness. There are six realms of existence in the World of Desire: those of the gods, asuras, humans, animals, hungry ghosts, and hell beings. A person is reborn after death in accordance with his karma. Good karma leads to rebirth into one of the first three realms, whereas bad karma leads to rebirth into one of the latter three realms. Karma means deed, but it also includes thought and speech. Unlike other Indian religions that also believe in karma, Buddhism puts special emphasis on a person's intention. If a person has the intention to harm someone, even if he does not carry out the action, he has already created bad karma, although it is less grievous than the karma that would result from his actually harming that person. As long as one is not enlightened, one creates karma and will continuously be reborn. This endless cycle of birth, death, and rebirth is samsara, a constant wandering through the six realms. All Indian religions regard this as a painful process. Since each birth ends in death, a person must die not once but endlessly. No wonder it is said that we are caught in a hangman's noose. Any rational person will naturally want to be freed from this condition. The end of samsara is nirvana. This was what the Buddha achieved at death and the goal to which he hoped all Buddhists would aspire. The core teaching of early Buddhism was the Buddha's first sermon on the Four Noble Truths. He delivered it in the Deer Park to the five ascetics who had once practiced austerities with him. The Four Noble Truths state:

1. Life is suffering (*duhkha*).
2. Suffering is caused by craving.
3. Nirvana is the end of suffering.
4. The Noble Eightfold Path leads to the end of suffering.

The first Noble Truth is the diagnosis, and the second Noble Truth provides the etiology. The third Noble Truth is the prognosis, while the fourth Noble Truth is the prescription. Human beings were the patients and Buddha the physician. Looked at another way, the sermon was an application of the Law of Dependent Origination in a condensed form. The second Noble Truth is the cause, and the first Noble Truth is the effect. Similarly, the fourth Noble Truth is the cause, and the third noble truth is the effect.

The Sanskrit word *duhkha* is generally translated as suffering. But it has a wide range of meanings. It denotes that something is unsatisfactory or "dis-ease." It is painful to grow old, become sick, and die, but to be separated from people and things one loves or forced to be with people and things one dislikes is also painful. Life consists of physical as well as psychological and spiritual suffering. The first Noble Truth of suffering connects with two other insights: impermanence and no self (*anātman*). Because everything in the world constantly changes, trying to hold on to and refusing to let go of a person or thing one loves can only cause suffering. On a more profound level, the conviction that each person has an unchanging self (*ātman*) within is the basic reason one suffers. Instead of a permanent self as advocated by Hinduism, Buddhism teaches that we are formed by five aggregates (*skandas*), or five physical and mental components that are in constant flux. They are:

1. Material form (*rūpa*)
2. Feelings and sensations (*vedanā*)
3. Perception (*samjñā*)
4. Constructing activities (*samskāra*)
5. Consciousness (*vijñāna*)

Failing to realize the true situation and holding on to the illusion of a self, we say, "I," "me," and "mine." This is the basis of egoism, the root cause of selfishness. Self is no more than a figure of speech that has no corresponding reality. In a famous example given by the monk Nāgasena, who explains this idea to a king, he compares a person to a carriage. Just as a carriage is made up of its body, wheels, and other parts, so is a person formed by the five aggregates. There is no "carriage" existing outside these parts. "Carriage," like "self," is no more than a name.

The second Noble Truth says that the cause of suffering is craving. We crave because we are ignorant. The causal circle of ignorance, craving, and suffering is a condensation of the Law of Dependent Origination (*pratītya-samudpāda*), which is formulated by twelve links:

1. Ignorance *(avidyā)*
2. Constructing activities (*samskāra*)
3. Consciousness (*vijñāna*)
4. Name and form (*nāma-rūpa*)
5. Six sense spheres (*sad-āyatana*)
6. Contact (*sparśa*)
7. Feelings (*vedanā*)
8. Craving (*trṣṇā*)
9. Grasping (*upādāna*)
10. Becoming *(bhava)*
11. Birth (*jāti*)
12. Old age and death (*jarā-marana*)

There is no creator or first cause in time. The series of causal links tie together not only suffering, craving, and ignorance but also our bodies, sense perceptions, feelings, and consciousness. The causal links are responsible for the process of rebirth itself. Everything is conditioned as well as conditioning. This is the Middle Way because it rejects the two extremes of absolute determinism and absolute nondeterminism, theories current during the Buddha's time. God does not determine the workings of the world and human life. However, it is not true that things happen randomly and without cause. The twelve links are usually depicted on the outer rim of the wheel of life with the six realms of rebirth. Craving, link number 8, is traced back to ignorance, link number 1. One must become free from craving and ignorance in order to break the cycle of samsara. The eradication of craving and ignorance is nirvana, the third Noble Truth. This is possible because the fourth Noble Truth provides the path to achieve it. Through moral and mental training, one gains the wisdom that eliminates ignorance and thus destroys craving. The fourth Noble Truth, called the Noble

Eightfold Path, consists of three kinds of training—morality (*śīla*), meditation (samadhi), and wisdom (*prajña*). Buddhism is often symbolized by the Dharma Wheel, which is a wheel with eight spokes. The eight spokes represent the eight parts of the Path:

1. Right view
2. Right resolve
3. Right speech
4. Right action
5. Right livelihood
6. Right effort
7. Right mindfulness
8. Right meditation

One begins with moral training, which covers 3–5. The essential requirement is nonharming. In the words of the Buddha, the kernel of morality is "Not to commit any evil, to do good, and to purify one's own mind." With a sound moral foundation, one embarks on the mental training, which is 6–8. Success in meditation is gaining the liberating wisdom. A person who successfully travels the path enters nirvana and is no longer subject to rebirth. Nirvana literally means extinction and is compared to a fire that goes out when there is no more fuel. This is a very apt metaphor. The Buddha once gave what is called the "Fire Sermon," declaring that every part of us is being burned with the fire of desire. Samsara is like the passing of one fire to another fire in another location, and karma is the fuel. There are two kinds of nirvana: with remainder and without remainder. When the Buddha achieved enlightenment, he was supposed to have reached nirvana with remainder, because the karma from his previous lives had not been exhausted. When he died, he entered nirvana without remainder because he had not only eliminated all the previous karma but also stopped creating new karma after his enlightenment. The death of the Buddha is called *parinirvana* or complete nirvana. In early Buddhism, under the Buddha there were said to be four levels of noble beings, depending on how many times one must be reborn before entering nirvana: the stream enterer, who will attain nirvana after seven more rebirths in this world; the once returner, who will attain nirvana after being reborn only one more time; the nonreturner, who will be reborn in a heavenly realm instead of in this world and will attain nirvana there; and the highest, the arhat (worthy one), who attains nirvana in this life and will never be reborn again. Although there were nuns who attained the status of arhat, the majority were monks. By creating merit through supporting the monastics, laypeople hoped to eventually come back in future lives as monks and strive toward this goal.

Mahayana and the Spread of Buddhism

The teachings of the Buddha were transmitted orally until they were written down in Pali around the second century BCE. By then, many schools of Buddhism had appeared, each proposing its own doctrines. A new movement identified as Mahayana (Great Vehicle) arose between 150 BCE and 100 CE. To differentiate themselves, the Mahayanists called the earlier Buddhism Hinayana (Small Vehicle). There are said to have been eighteen Hinayana schools, of which Theravada (Teachings of the Elders) is the only one that has survived; its adherents are found in Sri Lanka and Southeast Asia, except for Vietnam. Tibet, China, Japan, Korea, and Vietnam follow the Mahayana tradition.

The origin of Mahayana is an unsolved mystery. There is still no consensus about when or where it began, although most theories put the time as around the first century CE and the place as regions in the northwest and south of India. The Mahayana movement is connected with the sudden appearance of many new sutras claimed to be the "word of the Buddha" (Buddhavacana). A traditional theory is that Mahayana was a lay-oriented reform movement. Some scholars suggest that it started with communities centering on the worship of stupas, the burial mounds housing the relics of the Buddha and other saintly monks. Others propose that instead of the "cult of the stupa," the movement was connected with the "cult of the book," because all the Mahayana sutras asked the reader to worship and treat them as stupas. Mahayana promoted the ideal of the bodhisattva, a being who chooses to delay his entry into nirvana for the sake of helping others. While some sutras advocate an ascetic forest-dwelling lifestyle for monks, others put more emphasis on believers' faith and devotion to buddhas and bodhisattvas.

Although there is no conclusive proof, there is an emerging consensus that Mahayana was a reform movement initiated not by laypeople but by monks. Moreover, Mahayana monks did not institute a separate community but lived in the same monasteries with their non-Mahayana brethren and observed the same Vinaya or monastic rules, as witnessed by Faxian, the famous Chinese pilgrim who visited holy sites and monasteries in India from 399 to 412. Since the identity of the Mahayana monks was represented by their new messages promulgated in the Mahayana sutras, it would have been natural for the writers of the sutras to emphasize the central importance of copying, reciting, and expounding on these texts, for this was the main mechanism by which the new message could be spread. As the Mahayana teachings became better known, they developed into a separate school, and its missionaries began to spread beyond its base to Central Asia and eventually China.

Mahayana sutras present themselves as new revelations from the Buddha. They were translated into Chinese in the second and third centuries of the Common Era. We find in them three new ideas that are absent from the writings in the Pali canon. The first is that nothing has an intrinsic nature because everything is dependent on causes and conditions. *Śūnyatā* (emptiness) is the term used to refer to this true state of everything. This is a further development of the teaching of no self. As we have seen, early Buddhism denies the existence of the self but recognizes that of the five aggregates. Scholastics further broke down the aggregates into the so-called dharmas, the irreducible existential elements or building blocks of existence, comparable to atoms. For them, self was empty but dharmas were real. The earliest group of Mahayana sutras, known collectively as the *Perfection of Wisdom* scriptures, declares that both the self and the dharmas are empty.

The second distinctive idea is that the Buddha is eternal and everybody can achieve buddhahood. This is the central teaching of the *Lotus Sutra,* discussed in the next chapter, which was destined to become the most popular Mahayana sutra in China as well as the rest of East Asia.

The third idea, proclaimed by yet another group of early Mahayana scriptures known as *Sukhāvativyūha* (The Land of Bliss), is that through faith and devotion one can be reborn in a paradisiacal Pure Land created by the compassionate vows of Amitābha Buddha. Mahayana sutras held enormous appeal for the Chinese. As later chapters will show, the teaching of *śūnyatā* reminded them of *wu* (nothingness or nonbeing), taught by Laozi and Zhuangzi. The optimistic message that everyone can become a buddha echoes Mencius's teaching about the goodness of human nature. Finally, the fact that not only the Buddha but also many new buddhas and bodhisattvas appear as saviors gave hope to ordinary men and women and encouraged them to practice Buddhism. The philosophical explanation for the new devotionalism was that because Buddhas and bodhisattvas can transfer their overabundant merit to the devotees to ferry them across the sea of samsara. Karma is no longer individual but collective. This was another dramatic transformation of early Buddhism wrought by the authors of Mahayana sutras.

Two emperors were great patrons of Buddhism and transformed it into a world religion. The first was Emperor Aśoka (c. 268–239 BCE), who promoted Buddhism just as the Roman emperor Constantine did Christianity. Buddhist monks not only spread the teaching across the Indian subcontinent but also traveled abroad as missionaries. During his reign, Buddhist monks went east to what became lower Burma and central Thailand. Another mission headed by Aśoka's son went to Sri Lanka in 250 BCE. The Theravada tradition has been preserved in these countries up to now. Kanishka I, the third ruler of the Kushan dynasty, made a similar contribution to the spread of Buddhism. The Kushans were originally Scythians who lived in present-day Gansu province in northwest China. They were forced to emigrate west during the Former Han dynasty and arrived in Bactria about 135 BCE. Under Kanishka I, who ruled in the first century of the Common Era, Buddhist missionary activities received much support. As a result, city-states along the Silk Road became Buddhist. China had already had contact with Central Asia, or what the Chinese called the Western Regions, before this time. The Han general Zhang Qian traveled to Ferghana, Samarkand, and Bactria, returning in 126 BCE. He led a mission ten years later to form connections with Parthia, India, and Khotan. The early translators of Buddhist scriptures into Chinese were not natives of India proper, but Parthians, Scythians, Sogdians, and other residents of this region. It was along the Silk Road that Buddhism was introduced into China.

The Silk Road broke into two routes, the northern and southern, separated by the Taklamakan Desert. The two routes converged in Dunhuang in present-day Xinjiang Province. For a long time, only the northern Silk Road received much scholarly attention. But in recent decades two other Silk Roads have received increasing emphasis. One is the southern Silk Road, which connected Sichuan to India by way of Yunnan and Myanmar. The other is the maritime Silk Road linking the coast of southeast China to India through Southeast Asia. Although the northern Silk Road was the main entryway for Buddhism into China in the early stages, the other two also played important parts in later history.

Han Religion

The Chinese were not introduced to Buddhism in a systematic manner. Depending on the background and training of the missionary monks, scriptures representing either Hinayana or Mahayana teachings were translated into Chinese. By the time Buddhism arrived in the beginning of the Common Era, the Chinese people had firmly held many religious beliefs for over a millennium. In many ways they were sharply different from the Buddhist views of the world and life. The greatest difference was the absence of the belief in rebirth and the related concept of karma. The world in which human beings live is called, in Chinese, Heaven and Earth. Chinese religion does not have a creator god. As seen in the *Book of Changes* (Yijing), one of the basic Confucian classics and a divinatory handbook of great antiquity, Heaven and Earth is the origin of everything in the universe, including human beings. The creating and sustaining force, otherwise known as the Dao or the Way, is seen as good. Human beings are thought to live only one life, with the goal of following the Dao or the Way. There is no God transcendent of and separate from the world. The *Book of Changes* contains sixty-four hexagrams that are made up of eight trigrams. The first and second trigrams, known as *qian* and *kun,* represent the two prime principles of yang and yin, which constitute the Dao, as well as Heaven and Earth, the physical representations of these principles.

Although these ideas are datable to the Zhou dynasty (c. 1100–221 BCE), they received further refinement during the Han, particularly from Confucian thinker Dong Zhongshu (c. 179–c. 104 BCE) and his contemporaries. According to them, all living and nonliving things are constituted of qi, which has been translated as vital force, material force, or life force. Qi refers to yin and yang and the five phases of wood, fire, earth, metal, and water, which evolve from the interaction of the two. This is the worldview shared by all Chinese religions. Because human beings are of the same substance as the rest of the universe, there is the possibility of communication between our environment and ourselves. This belief is implied by the concept of the Mandate of Heaven, the foundation for the Chinese belief in the correspondence between microcosm and macrocosm: a person is a small universe, replicating the greater universe without.

The Mandate of Heaven was originally used by the Zhou founders to justify their rebellion against the previous Shang dynasty (c. 1600–c. 1100 BCE). According to them, the last two Shang rulers lost their mandate because they were deficient in virtue. The mandate went to the Zhou founders because they were virtuous. Heaven not only gave and took away its mandate, it also sent blessings or warnings before it did so. The ruler was the Son of Heaven and formed a triad with Heaven and Earth. The Chinese believed in omens and portents, taking them to represent Heaven's responses to the behavior of humankind. Officials specializing in astrology kept track of unusual happenings in nature. Chinese philosophers were very interested in cosmology and the workings of the natural world.

Confucianism was adopted as the state ideology in the Han and remained so throughout imperial history, although individual emperors might have favored Daoism or Buddhism. Confucianism is based on the teachings of Confucius (551–479 BCE), who lived earlier than the Buddha. According to tradition, he was the first teacher who taught as many as three thousand students from different walks of life. Before his time, only sons of the rulers and aristocracy could receive an education. For this reason, his birthday (September 28) is celebrated as Teacher's Day today. Confucius believed that everyone could become a virtuous person or a noble person (*junzi*) by cultivating benevolence (*ren*) and conducting himself with propriety (*li*). To be humane is to treat others as oneself. This is the same as the "golden rule": treat others as you wish to be treated. Benevolence should be practiced together with *li* or propriety. *Li* is not just good manners or etiquette; it is also translated as ritual. Being a humanist, Confucius concentrated on teaching people how to be virtuous in this life. He did not say much about gods, ghosts, or life after death. However, he believed it was important to conduct the religious rituals to one's ancestors, for ancestor worship was a distinctive feature of Chinese religion as early as the Shang. To embody *li* is to apply the same kind of respect and sincerity directed to ancestors and the spirit world to our daily interactions with our fellow humans. Confucius further believed that virtue should be cultivated through five fundamental human relationships: ruler and subject, father and son, husband and wife, older brother and younger brother, friend and friend. These are hierarchical relationships except for the last one. Ruler, father, husband, and older brother are superior to subject, son, wife, and younger brother. Reflecting the historical and social conditions of his time, Confucius taught men only, and Confucianism was a patriarchal system. He did not believe a man could become virtuous if isolated from his community and rejected the ascetic model favored in India. This justified Confucian thinkers' perennial criticism of the Buddhist monastic order. But on the other hand, the Confucian emphasis on benevolence, correct behavior governed by *li,* and the family system based on lineage were contributing factors that enabled Buddhism, an originally Indian religion, to become a thoroughly Chinese religion.

Mencius (c. 372–289 BCE) is the second most important Confucian thinker. He was the first to identify the Mandate of Heaven with the innate goodness of human nature. According to him, human nature is good because it is bestowed by the Dao. To follow our inborn moral nature and cultivate it to its fullest potential through study and emulation of sagely models should be the goal of humankind.

There was a countercurrent to Confucianism known as Daoism, represented by the thought of Laozi and Zhuangzi (c. 368–286 BCE). Scholars cannot be sure when Laozi lived or if he was even a real historical person, for Laozi, which means Old Master, is not a family name, but Zhuangzi was a contemporary of Mencius. The well-known *Daode jing* was supposedly written by Laozi. In fact, in China, the text was also known as *Laozi.* Legends say that this text consisted of five thousand words was given by Laozi to the keeper of the pass when he left China for the west.

Although the Dao is a central idea for both Confucianism and Daoism, it is understood differently in each. The method for humankind to attain the Dao also differs in the two traditions. According to the *Daode jing,* the Dao transcends language and morality and is not particularly concerned with human beings. Its first line declares, "The Way that can be spoken of is not the constant way." It uses metaphors to describe the Dao, comparing it to the mother, water, and the female because the Dao is life-giving, soft, yielding, yet everlasting. Instead of study and moral cultivation, it is through unlearning and nonaction (*wuwei*) that we can access the Dao. This is because knowledge leads to desire and discrimination, and action leads to reaction. For Laozi, the present is already perfect, and any human interference with either nature or society can only make things worse. Civilization is thus a fall from the original unity with the Dao. Zhuangzi speaks of "fasting of the mind," a meditative process wherein one does away with the conventional dichotomies, or "pairs of opposites," created by discriminatory thinking. Such distinctions between good and evil, beauty and ugliness, true and false, life and death, self and others all arise from the partial view of humankind. From the perspective of the Dao, all things are equal, for each creature and everything comes from the Dao. The Dao is nature (*ziran,* "self-so," in Chinese), for nature in its state free from human meddling demonstrates its perfect working. Thus, if Confucianism is yang and humanism, Daoism is yin and naturalism.

During the first century of the Common Era, new beliefs appeared and led to new religious movements. The Chinese traditionally believed that human beings have two souls, *hun* and *po,* corresponding to yang and yin. While *hun* is spiritual and controls our intellect and thinking, *po* is physical and responsible for our emotions and sensations. When we are alive, our body holds the two together. When we die, they separate. *Hun,* being yang, ascends upward to Heaven, while *po,* being yin, sinks down to earth, to a place called Yellow Spring. Although neither Heaven nor Yellow Spring was clearly defined, it was believed that the dead continued to lead a life similar to the one on Earth. That was why tombs were furnished with food, drink, and other necessities of life. That was also why people were to offer cooked food as sacrifices to their ancestors at home on New Year's Eve and the anniversary of the day their ancestors died. They would also visit the tombs on the Clear and Bright Festival in the spring. Meanwhile, as early as the time of Zhuangzi, there was the belief that some people do not die but become immortals, depicted in art as figures covered with feathers and flying through the air. There were different ways to achieve this goal. The most efficacious way was to ingest a magical plant found in Penglai, the Isles of Immortals, lying in the Yellow Sea, or a magical peach growing in the garden of the Queen Mother of the West on top of Mount Kunlun on China's western border. Since these were very difficult to obtain, other methods included adopting a special diet excluding grains, doing gymnastics, following a special sexual regimen, and drinking an elixir produced through alchemical manipulation. The First Emperor of Qin (r. 246–210 BCE) and Emperor Wu (r. 136–88 BCE) of the Former Han were fervent believers in the cult of immortals.

Laozi was deified and worshiped together with the Yellow Emperor, the legendary founder of Chinese civilization, as gods in religious Daoism. Not only did Laozi never die, he had also transformed himself eighty-one times in order to teach humankind. Religious Daoism began as the Way of Celestial Masters when Laozi, as a god, revealed himself to the first Celestial Master, Zhang Daoling, in Sichuan in 142 CE. The movement was noted for its parish organization (in which both men and women held leadership roles), moral codes, collective confession, and petitioning rituals (to invoke divine powers to heal disease). Daoism competed with Buddhism for royal patronage, and the two religions frequently came into open conflict. The most famous example was the controversy created by a text titled "Laozi Converting the Barbarians." Based on the legend that Laozi left China and went to the West, it claimed that he actually went to India and taught people there a debased form of Daoism because they could not understand its profundity. Buddhism was therefore a lower form of Daoism. Writers of Buddhist apocrypha came up with a counternarrative claiming that Laozi was actually the Buddha's disciple Kāśyapa and Confucius was a bodhisattva. Although several emperors in previous dynasties had issued edicts prohibiting the circulation of "Laozi Converting the Barbarians," it was not until the thirteenth century, during the Yuan dynasty (1260–1368) under the Mongols, that the emperor ordered all the printing blocks of this text to be destroyed. This happened because the Buddhists won a debate with the Daoists held at the court. The Mongol rulers patronized Tibetan Buddhism.

The Coming of Buddhism

There are several legends about the arrival of Buddhism in China. The most famous one concerns the dream of Emperor Ming (r. 58–75). In the dream he saw a very tall golden man flying into the palace. When he asked his ministers for an interpretation, he was told that there was a sage in India known as the Buddha who could fly, and his body had a golden hue. The emperor then sent a mission to India in 60 (or one of the variant dates: 61, 64, 68), which returned three years later with two monks, Kāśyapa Mataga and Dharmaratna, who also brought the *Scripture in Forty-two Sections* on a white horse. The emperor housed the missionaries in a temple named after the horse, the White Horse Temple, in Luoyang, the capital. This story provides an attractive narrative, for it furnishes a royal pedigree to the arrival of Buddhism. But it has no historical basis, for the earliest reference to the White Horse Temple, which served as a center for translation, is from the third century. The scholarly consensus is that the *Scripture in Forty-two Sections* is a compilation of Buddhist teachings made in India, Central Asia, or China, but not a translation from any scripture. As time went by, more details were added to the legend, and it became firmly established by the fifth century.

We do know, however, that Buddhism was definitely already present in China during the first century of the Common Era, although it would take another three centuries to become what we can speak of as Chinese Buddhism, a religion understood and practiced by Chinese Buddhists.

The earliest historical reference to the Buddha is an edict of 65 in which Emperor Ming granted amnesty to those who were sentenced to death if they paid a certain number of rolls of silk as ransom. Prince Ying of Chu was the half brother of the emperor and lived in Pengcheng (present-day Xuzhou, Jiangsu). He offered thirty rolls of silk as atonement for some offense he had committed. But the emperor refused to accept the silk and instead praised the prince for his worship of the Yellow Emperor, the deified Laozi, and the Buddha. The prince then used the ransom money to prepare a vegetarian feast for the Buddhist monks and laymen living in the city. The Buddha was also worshiped at court together with the Yellow Emperor and Laozi, for in a memorial submitted by a minister in 166, Emperor Huan was castigated for failing to follow their teachings because of moral turpitude. Historical sources mention three Buddhist communities, Pengcheng in the lower Yangzi region, Luoyang in central China, and Jiaozhou in present-day northern Vietnam. Pengcheng was a center of commerce, linking the Silk Road with Shandong and Canton. The author of the treatise "Mouzi Resolving Doubts," one of the earliest Buddhist apologetics, came from Jiaozhou. Buddhism was mainly a foreign religion. New immigrants and naturalized foreigners made up these early Buddhist communities.

Buddhism was at first poorly understood. The Buddha was regarded as a deity who could teach the secrets of immortality. Art provides another example of how Buddhism was initially grafted onto indigenous beliefs. The Queen Mother of the West, the most important Daoist goddess of the immortality cult, was the first Chinese deity represented in art. By the first century of the Common Era, the Chinese carved her image on stones or bricks to adorn the tombs of wealthy people. The image would be situated along the upper part of the tomb wall below the ceiling, indicating a heavenly space. When the Chinese began to create the image of the Buddha, they made him resemble the Queen Mother of the West. Images of the Buddha were found in tomb reliefs in Maohao and Shiziwan in Leshan, Sichuan, dated to the late second century. Both the iconography and the location of the Buddha image in the tombs were the same as those of the Queen Mother of the West. The Buddhist teaching of rebirth presented a great problem of understanding for the Chinese. The only way that they could make sense of rebirth was by positing that Buddhism taught the continued existence of a soul after death, an idea completely contrary to the central Buddhist teaching of no self.

Scripture in Forty-two Sections

What Buddhist teachings are found in the *Scripture in Forty-two Sections,* the legendary first scripture brought to China by the two Indian monks on a white horse? This text is often included in the assigned readings of Buddhist seminaries in Taiwan today. Despite its questionable historicity, it has clearly achieved a commonly acknowledged authority among Chinese Buddhists. It consists of pithy aphorisms and striking parables. Unlike Buddhist sutras, the format is similar to that of the Confucian classic the *Analects,* which consists of dialogues between Confucius and his disciples. This is probably one of the reasons the *Scripture* holds such a perennial appeal. There are sections exhorting benevolence and spiritual practice similar to those found in the *Analects:*

> (5) The Buddha says: "Should a man malign me and seek to do me harm, I counter with the four virtues of benevolence, compassion, joy, and equanimity. The more he approaches me with malice, the more I reach out with kindness. The forces (qi) of benevolent virtue lie always with this, while harmful forces and repeated misfortune will revert to the other."

> (15) The Buddha says: "What do I contemplate? I contemplate the Way. What do I practice? I practice the Way. Of what do I speak? I speak of the Way. I contemplate the true Way, never neglecting it for even an instant."

But more sections are about the Buddhist central emphasis on right view and right behavior.

> (18) The Buddha says: "Ardently contemplate the four primary elements that comprise the body. While each has a name, they are all devoid of self. [The sense of an] 'I' emerges from the aggregates, but it is not long lived and is really but an illusion."

> (20) The Buddha says: "Riches and sex are to men what sweet honey on the blade of a knife is to a young child: before he has fully enjoyed a single bite, he must suffer the pain of a cut tongue."

> (22) The Buddha says, "The misery of being shackled to wife, children, wealth and home is greater than that of being shackled in chains and

fetters and thrown in prison. In prison there is the possibility of pardon, but even though the desire for wife and children is as perilous as the mouth of a tiger, men throw themselves into it willingly. For this crime there is no pardon."

(27) The Buddha told a śramaṇa: "Take care not to look at a woman. If you meet one, look not, and take care not to converse with her. If you must converse, admonish the mind to right conduct by saying to yourself: 'As a śramaṇa I must live in this befouled world like a lotus, unsullied by mud.' Treat an old lady as if she were your mother, an elder woman as your elder sister, a younger woman as your younger sister, and a young girl as your own daughter. Show respect for them through your propriety. Remember that you see only the outside, but if you could peer into the body—from head to foot—what then? It is humming with foulness. By exposing the impure aggregates [that compose the body] one can free oneself from [impure] thoughts."[1]

Although we do not know how this scripture was used in the early period or among what circles it was circulated, the ascetic ideal it promotes is typical of scriptures of the Hinayana tradition. The strong misogyny displayed in the passages offends our modern sensibility. But this serves a pedagogical function. Since sexual desire and sensual enjoyment, including domestic life, are the greatest threats to a monastic career, it is perhaps not too surprising that these are projected onto women and turn them into fearful and feared temptresses. Such sentiment is absent in the Mahayana sutras, which were introduced to China at the same time.

Translation of Buddhist Scriptures

A key way that Chinese people learned about Buddhism was through reading and listening to the exposition of Buddhist sutras. For this reason, the energies of early missionaries and their Chinese collaborators were concentrated on the translation of Buddhist scriptures. Depending on the personal backgrounds and interests of the translators, the sutras chosen for translation could be from early Buddhist or Mahayana traditions. In this way, the Chinese were exposed to a whole range of Buddhist literature, from the stories of the Buddha's previous lives to meditation manuals and the philosophical teaching of *śūnyatā* (the lack of inherent nature of all things), expounded in the *Perfection of Wisdom* scriptures. This accounts for the ecumenism of Chinese Buddhism, a very significant feature of the tradition. Because the Chinese accepted all the sutras translated as the "word of the Buddha," they were forced to find a way to reconcile the many different ideas found in them. This led to the creation of doctrinal classifications in the Sui (581–618) and Tang (618–907) dynasties, a hierarchical ordering of the doctrines found in the sutras. This was a major achievement. At the same time, singling out one sutra for special emphasis, new Chinese Buddhist schools not found in India came into being.

Most translators of the early period came from Central Asia, although some also came from India. This is attested by their surnames. A foreign monk would use the first character of the country from which he came as his surname. It was an ethnic identifier and not a family name. For instance, many translators were known this way: *Kang* for Sogdia, *An* for Parthia, *Zhi* for Scythia, *Yu* for Khotan, *Bo* for Kucha, and *Zhu* for India. It was the monk Daoan (312–385) who started to use the first character of Śākyamuni's transliterated name, *Shi,* as the family name of all Chinese monks, making the Buddha the ancestor of their lineage.

Hinayana and Mahayana were introduced to China at about the same time. The former was represented by the work of Anshigao, the latter by Lokakṣema. Anshigao was a Parthian who arrived in Luoyang in 148 and translated many Hinayana scriptures in twenty years. Most are on meditation methods, concentrating on mindfulness of the breath. Since meditation was one of the Daoist methods to achieve immortality, these scriptures were favorably received. Anshigao's student, Yan Fotiao, was the first Chinese monk. Lokakṣema was a Scythian and a contemporary of Anshigao, active 168–188. He was the first translator of Mahayana sutras, chief among which are the *Perfection of Wisdom in 8,000 Lines* and *Scripture of Prolonged Samadhi* (Banzhou sanmei jing). The former introduces the concept of *śūnyāta* (emptiness), a seminal Mahayana teaching that proclaims that not only is a person empty of a self, but all phenomena are also empty of intrinsic nature. The latter teaches a method of meditation that enables one to see the Buddha face-to-face.

Unlike Anshigao and Lokakṣema, Dharmarakṣa (c. 266–308) was a naturalized Scythian living in Dunhuang, the terminus of the Silk Road, and he knew Chinese. He became a monk at the age of eight (c. 239) and translated some of the most important Mahayana sutras. The *Lotus Sutra* teaches the good news of universal buddhahood and that the Buddha is the eternal savior. It also glorifies and gave rise to the cult of the bodhisattva.

He also translated the *Perfection of Wisdom* scriptures and the *Vimalakīrti Sutra*. The fact that he knew both Chinese and foreign languages must be one reason he was so prolific. Because of the central importance of these Mahayana sutras, different translators chose to retranslate them. But the translations by Kumārajīva after he came to China in 401 replaced earlier versions and became the standard not only in China but also throughout East Asia. In the next chapter I will discuss in more detail these scriptures and why they became so popular in China.

The translation projects of the early centuries were not sponsored by the state (as were the cases of Kumārajīva and, later, Xuanzang). Rather, they were individual projects carried out by the foreign monks with the assistance of their Chinese collaborators. Some missionary monks brought a written text, but very often they recited and explained from memory because copies of scriptures were not easily come by. Moreover, Buddhist monks received superb training in memorization. For instance, Dharmarakṣa was reported to have memorized ten thousand words in one day. Sutra translation was the collective work of a team. The foreign monk would read out the text or recite it from memory. Another person who understood the language would write it down. A third person would translate it into Chinese. Sometimes a fourth person whose Chinese was good would polish the translation. Finally, the finished translation was read back to the foreign monk for verification. It was also possible that the Chinese sutra was not an actual translation from an original text but sermons given by the foreign master, recorded by his disciples, and then edited by the master afterward. The translation of Buddhist sutras is a major event in the history of Chinese Buddhism, carried out with enormous human and financial resources over many centuries.

Buddhism during the Period of Disunity (220–581)

The Han dynasty lasted four hundred years, making it one of the longest in Chinese history. This is the reason the Chinese people refer to themselves as Han, although there are many ethnicities besides the Han in China. The last decades of the dynasty were marked by inept rulers, some of whom ascended the throne as teenagers. There were mass rebellions, such as the Yellow Turban Rebellion, which devastated large parts of the country. After the Han fell in 220, China underwent more than three hundred years of division until it was united under the Sui dynasty. During these years of disunity and instability, Buddhism began to be established on Chinese soil.

For most of this period China was divided between the north and the south. Buddhism in North China, which was ruled by non-Chinese rulers, enjoyed imperial patronage. Buddhist devotion took concrete forms such as the large-scale rock sculptures at Yungang Caves near Datong and Longmen Caves near Luoyang, capitals of the Northern Wei. Among the foreign monks who contributed to the flourishing of Buddhism in the north, Fotudeng demands special mention. He was from Kucha and educated in Kashmir, trained in the Sarvastivada school of the Hinayana tradition. He arrived in Luoyang around 310 and converted the Latter Zhao rulers Shi Le and his son, Shi Hu, to Buddhism. Fotudeng impressed Shi Le by the display of magic. He produced a lotus flower out of a bowl of water and used toothpicks to draw water from a dry well. He had the ability to produce rain and predict future events and the outcome of military expeditions. He gained the confidence of Shi Le and served him for over two decades as imperial adviser. He was equally trusted by Shi Hu and tried to make him a compassionate ruler by stressing the first precept of nonkilling. The emperor said that as a ruler he could not avoid killing and asked what he should do to follow the Dharma. Fotudeng told Shi Hu that when a person commits a crime, he must be punished and even executed. But if the ruler is tyrannical and kills innocent people, he will create serious negative karma even if he follows the Dharma. This is a good example of early missionary monks teaching Buddhism through the display of magical power and persuasive argument.

Buddhism in the south was characterized by philosophical speculation and participation by members of the aristocratic classes. Its spread was helped by renewed interest in the thought of Laozi, Zhuangzi, and the *Daode jing*. Scholars called the new movement Neo-Daoism. Though related to Daoism, it was represented by two distinctive trends. As philosophy it was known as Dark Learning, and as a way of life, it was known as Pure Conversation. Dark Learning provided the vocabulary and framework for the educated elites to interpret some of the newly introduced Buddhist philosophies. For this reason, Buddhism in the south has commonly been called gentry Buddhism. The movement was named "dark" because it dealt with the mystery of the Dao. *Śūnyatā*, described in the *Perfection of Wisdom* scriptures, was equated with nothingness or nonbeing (*wu*) in the *Daode jing*. The five precepts of Buddhism not to kill, not to lie, not to steal, not to have improper sex, and not to drink were equated with the five cardinal virtues of benevolence, righteousness (*yi*), propriety, wisdom (*zhi*), and trustworthiness (*xin*), which prescribe the correct conduct governing the five relationships of Confucianism. Nirvana was equated with nonaction (*wuwei*), while Suchness (*tathatā*), the Buddhist ultimate reality, was translated as original nothingness (*benwu*). The practice of pairing concepts from Buddhism with those from the indigenous traditions was called "matching of concepts" (*geyi*). It matched the scriptural categories with secular books. This became a favorite way of making Buddhist ideas familiar to educated adherents. Although it was an efficient expediency, it was abandoned when a better understanding of Buddhism was made possible by the masterful translator Kumārajīva.

The practitioners of Pure Conversation celebrated living spontaneously. The Seven Sages of the Bamboo Grove were friends who often met in a bamboo grove to engage in conversation not tainted by worldly interests and concerns. They typified this distinctive lifestyle characterized by clever repartee and unconventional behavior. Several anecdotes serve as good examples.

Liu Ling (c. 221–c. 300), one member of this group, had the habit of being completely naked when he was in his room. He was criticized for this lack of propriety. He responded, "I take the whole universe as my house and my own room as my clothing. Why, then, do you enter here into my trousers?" Ruan Ji and his nephew Ruan Xian, two other members, were great drinkers. When they met, they sat by a large jar and drank from it, not bothering with cups. If pigs came by, they would drink together with the pigs. Such unconventional behavior was admired as "pure" precisely because it was against the social norm. Other stories celebrated individuals who followed impulse. Wang Huizhi, son of the greatest calligrapher, Wang Xizhi, woke up one night and saw the bright whiteness after a heavy snowfall. He had a sudden impulse to visit his friend Dai Gui, the sculptor, and immediately had servants get a boat ready for a trip that took all night. But when he reached Dai's home and was at the point of knocking on the door, he suddenly changed his mind and returned home. Later, when asked why, he said, "I came on the impulse of my pleasure, and now it is ended, so I go back. Why should I see Dai?"[2]

Kumārajīva

Of the many translators of Buddhist scriptures, Kumārajīva (344–413) is undoubtedly the greatest. He had a very unusual background and led an extraordinary life. He was a native of Kucha. His mother was a princess, and his father came from the priestly caste. After he was born, his mother wanted to become a Buddhist nun, but his father would agree only after she gave birth to another son. When he was seven, the mother and son entered the Buddhist order. They first went to Kashmir to study Hinayana Buddhism. At this young age, Kumārajīva was reputed to have already shown his brilliance at debate. In addition to Buddhist sutras, he also studied the Vedas and texts on astronomy, mathematics, and occult sciences. After three years they went to Kashgar for one year, and he was converted to Mahayana after being introduced to its literature. His fame reached Yao Xin, the ruler of the Former Qin dynasty, in 379, and Yao dispatched a general to take him to the capital, Chang'an. Unfortunately, because the general was hostile to Buddhism, he kept Kumārajīva captive for seventeen years in Liangzhou, a northwest border town. Finally, only after the general was subdued in 401, Kumārajīva was taken to Chang'an.

Kumārajīva was honored as National Preceptor and a translation center was established at the Garden of Leisure. He carried out translation activities with a thousand monks in attendance. Unlike other translators, he knew Chinese, which he had learned during his long stay at Liangzhou. From his arrival in Chang'an until his death in 413, with the help of his able Chinese disciples, he translated a large body of Buddhist sutras, some of which superseded earlier versions and became the classics of East Asian Buddhism.

Kumārajīva did not write much. He was said to hold a Sanskrit text in one hand while rendering its meaning orally. Translation was carried out together with exposition and sermonizing. He was very skillful in using stories to illustrate Buddhist teachings. The stories are built on metaphors, similes, and parables. We can get a sense of how this was done. There are quite a number of such stories in his commentary on the *Vimalakīrti Sutra*. For instance, in commenting on the line in the sutra that compares the body to a well on a hillock, he tells the following story:

> Long ago there was a man who offended the king. Afraid of the consequences of his offense, he fled. The king ordered that a drunken elephant pursue him and, in a panic, the man threw himself into a dried-up well. As he was halfway down, he saw a blade of rotten grass and grabbed it. Below, a ferocious dragon was spitting its venom at him. Around him, five poisonous serpents were attempting to injure

him. Two rats, one black and one white, were gnawing at the grass, which was about to snap. At the same time, the elephant above was trying to get at him. The anguished man was in extreme peril, and he was utterly horrified. Above his head stood a tree from which honeylike liquid dripped down into his mouth from time to time. Because he was enticed by the sweet flavor, the man forgot about his fear.

The dried-up well is a metaphor for samsara or life and death; the drunken elephant, for impermanence. The venomous dragon is a metaphor for the evil destinies; the poisonous serpents, for the five aggregates. The rotten grass is a metaphor for the root of life. The white rat is a metaphor for the sun and the black one for the moon (i.e., time). The honeylike globules are a metaphor for the five sensuous pleasures. Forgetting about fear because of them is a metaphor for the fact that sentient beings, when they taste the sweetness provided by the five sensuous pleasures, are not afraid of suffering.[3]

The sutra implies only obliquely that the well will soon dry up because of its precarious location. It uses this metaphor to illustrate the impermanence of human life. But Kumārajīva framed the moral with this elaborate story and left readers with this indelible image of the human condition. It is no wonder that the story was often retold and became the favorite theme of sermons used by later Chan masters.

Chinese Masters: Daoan and Huiyuan

Although Daoan (314–365) and Huiyuan (334–416) were not among the Chinese monks who studied under Kumārajīva in the capital, both had significant contact with and were highly praised by him. He called Daoan "the sage of the east" and Huiyuan "the bodhisattva protector of the law in the east." Daoan was the most famous disciple of Fotudeng. Unlike most monks and lay believers at that time, he was orphaned young and did not come from an aristocratic background. In his youth, he begged scriptures from his teacher to study, which indicates the difficulty of possessing copies of one's own. He received early training in Hinayana, was interested in the meditation sutras translated by Anshigao, and studied the Agamas and Abhidharma literature. However, he was equally enthusiastic about the *Perfection of Wisdom* scriptures. In this respect, Daoan was the ideal Buddhist practitioner, proficient in both meditation and wisdom. He was also typical of Chinese monks, learning from both the Hinayana and

Mahayana traditions. This nonsectarian approach is exemplified by the creation of Chinese Buddhist schools in a later period.

Daoan attracted as many as five hundred disciples. He understood the central importance of the Vinaya, or monastic discipline. However, because there was no translation of any Vinaya text yet, he created rules for his own community. Even after the existing texts had all been translated into Chinese, various new monastic rules known as "pure rules" were created from the Song dynasty (960–1279) onward. They served as the real guides for how monasteries should function. Daoan's rules were supposed to be followed by other monasteries during his lifetime; they might be considered the prototype of the later pure rules. Known as *Regulations for Monastics,* his set of rules did not survive, although parts of it were quoted by Daoxuan (596–667), a specialist in the Vinaya. These rules governed three procedures for collective living: (1) offering incense, taking one's seat, and reciting scriptures while circumambulating in the Buddha hall; (2) daily practice performed at six periods of the day (morning, noon, evening, and the first, second, and third watches of the night), including circumambulating the Buddha's image, eating meals, and chanting at mealtimes; and (3) semimonthly confession and the ritual of repentance. Daoan was the first Buddhist master who established monastic regulations for his community. Studying the sutras has a high priority in this list. For Daoan, wisdom was emphasized as much as monastic discipline in the training of a monk.

Daoan was the first to compile a catalogue of Buddhist sutras, an important genre of Buddhist historiography. He compiled the *Comprehensive Catalogue of Scriptures,* a bibliography of all the Buddhist scriptures translated up to his time, in 374; it is also no longer extant. Compiling these catalogues was a major undertaking of Buddhist exegetes. Up until the eighteenth century, there were seventy-six such catalogues. The purpose was to pass judgment on the authenticity of sutras and separate the translated ones from those composed in China, which were called spurious or suspicious. Daoan used the term *non-Buddhist scriptures* to refer to twenty-six texts listed in his record. This tells us that forged sutras had appeared as early as the fourth century. Daoan was distressed by the indiscriminate mixture of the genuine with the false and regarded the latter as despicable, as did all compilers after him. However, in recent decades scholars have alerted us to the positive value of these texts. Instead of dismissing them as "forgeries," they regard them as valuable documents revealing contemporary understandings of Buddhism. These texts are creative attempts to synthesize Buddhist teachings and adapt them to the native milieu.

Just as meditation and wisdom are jointly exalted, Chinese Buddhist masters often combined piety and scholarship. Daoan was a devotee of Maitreya, the future Buddha. Together with eight disciples, he made a vow in front of an image of Maitreya, praying to be reborn in Tushita Heaven. This is the heaven where Maitreya is now living, waiting to descend to Earth to renew Buddhism in the future.

Huiyuan was twenty years old when he became Daoan's disciple in 354, when the latter was already a very famous Buddhist master. In many ways Huiyuan shared his teacher's interests and was the prime representative of southern Buddhism. He had been educated in Confucian classics and the Daoist thought of Laozi and Zhuangzi before he converted to Buddhism. He was an expert in both the *Perfection of Wisdom* philosophy and meditation literature. He emphasized strict observation of monastic discipline, and his personal life served as a good example. When he settled at Mount Lu in present-day Jiangxi province, around 386 at the age of thirty-two, he declared that he would never go beyond the stream that marked the boundary of the monastery. He carried out long-distance correspondence with Kumārajīva and discussed abstract Buddhist doctrines such as the nature of Dharmakāya (Body of the Buddha) and the difference between a bodhisattva and an arhat.

During the fourth century in southern China, intellectuals hotly debated the Buddhist concepts of karma and rebirth. Huiyuan's writings on these topics make us understand the concerns of his contemporaries. To those who had doubts about karma, he wrote:

> The sutra says that karma has three kinds of response: first, in the present life; second, in the next life; and the third, in later lives. In the first, good and bad deeds originate in this present life and are rewarded in this life. In the second, the deeds are rewarded in the next life, while in the third, the deeds are rewarded in the third, hundredth, or thousandth life afterward. . . . In this world there are people who have good karma and yet collect disaster. Perhaps there are cruel and evil ones who arrive at good fortune. This is all because the karma that should be rewarded in the present life has not yet manifested, while that of former lives is bearing fruit.

Many people in his time had trouble accepting the idea of reincarnation. In order to prove the validity of rebirth, Buddhists upheld the theory of the indestructibility of the soul. Huiyuan wrote: "The transmission of fire to firewood is like that of the soul to the body. The transmission of fire to another piece of firewood is like that of the soul to another new body. . . . The former body is not the latter body, and we therefore know that the interaction between feelings and destiny is profound. A deluded person, seeing the body destroyed in one life, assumes that the soul and feelings also perished with it, as if fire would be exhausted when a piece of wood is burned."[4]

While Daoan was a devotee of Maitreya, the future Buddha, Huiyuan worshiped Amitābha Buddha. In 402, he gathered 123 followers, both lay and monastic, and together they made a vow in front of an image of Amitābha for rebirth in the Pure Land or Western Paradise. This group came to be called the White Lotus Society, and Huiyuan was retroactively regarded as the first patriarch of the Pure Land school by later Buddhists. They vowed to be reborn in Amitābha's Pure Land because they hoped to become enlightened there by listening to Amitābha's teaching. They also vowed that when one of them became enlightened, he would return or reveal himself in some form to help the others. The White Lotus Society was a Buddhist counterpart of the Seven Sages of the Bamboo Grove celebrated in Dark Learning circles. The Buddhist wish to be reborn in the Western Paradise of Amitābha echoed the Daoist cult of immortality. As early as the First Emperor of Qin, the search for an elixir of immorality had obsessed rulers. By the Common Era, not only emperors and the ruling elite but also people of humbler birth were interested in becoming immortals who would live in wondrous realms above the earth. During the first four centuries after the introduction of Buddhism into China, there were parallel developments in new philosophical inquiry as well as religious innovation by both Buddhists and Daoists. It is therefore not surprising that the two traditions stimulated each other. It is also not surprising that there were mutual borrowings as a result of this interaction.

Why single out these two early Chinese monks? A Buddhist is supposed to be proficient in three areas: morality, concentration, and wisdom. He or she is also encouraged to cultivate both blessing and wisdom. The latter refers to the study and observation of the Vinaya or monastic discipline, mastery of meditative training, and gaining of true insight. The former stresses the necessity of cultivating religious merit in addition to gaining wisdom. There are different ways of generating merit, including making offerings to the monastic community, feeding the monks, building temples, and casting Buddha images. The basic motivating force behind all these activities comes from a heart of faith and devotion. Daoan and Huiyuan combined both sets of ideals through their life and work. Because of this they have been celebrated down the ages.

Discussion Questions

1. What are some of the differences between Hinayana and Mahayana Buddhism?
2. Who were some of the early Buddhist translators? How was the translation carried out?
3. What Buddhist ideas were most difficult for the Chinese to understand and why?
4. What was the "matching of concepts," and why was this method of explaining Buddhism abandoned?
5. What monastic ideals did Huiyuan embody?

Further Reading

Ch'en, Kenneth. *Buddhism in China: A Historical Survey.* Princeton, NJ: Princeton University Press, 1964.

Lau, D. C., trans. *Lao Tzu: Tao Te Ching.* London: Penguin, 1963.

———, trans. *Confucius: The Analects (Lun Yü).* Penguin Classics. Harmondsworth: Penguin, 1979.

Mitchell, Donald W., and Sarah H. Jacoby. *Buddhism: Introducing the Budddhist Experience*, 3rd ed. New York: Oxford University Press, 2013.

Schwartz, Benjamin I. *The World of Thought in Ancient China.* Cambridge, MA: Harvard University Press, 1985.

Strong, John S. *The Buddha: A Short Biography.* Oxford: Oneworld, 2001.

Williams, Paul, and Anthony Tribe. *Buddhist Thought: A Complete Introduction to the Indian Tradition.* London: Routledge, 2000.

Wright, Arthur F. *Buddhism in Chinese History.* Stanford, CA: Stanford University Press, 1959.

———. *Studies in Chinese Buddhism.* Edited by Robert M. Somers. New Haven, CT: Yale University Press, 1990.

Notes

1 Robert H. Sharf, "The Scripture in Forty-two Sections," in *Religions of China in Practice,* ed. Donald S. Lopez Jr. (Princeton, NJ: Princeton University Press, 1996), 365–369.

2 Fung Yu-lan, *A Short History of Chinese Philosophy,* ed. Derk Bodde (New York: Macmillan, 1960), 235–237.

3 Yuet Keung Lo, "Persuasion and Entertainment at Once: Kumārajīva's Buddhist Storytelling in His Commentary on the Vimalakīrti-sūtra," *Chinese Literature and Philosophy Quarterly* 21 (September 2002): 101–102.

4 Ch'en, *Buddhism in China,* 111–112.

CHAPTER 1

Major Buddhist Sutras and Treatises of Chinese Buddhism

The Chinese Buddhist canon is a vast collection of many translated scriptures from both early and Mahayana traditions. In this chapter, I shall discuss some of the most important ones.

The Perfection of Wisdom Scriptures

As we read in the previous chapter, Lokakṣema was the first translator of the *Perfection of Wisdom in 8,000 Lines,* the earliest Mahayana sutra teaching *śūnyāta* (emptiness). The insight of *śūnyāta* is the perfection of wisdom, which constitutes enlightenment and buddhahood. Most *Perfection of Wisdom* scriptures are named in accordance with their length. Aside from the *Perfection of Wisdom in 8,000 Lines,* there are the *Perfection of Wisdom in 25,000 Lines* and the *Perfection of Wisdom in 100,000 Lines,* but also the *Perfection of Wisdom in One Letter.*

The *Heart Sutra* and the *Diamond Sutra* belong to the same group of *Perfection of Wisdom* scriptures. The *Heart Sutra* is chanted daily in the morning service by monastics. It is a very brief scripture of one page in English translation. The opening lines state that the bodhisattva Avalokiteśvara (Guanyin) in deep meditation looks down from on high and sees that "Form is emptiness and the very emptiness is form; emptiness does not differ from form, nor does form differ from emptiness; whatever is form, that is emptiness; whatever is emptiness, that is form."[1] Form is the first of the five aggregates and refers to the body. If we think that form has an intrinsic nature, we are deluded. But if we think that emptiness exists apart from form and is a higher reality than form, we are equally deluded, because in either case we are engaged in discrimination and thus create attachments to either form or emptiness. The

Heart Sutra refers to this as "thought coverings." There is a reason the sutra makes a fourfold equation between form and emptiness. As Zhuangzi pointed out, we are accustomed to thinking in dichotomies. Our natural tendency is to contrast form with emptiness and make a distinction between the two. But with the fourfold equation, we are prevented from doing this and are led to the insight of nonduality. When we realize that the true nature of form is emptiness, form is not negated but is seen in its newly revealed, expansive fullness. The psychological effect of this spiritual insight is freedom from fear. The sutra describes someone who has achieved this realization this way: "through his having relied on the perfection of wisdom, he dwells without thought-coverings. In the absence of thought-coverings he has not been made to tremble, he has overcome what can upset, in the end sustained by Nirvāṇa."[2] It was said that the famous pilgrim Xuanzang (ca. 596–664) recited this sutra when he crossed the dangerous Taklamakan Desert on his way to India.

The *Diamond Sutra* is also famous for its protective power. Many miracle stories have been collected throughout centuries about people who escaped all kinds of danger by reciting it. Although it also speaks of nonduality from the standpoint of emptiness, the language it uses is dramatically different from the *Heart Sutra*. Instead of proclaiming this truth based on an ecstatic vision, it uses paradoxes to drive this home. In the sutra, the Buddha teaches Subhūti, the disciple most famous for his knowledge, about the perfection of wisdom. In a series of questions and answers, the Buddha turns the most common Buddhist concepts, such as living beings, bodhisattva, and nirvana, on their heads.

> The Blessed One said: "Here, Subhūti, one who has set out on the way of a bodhisattava should produce a thought in this manner: 'All living beings should be led by me to final nirvana in the realm of nirvana which leaves nothing behind. But after having led living beings thus to final nirvana, there is no living being whatsoever who has been led to nirvana.' And why is that? If, Subhūti, a conception of a living being were to occur to a bodhisattva, a conception of a personal soul, or a conception of a person, he is not to be called 'a bodhisattva.' And why is that? Subhūti, that which is called 'one who has set out on the way of a bodhisattva,' that is not a thing."[3]

Why does the Buddha first declare that the bodhisattva leads a living being to nirvana and then deny that this is precisely what he does?

Although the sutra does not mention *śūnyāta,* it is firmly based on this understanding of reality. Conventionally we take a "living being" and "bodhisattva" as really existing and having a "self." But this is actually not the case, because both are without any intrinsic self, being dependent on causes and conditions. But this insight is difficult to express through language. It can only be expressed by the formula "A is in fact not A, therefore it is called A," used here and throughout the sutra. Here is another more explicit example: "The Blessed One said: 'They, Subhūti, are neither living beings nor non-living beings. Why is that? "All living beings," Subhūti, they are said to be not living beings by the Tathāgata. In that sense "all living beings" is used.'"[4]

Mahayana does not negate the existence of people or things, but it tells us that they are not what we think they are. They exist conditionally but are devoid of essence. Therefore, we should see them with a double vision and uphold simultaneously the two truths. To see all phenomena as real is the conventional truth, and to see them in their empty nature is the ultimate truth. The famous second-century philosopher Nāgārjuna founded the Madhyamaka (Middle Way) school based on the *Perfection of Wisdom* literature. The middle way as taught by the Buddha is originally represented by the Noble Eightfold Path, an ethical life of neither austerity nor indulgence. It now refers to an epistemological middle way of neither affirmation nor negation. We can have a glimpse of such a vision of reality described in these similes beloved by the Mahayana writer:

> As stars, a fault of vision, as a lamp,
> A mock show, dew drops, or a bubble,
> A dream, a lightning flash, or cloud,
> So we should view what is conditioned.[5]

The dialectic language used in these two sutras serves a soteriological function. Edward Conze, a scholar who spent his entire career on the study of the *Perfection of Wisdom* (*prajñapāramitā*) literature, describes it this way: "The thousands of lines of the prajñapāramitā can be summed up in the following two sentences. (1) One should become a bodhisattva (or buddha-to-be), i.e., one who is content with nothing less than all-knowledge attained through perfection of insight for the sake of all beings. (2) There is no such thing as a bodhisattva, or as all-knowledge, or as a 'being,' or as the perfection of insight, or as an attainment. To accept both these contradictory facts is to be perfect."[6] When the reader is asked to accept these two contradictory positions simultaneously, she has to go beyond the opposition between them. The middle way receives a new interpretation. Instead of avoiding the opposition between indulgence and austerity, one is urged to dwell in nonduality, beyond either affirmation or negation.

In terms of lasting fame and influence, there are two scriptures that tower above the rest: the *Lotus Sutra* and the *Vimalakīrti Sutra*. They were translated several times by different translators, but those by Kumārajīva are considered the best. As explained in the previous chapter, the translation was always done by a committee headed by a foreign monk. For this reason, although Kumārajīva is listed as the translator, he was assisted by his Chinese disciples, some of whom were highly accomplished both in Buddhist thought and in literary ability. To make the translation accessible, Kumārajīva chose to convey the meaning of the host text instead of faithfully rendering it word by word. The result is a distinctive mixture of classical and vernacular Chinese. His translations of these two sutras became the standard not only in China but also throughout East Asia. English translations were also based on the versions produced by him.

The *Lotus Sutra*

Like all Mahayana sutras, the *Lotus Sutra* claims that it is a record of the preaching of the historical Buddha. It opens with the statement: "This is what I have heard: At one time the Buddha was in Rajagriha, staying on Mount Gridhrakuta." These are the same words used in the sutras of the Pali canon. The "I" refers to Ānanda, Buddha's close disciple, who is known for his superior memory. The setting is the traditional place where the Buddha preached as recorded in the Pali sutras. And so, the sutras in the Pali canon are presented as the record of what Ānanda heard the Buddha preach. By using the same phrase, the *Lotus Sutra* presents itself as a faithful record of a sermon, although it was written by authors living several hundred years after the Buddha's death. Scholars believe that the scripture was composed in three different stages at different times and by different authors between 100 BCE and 100 CE.

Despite the effort of the writers to make the *Lotus Sutra* appear to be a traditional sermon by the Buddha, the narrative immediately alerts us that we are in a totally different world, where our ordinary sense of time and space is drastically transformed. The audience in the *Lotus Sutra* and its listener or reader are presented with a miraculous scene. The dazzling light issued by the Buddha first illuminates innumerable other worlds previously unknown to the audience. Then, empowered by the Buddha, the assembly sees the buddhas in each of those worlds, hears their teachings, and witnesses the entire religious careers of buddhas, bodhisattvas, monastics, and laypeople in the span of a short time. This extraordinary vision is a prelude to the similarly extraordinary teachings the Buddha is about to reveal next. The setting is of course designed by the Mahayana authors to glorify the Buddha. But equally significant, it is an effective way to stretch the imagination of the audience by shattering their conventional views about reality.

Once the mind and consciousness of the audience are transformed, they are ready to receive the teachings. It becomes immediately clear that the teachings have little resemblance to what the disciples have learned from early Buddhism. The *Lotus Sutra* also reveals the identity of the Buddha, who is really not the one presented in the early Hinayana scriptures. These are the two major revolutionary messages: Buddhism is the one universal vehicle enabling everyone to achieve buddhahood, and Śākyamuni is the primordial Buddha instead of a historical person who attained buddhahood under the Bodhi tree. Traditionally, Buddhist scriptures speak of Buddhist ideals and the three corresponding vehicles that will transport a person to those ideals. They are *śravākas* (voice hearers), *pratyekabuddhas* (private buddhas), and bodhisattvas. *Śravākas* are the disciples of the Buddha who achieve enlightenment by listening to his teaching. The goal of this vehicle is to achieve arhatship and attain nirvana at the end of this life.

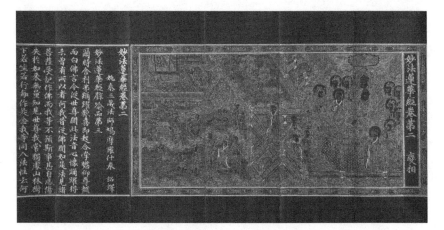

Illustrated Manuscript of the Lotus Sutra. Ca. 1340. Korea. Metropolitan Museum of Art

*Pratyekabuddha*s are those who attain buddhahood without listening to the Buddha's teaching and do not teach others. These two vehicles belong to the Hinayana tradition. Separated from and superior to them are the bodhisattvas, who represent the ideal of the Mahayana. The goal of the bodhisattva vehicle is to become a buddha, teach sentient beings, and help them achieve enlightenment as Śākyamuni did.

The path of the bodhisattva is a long one. It begins with the thought for enlightenment and making vows to benefit sentient beings. She then practices the six perfections of giving, morality, vigor, patience, meditation, and wisdom. While morality, meditation, and wisdom are also mentioned in the Noble Eightfold Path of early Buddhism, this is a far more intense and demanding physical, ethical, and spiritual training. Two features require our attention. The first is that unlike the Noble Eightfold Path, the bodhisattva's path starts with giving. Mahayana speaks of three kinds of giving: giving of material things, giving of Dharma, and giving of the body. Following the models set by the Buddha in his previous lives, which are compiled in the *Jātaka* tales, a bodhisattva willingly offers her eyes, hands, head, and life for the sake of saving others. It is only by performing this kind of giving that she becomes perfect. Furthermore, in light of *śūnyatā,* the ideal giving is carried out in the manner of triple emptiness. In giving, one is not self-consciously aware of the giver, gift, or recipient. The same implication of complete fulfillment applies to the other five perfections. Traditionally, the completion of the bodhisattva path covers ten stages and takes three incalculable eons.

The One Vehicle and Expedient Means

In the *Lotus Sutra* the Buddha makes the astonishing declaration that there are not three vehicles with their different goals as traditionally understood but in fact only one vehicle that leads everyone, not just bodhisattvas, to buddhahood. He states that the reason he was born in this world is solely to announce this good news. Such a novel teaching naturally raises doubt among his audience, which consists of *sravāka*s and bodhisattvas as well as gods, humans, and nonhumans. The Buddha says that he teaches the three vehicles to suit the intellectual and spiritual capacities of his listeners. Since beings are not the same due to their different karma, a good teacher adapts the teachings accordingly by using *upāya* (expedient means). *Upāya* is a central Mahayana idea used to reconcile many differences in doctrines and practices. According to the concept of *upāya,* an enlightened being—a buddha or a bodhisattva—possesses a special ability and prerogative to use whatever teaching method is best suited to the karmic dispositions of the student. Only his superior insight ensures the appropriateness of any one method to the situation at hand. This pedagogical skill is a unique quality of the Buddha. Now he reveals the one vehicle because the audience is mature enough to hear it.

> Up to now I have never told you
> That you were certain to attain the Buddha Way.
> The reason I never preached in that manner
> Was that the time to preach so had not yet come.
> But now is the very time.[7]

The *Lotus Sutra* employs several parables to illustrate how the Buddha makes use of this powerful device. What appear to be lies are expedient devices that Buddha the father uses to save us, who are his sons. This is a point the Buddha emphasizes throughout the scripture.

These parables have become well known through repeated storytellings and sermons. They are alluded to in poetry and depicted in paintings. Chinese Buddhists come to understand the teaching of the Buddha in the *Lotus Sutra* through these parables, just as many Christians come to understand the teaching of Christ through the parables in the New Testament.

Parables

The parable of the burning house in chapter 3 is undoubtedly the most famous. The father wants to save the children who are playing obliviously in a house that has caught fire. Knowing that they are too young to understand the danger of fire, he uses *upāya* to get them out. The father tells them that he has prepared three different carts, which each child has always wanted. They are carts drawn by deer, goats, and oxen. But when the children leave the house safely, the father gives each of them a great, beautiful white cart drawn by a bull instead of the three different carts he has promised. After the Buddha tells the story, he says that he is the father, the children are us human beings, the burning house is the world of samsara, and the three carts represent the vehicles of *śravāka*s, *pratyekabuddha*s, and bodhisattvas, respectively. The great white cart drawn by a bull given to each child is the one universal vehicle that leads everyone to buddhahood. Scholars put forward varying explanations about the relationship between the three vehicles and the one vehicle. Is the oxen cart representing the bodhisattva vehicle the same as the great white cart drawn by a bull representing the buddha vehicle? Or are there in fact four vehicles, the great white cart drawn by a bull being different from the others promised earlier? One way to answer the question is to regard the three carts as provisional and the great white cart drawn by a bull as final, reflecting the conventional versus the ultimate truths. Instead of the three different vehicles, they are in fact one, for all are destined to become buddhas, as the Buddha gives the prediction to the entire assembly in chapter 9.

The theme of the Buddha as the father reappears in two other parables. Chapter 4 tells the story of the prodigal son. The son leaves home and becomes impoverished in his wandering. The father searches for the son and eventually settles in a different city and becomes very rich. One day the son comes to beg at the father's big mansion without realizing that it is his father's home. The father, however, immediately recognizes his son, even though he is wearing rags and covered with dirt. Instead of revealing his identity and welcoming the prodigal son as the father does in the Bible, he uses *upāya* and chooses to do so in stages. He first hires the son to gather dung and do other lowly manual labor. After the son proves himself a hard and diligent worker, he is promoted to manage the estate. Years later, when the father is near death, he finally reveals who he really is and bequeaths the entire estate to the son. The Buddha is the father and we are his son. The jobs assigned to the son are the three vehicles and the estate is the one vehicle. The work of carrying dung in the son's early employment is comparable to the training undertaken by the disciples. Astonishingly, nirvana, the highest goal in early Buddhism, is compared to the daily wages. The advanced disciples announce, "We were diligent and exerted ourselves in this matter until we had attained nirvana, which is like one day's wages. And once we had attained it, our hearts were filled with great joy and we considered that this was enough" (p. 86). But if nirvana is no longer the goal worth pursuing, what about the Buddha's nirvana? When the one vehicle of buddhahood becomes the new gospel, the *Lotus Sutra* also overturns the meaning of nirvana.

The third parable of the Buddha as the father is found in chapter 16. This is a very crucial chapter, for it reveals the identity of Śākyamuni as the primordial Buddha. Naturally, in this new light, nirvana is also understood differently. The parable is again about a father and his sons who, unlike those in the burning house parable, are adults. The father is a physician, and while he is away on some business, the sons drink poison and become very ill. When the father returns, he makes a potent medicine and gives it to the sons. While some take it, those who have lost their senses due to the severity of their suffering refuse to do so. Eager to cure all the sons, the father resorts to *upāya*. He tells the sons that he must go away again and hopes they will take the medicine he leaves behind. After he leaves, he sends a messenger back to report that he has died. Overwhelmed with grief, the sons remember the medicine the father left for them and take it. When they recover, the father returns, to their great joy. Nirvana is compared to the father's fake death. Passing into nirvana is thus a show, and so are Buddha's birth and enlightenment. The Buddha explains:

> Why do I do this? Because if the Buddha remains in the world for a long time, those persons with shallow virtue will fail to plant good roots but, living in poverty and lowliness, will become attached to the five desires and be caught in the net of deluded thoughts and imaginings. If they see that the Thus Come One is constantly in the world and never enters extinction, they will grow arrogant and selfish, or become discouraged and neglectful. They will fail to realize how difficult it is to encounter the Buddha and will not approach him with a respectful and reverent mind. (227)

The Buddha is shown here as a keen observer of human nature. If the sons see the father all the time, they will take him for granted and will not pay attention to his instruction.

Nirvana is compared to the wages of one day or, like here, a show. In chapter 7, it is compared to a conjured city that serves as a temporary resting place on the way to the place of true treasures symbolized by buddhahood. In this parable, the Buddha is the leader of travelers who are journeying to a distant place of many treasures. They become tired and wish to turn back. To spur them on, the leader conjures up a phantom city as a goal. After they have a good rest, the leader "wipes out the phantom city and says to the group, 'You must go now. The place where the treasure is is close by. That great city of a while ago was a mere phantom that I conjured up so that you could rest'" (136). This parable makes it very clear that the nirvana sought by the arhat is the phantom city, and buddhahood attained by the bodhisattva is the treasure trove. It implies that the traditional goal of self-enlightenment advocated by Hinayana is inferior to the new Mahayana goal of universal enlightenment.

Just as the city is not real, the nirvana promised by early Buddhism is also not the true one. But what is the real goal if it is not nirvana? The Buddha says,

> When I know they have reached nirvana
> and all have attained the stage of arhat,
> then I call the great assembly together
> and preach the true Law for them.
> The Buddha through the power of expedient means
> makes distinctions and preaches three vehicles,
> but there is only the single Buddha vehicle—
> the other two nirvanas are preached to provide a resting place.
> Now I expound the truth for you—
> what you have attained is not extinction. . . .
> If you gain enlightenment in the Law of the Buddha
> with its comprehensive wisdom and ten powers
> and are endowed with the thirty-two features,
> then this will be true extinction.
> The Buddhas in their capacity as leaders
> preach nirvana to provide a rest.
> But when they know you have become rested,
> they lead you onward to the Buddha wisdom. (142)

The *Lotus Sutra* boldly makes universal buddhahood the ultimate goal for everybody instead of nirvana. But what about the early teaching? Did the Buddha lie? The parable of the medicinal plants in chapter 5 provides an answer. The Dharma taught by the Buddha is compared to the rain falling from a great cloud on all vegetation without making any distinction. The plants, trees, thickets, groves, and medicinal herbs represent those who listen to the Dharma. Although all of them grow on the same earth and receive the same moistening rain, each grows and sprouts differently in accordance with its own nature. Similarly, sentient beings gain different understandings of the Dharma based on their capacity. The Buddha does not create the hierarchy of the Buddhist community. Rather, it is generated by the community itself. In this verse, the Buddha compares the whole range of beings, beginning with gods and humans and leading all the way to the bodhisattvas, to different types of medicinal herbs and trees. Each obtains benefit from the Dharma rain only to the extent they are capable. While some understand that the Buddha teaches buddhahood as our destination, others take it to be nirvana.

When all the various living beings hear the Law,
they receive according to their powers,
dwelling in their different environments.
Some inhabit the realm of human and heavenly beings,
of wheel-turning sage kings,
Shakra, Brahma and the other kings—
these are the inferior medicinal herbs.
Some understand the Law of no outflows,
are able to attain nirvana,
to acquire the six transcendental powers
and gain in particular the three understandings,
or live alone in mountain forests,
constantly practicing meditation
and gaining the enlightenment of pratyekabuddhas—
these are the middling medicinal herbs.
Still others seek the place of the World-Honored One,
convinced that they can become Buddhas,
putting forth diligent effort and practicing meditation—
these are superior medicinal herbs.
Again there are sons of the Buddha
who devote their minds solely to the Buddha way,
constantly practicing mercy and compassion
knowing that they themselves will attain Buddhahood,
certain of it and never doubting—
these I call the small trees.
Those who abide in peace in their transcendental powers
turning the wheel of non-regression,
saving innumerable millions
of hundreds of thousands of living beings—
bodhisattvas such as these
I call the large trees.
The equality of the Buddha's preaching
is like a rain of a single flavor,
but depending upon the nature of the living beings
the way in which it is received is not uniform. (103–104)

In chapter 8, buddhahood is symbolized by a hidden jewel sewn secretly inside the lining of a man's robe by a rich friend. When the man wakes up from a drunken slumber, he goes on his way. Years go by and they meet again by chance. The man has been working hard to earn a living, unaware of the jewel he has inside his robe. The rich friend is sorry to see him in this state and tells him the truth. The jewel is the buddhahood we are endowed with, although, like the drunken man, we are oblivious of the fact.

The Primordial Buddha

According to early Buddhism, there is only one Buddha in the world at a time. Before Śākyamuni achieved buddhahood, he practiced the six perfections in many lifetimes as a bodhisattva. There were six buddhas before him, and Maitreya is the future Buddha. The *Lotus Sutra* revolutionizes this traditional understanding of who the Buddha really is. Three chapters play a central role in putting forward this new idea.

We are shown several fantastic miracles in chapter 11. It opens with the emergence of the Treasure Tower that houses the Buddha of Many Treasures (who is supposed to have entered nirvana a long time ago). He announces that he has come to listen to the Buddha's preaching of the *Lotus Sutra* because of the vow he has made. "If, after I have become a Buddha and entered extinction, in the land in the ten directions there is any place where the *Lotus Sutra* is preached, then my funerary tower, in order that I may listen to the sutra, will come forth and appear in that spot to testify to the sutra and praise its excellence" (171). The Buddha performs the miracle of illuminating the eastern quarter of the world system by issuing a bright light from a tuft of white hair between his eyebrows. In all the lands many buddhas who are said to be emanations of Śākyamuni Buddha are seen preaching the *Lotus Sutra*. This is followed by yet another miracle. When Śākyamuni Buddha opens the Treasure Tower, the Buddha of Many Treasures is shown seated as if in meditation with his body whole and unimpaired. The latter offers half a seat to the Buddha and the two of them sit side by side. This is one of the most frequently depicted scenes in Chinese Buddhist art. The Buddha performs a final miracle of lifting the entire assembly into midair so that they can be at eye level with the two buddhas in the tower. The symbolic meaning of these spectacular scenes cannot be lost on the reader. Śākyamuni Buddha is extraordinary not only because he creates innumerable emanations but also because he, like the Buddha of Many Treasures, is primordial. In fact, they are of the same nature.

The new status of Śākyamuni Buddha as the primordial Buddha is further affirmed in a miraculous event in chapter 15 in which bodhisattvas "equal in number to the sands of sixty-thousand Ganges rivers" emerge from under the earth and pay obeisance to the two Buddhas seated together in the Treasure Tower. When Śākyamuni Buddha declares that all these bodhisattvas trained under him, the audience cannot understand how this is possible because the Buddha attained enlightenment only some forty years before. Maitreya, speaking on behalf of the assembly, asks, "Suppose, for example, that a young man of twenty-five, with ruddy complexion and hair still black, should point to someone who was a hundred years old and say, 'This is my son!' or that the hundred years old man should point to the youth and say, 'This is my father who sired and raised me!' This would be hard to believe, and so too is what the Buddha says" (221). The Buddha gives the answer in chapter 16, which is titled "The Life Span of the Thus Come One." This is the highlight of the *Lotus Sutra* because it reveals the identity of Śākyamuni Buddha. "Life span" in the chapter title refers to the length of time since he has become enlightened. The Buddha says, "It has been immeasurable, boundless hundreds, thousands, ten thousand, millions of nayutta and asamkhya kalpas since I attained Buddhahood. But for the sake of living beings I employ the power of expedient means and say that I am about to pass into extinction" (229). The Buddha is therefore eternal. His birth, home leaving, religious practice, awakening, and nirvana are all expedient devices for the sake of teaching us. Not only is the Buddha using *upāya* as a teaching method, his entire life is a demonstration of *upāya*.

Medium without Message

Scholars often describe the *Lotus Sutra* as being a medium without message because it is self-referential. As we saw above, the *Lotus Sutra* glorifies Śākyamuni Buddha, but it glorifies itself just as much. Throughout the sutra, it refers to itself as the most excellent and unsurpassed teaching given by the Buddha. It encourages people to "listen to the preaching of the sutra, accept and uphold it, preach it oneself, copy it, cause others to copy, and treat the copies with reverence, respect and praise" (204). If a person performs these new rituals, then it is not necessary for him to "erect towers or temples or build monks' quarters or offer alms to the community of monks" (241). Worship of the *Lotus Sutra* replaces traditional Buddhist devotional activities. The sutra is highly laudatory about itself. One should not only recite and promulgate the scripture but also worship it as if it were the Buddha himself with offerings of flower, perfume, incense, canopies and banners, garlands and music. The preacher of the *Lotus Sutra* receives special praise, and those who have faith in the *Lotus Sutra* will be born with intelligence and physical perfection. Moreover, in all future rebirths, they "will always be born as a human being, see the Buddha, hear and have faith in the Dharma" (248).

Although the *Lotus Sutra* does not spell out the ideas in a systematic fashion, important themes emerge in the form of parables and saintly models. Besides *upāya* and the primordial Buddha, there are a few other themes. One is the anticipated persecution met by a preacher of the new message of universal buddhahood. Together with extravagant self-exaltation, the *Lotus Sutra* expresses a sense of great urgency. We find in chapter 20 a kind of Buddhist eschatology, anticipating the tripartite division into the Age of True Dharma, the Age of Counterfeit Dharma, and the Age of Decline of the Dharma. It predicts that in the future after the Age of True Dharma passes away, there will be an Age of Counterfeit Dharma. Monks of "overbearing arrogance" will be in power. At that time Śākyamuni Buddha will appear as the bodhisattva monk named Never Disparaging. "This monk, whatever persons he happened to meet, whether monks, nuns, laymen or laywomen, would bow in obeisance to all of them and speak words of praise, saying, 'I have profound reverence for you. I would never dare treat you with disparagement or arrogance. Why? Because you are all practicing the bodhisattva way and are certain to attain Buddhahood'" (266–267). Instead of feeling joy when thus saluted with respect, people beat and abuse the monk, thinking that they are being made fun of. Failing to acknowledge their Buddha nature, humankind sells itself short, and the bodhisattva is made into a suffering savior.

The second theme is also related to universal buddhahood. The Buddha gives a prediction to the assembly that each person will become a buddha. In history, the Buddha's cousin Devadatta was a very evil person. He tried to kill the Buddha out of jealousy and also committed the grievous sin of creating schism within the monastic community. But in chapter 12 the Buddha tells the story of how in a past life Devadatta was a seer and he himself was a king. The seer came to the king and offered to teach him the *Lotus Sutra,* and as a result he became the Buddha. "The fact that I have attained impartial and correct enlightenment and can save living beings on a broad scale is all due to Devadatta, who was a good friend" (184). The

Buddha makes the prediction that Devadatta will attain buddhahood like the rest.

In the same chapter there is the story of the eight-year-old Dragon Princess, the daughter of the Dragon King. According to Mahayana lore, the Dragon King is the owner of priceless treasures, but also the keeper of Mahayana sutras until the time when humans are ready to accept them. After listening to the preaching of the *Lotus Sutra* by the bodhisattva Mañjuśrī, the Dragon Princess gives rise to the mind for enlightenment and becomes an advanced bodhisattva in an instant. When Mañjuśrī reports the event to the Buddha, the Dragon Princess suddenly appears. Śāriputra is an advanced disciple of the Buddha and represents the views of conservative Hinayana monks. He is scandalized and asks how it is possible that a female can attain buddhahood. According to tradition, a woman is subject to five obstacles: she cannot become a heavenly Brahma, Shakra, Mara, wheel-turning sage king, or Buddha (188). Upon hearing this, the Dragon Princess performs the miracle of first transforming herself into a man, and then carrying out all the practices of a bodhisattva quickly and attaining enlightenment. Fully endowed with the thirty-two major marks and eighty minor marks of a buddha, she as a man teaches the *Lotus Sutra* to living beings everywhere in the ten directions. Because the five obstacles prevent women from attaining worldly and spiritual heights available only to men, the Dragon Princess must undergo sexual transformation into a male before attaining buddhahood. This raises important issues about Buddhism and gender, a topic that will be explored further in chapter 9.

A third theme of the *Lotus Sutra* is the depiction of bodhisattvas as savior figures, thus giving rise to the cults of bodhisattvas. Chapter 23 celebrates the bodhisattva Medicine King and chapter 25 the bodhisattva Sound Observer (Guanyin). Many Chinese converted to Buddhism not so much from reading and studying the doctrines expounded in the *Lotus Sutra* but by being exposed to the call for faith and devotion found in these chapters. The chapter about Medicine King gave rise to the cult of self-immolation in China. According to Mahayana Buddhism, after a person gives rise to the aspiration for enlightenment, he embarks on the bodhisattva path by practicing the six perfections of giving, morality, vigor, patience, meditation, and wisdom. In practicing the perfection of giving, the gift of the body is superior to all kinds of material gifts. A bodhisattva practices giving in two ways: he either makes donations to help sentient beings or makes offerings to the Buddha. There are many stories glorifying bodhisattvas who sacrifice their lives to save sentient beings from starvation. Perfection of giving also includes making offerings to the Buddha. However, the case of Medicine King is different, for he performs self-immolation as an offering to a buddha in the past.

Anointing his body with fragrant oil, he appeared before the Buddha Sun Moon Pure Bright Virtue, wrapped his body in heavenly jeweled robes, poured fragrant oil over his head, and, calling on the transcendental powers, set fire to his body. The glow shone forth, illuminating worlds equal in number to the sands of eighty million Ganges. The Buddhas in these worlds simultaneously spoke out in praise, saying: "Excellent, excellent, good man! This is true diligence. This is what is called a true Dharma offering to the Thus Come One. Though one may use flowers, incense, necklaces, . . . presenting offerings of all such things as these, he can never match this! Though one makes donations of his realm and cities, his wife and children, he is no match for this! Good man, this is called the foremost donation of all. Among all donations, this is the most highly prized, for one is offering the Dharma to the Thus Come Ones!" (283).

Inspired by the legend of Medicine King in the *Lotus Sutra,* some Buddhist believers followed his example. Their stories are found in the *Accounts in Dissemination and Praise of the Lotus,* a collection of miracle tales compiled in the Tang (618–907). The stories are about monks and nuns who lived in the seventh century. This is a story about two nuns who were sisters.

> Their names have been forgotten, but they both recited the *Lotus Sūtra,* held a deep loathing for the physical body, and together conceived the desire to give up their lives [in offering to the Dharma]. [To this end,] they set restrictions on clothing and diet and prescribed for themselves a regimen of painful austerities. They ingested various perfumed oils and gradually reduced their intake of coarse rice, until they gave up grains altogether and took only fragrant honey. [Even then,] their energy and spiritual determination remained as vigorous and fresh as ever. They announced [widely] to the monks and laity [around them] that at an appointed time in the future they would immolate themselves.
>
> On the evening of the eighth day of the second month during the third year of the Zhenguan era [629], they set up two high seats in the middle of one of the large boulevards of Jingzhou. Then they

wrapped their bodies from head to foot in waxed cloth, leaving only their faces exposed. The crowds gathered like a mountain; their songs of praise filled the air like clouds. The two women together began to chant the *Lotus Sūtra*. When they reached the "Medicine King" chapter, the older sister first ignited the head of the younger sister, and the younger in turn lit the head of the older sister. Simultaneously the two blazed up, like two torches in the clear night. As the flames crept down over their eyes, the sound of their voices became even more distinct. But, as it gradually arrived at their noses and mouths, they grew quiet [and their voices were heard no more]. [They remained seated upright] until dawn, linked together on their two seats. Then, all at once, the fire gave out. [As the smoke and flame cleared,] there amidst their charred and desiccated bones lay two tongues, both perfectly intact. The crowd gasped in awe. [A short time later] a tall stūpa was constructed for them.[8]

This record provides a detailed description of the ritual of self-immolation. Many other tales follow a similar format. It describes the preparation the sister-nuns undertook: what kind of diet they followed and how the ritual was carried out. The ritual took place publicly, witnessed by many people. The story makes clear that they, like other self-immolators, modeled themselves on Medicine King. Their devotion and faith in the *Lotus Sutra* were finally confirmed by the miracle of their intact tongues. This miracle resulted from the sisters' constant chanting of the *Lotus Sutra,* an act of devotion extolled by the scripture itself. Indeed, a number of miracle tales are about the uncorrupted lips and tongues of those who chanted the *Lotus Sutra.*

Self-immolation is performed not only as a form of extreme devotion but also as a form of protest in defense of the Dharma. A famous example in recent times was the Vietnamese monk Thich Quang Duc, who in June 1963 burned himself to death on the streets of Saigon. He did so because President Ngo Dinh Diem favored Catholicism over Buddhism. More recently, Tibetan monks and nuns have immolated themselves to protest the treatment of Tibetan Buddhism by the Communist Chinese government.

Another favorite devotional practice was to carry out marathon chanting of the *Lotus Sutra. The Lives of Nuns,* compiled by Baochang in 516, includes stories of several nuns who were experts in chanting sutras and could chant the entire sutra within a very short period of time. For instance, Zhixian (c. 300–c. 370) was an expert in chanting the *Lotus Sutra*. Even in her old age, she could chant its entirety in only one day and one night. According to Kathryn Tsai, this would require chanting about fifty words per minute nonstop over a twenty-four-hour period. If she took any rest, she would have had to chant much faster. Another nun, Sengnian (415–504), also loved to chant the *Lotus Sutra*. She did it seven times in a day and a night. Since the *Lotus Sutra* contains approximately 500,000 words at a minimum, to chant the sutra seven times in a day and a night would require chanting approximately 20,800 words per hour, or 347 words per minute, or 5.7 words per second. Some nuns were famous not only for the speed but also for the frequency of their chanting. For instance, Daoshou chanted the *Lotus Sutra* three thousand times and frequently saw auspicious omens. In 439, on the seventh day of the ninth month, a jeweled canopy descended and hovered over her. To chant the sutra three thousand times would have taken her eight years, nonstop, one second per word.[9]

The *Lotus Sutra* is the foundational scripture of the Tiantai tradition, one of the two Chinese Buddhist doctrinal schools discussed in chapter 5.

The *Vimalakīrti Sutra*

Like the *Lotus Sutra,* the *Vimalakīrti Sutra* is one of the most influential and popular Buddhist scriptures not only in China but also in East Asia. Unlike the *Lotus Sutra,* the *Vimalakīrti Sutra* uses dialogues and paradoxes to convey some of the most central teachings of Mahayana Buddhism. This literary device made it a favorite text for monks and literati who were actively engaged in the Dark Learning and Pure Conversation movements in the fourth and fifth centuries. The sutra was translated six times into Chinese, the earliest version dated 225, but the version done by Kumārajīva in 406 is the most famous one. Its popularity is attested by the great number of commentaries written on the sutra and the many artistic depictions of the debate between Vimalakīrti and Mañjuśrī, an important theme of the scripture, on the frescos and sculptures in the cave temples of Dunhuang, Yungang, and Longmen. The scripture has remained a perennial favorite in the history of Chinese Buddhism. It exerted great influence on Chan Buddhism. The *Platform Sutra of the Sixth Patriarch,* to be discussed in chapter 6, for instance, quotes from it several times. The Chan myth about Bodhidharma's transmission of the mind Dharma to the second patriarch, who remained silent, recalls Vimalakīrti's own "lion's roar of

silence." Moreover, as chapter 9 shows, the Humanistic Buddhism promoted by contemporary Buddhist leaders in Taiwan advocates building the
Pure Land on earth based on the statement found in the first chapter of the
text: "When the mind is pure, the Buddha land will be pure."[10]

The sutra opens as the *Lotus Sutra* and many other Mahayana sutras
do, with an astonishing miracle. A huge assembly of disciples and bodhisattvas has gathered to hear the Buddha preach. A group of Licchavi youths
appears from the crowd and offers parasols to the Buddha. When the last
parasol is laid at the Buddha's feet, all the parasols are miraculously transformed into a single giant parasol that covers the many universes. The features of all the worlds are reflected on its underside, complete with the
buddhas of the ten directions preaching in their respective buddha fields.
The assembled multitude is filled with wonder and astonishment by this
cosmic vision. The Buddha uses magic as an expedient device to make ordinary people see that what they take as reality is in fact empty in nature.
Here the link among magic (or miracle), vision, expedient device, and emptiness is demonstrated with startling clarity.

What is emptiness? It is a translation for *śūnyatā* in Sanskrit and *kong*
in Chinese. The *Perfection of Wisdom* literature discussed in the introduction centers on this idea, for the insight that everything is empty is none
other than wisdom. *Śūnyatā* is compared to the empty space of the sky or
the zero point, the mathematic notion of zero signifying the absence of
discrimination, the state prior to the quantifying and divisive act of enu-
meration and numbering. It means that everything is not independent and
substantial. It does not have an intrinsic nature. However, the denial of
separate substantiality is united with a positive assertion of the interdependent nature of all things. What prevents us from seeing the true nature of
everything as empty is our dualistic way of thinking, which makes discriminatory distinctions. Therefore, not to engage in this way of thinking is
the path to salvation. The insight that everything in the world is *śūnya*
ironically leads to an active engagement with this world. It frees one from
being attached to a fixed way of behaving. That is why in the scripture the
enlightened protagonist, Vimalakīrti, uses all kinds of unconventional
methods, be they words or actions, to teach the Dharma.

The Buddha teaches this lesson by first making the paradoxical statement that the land is pure because, out of compassion for sentient beings,
bodhisattvas have already created a pure land here and now with their pure
mind. But Śāriputra, the spokesman for Hinayana tradition, is troubled

because he only sees a land full of impurities. The Buddha tells him that the reason he sees the land as impure is that "your mind has highs and lows and does not rest on Buddha wisdom" (30). The "highs and lows" refer to the mind that engages in making distinctions, or what the Daoist philosopher Zhuangzi calls "pairs of opposites." In contrast to ordinary people, the Buddha does not engage in this kind of thinking. He is said to be "In mind and action impartial, like the empty sky" (23). He is called the "Great physician king" not only because he is the "healer of old age, sickness and death" but also because he frees sentient beings from distorted views by expedient means. The main character, Vimalakīrti, is another skillful teacher who is an expert in using *upāya*. He is a living exemplar of someone who has successfully combined opposites by transcending them. He is a layman, yet also a bodhisattva. Titled "Expedient Means," chapter 2 is devoted to a description of this enigmatic figure. "Though dressed in the white robes of a layman, he observed all the rules of pure conduct laid down for monks, and though he lived at home, he felt no attachment to the threefold world. One could see he had a wife and children, yet he was at all times chaste in action; obviously he had kin and household attendants, yet he always delighted in withdrawing from them; he ate and drank like others, but what he truly savored was the joy of meditation. In a spirit of trust and harmony he conducted all kinds of business enterprises, but though he reaped worldly profits, he took no delight in these" (33).

For the sake of helping others, he engages in antinomian activities and visits casinos, brothels, and bars, all for the sake of teaching them Dharma. "If he visited the gambling parlors, it was solely to bring enlightenment to those there. . . . He entered houses of ill fame to teach the folly of fleshly desire, entered wine shops in order to encourage those with a will to quit them" (33).

Although he is a very successful married businessman, Vimalakīrti is far more advanced than the Buddha's foremost disciples, who are still bound by dualistic thought. He uses his illness as an expedient device to teach. When the Buddha asks his advanced disciples to visit Vimalakīrti and inquire about his illness, all of them decline, saying that they are not competent to do so because in the past the layman has shown them to be mistaken in their views. While the disciples adhere to the conventional Hinayana practices, Vimalakīrti overturns those practices by giving a new interpretation according to the Mahayana teaching of *śūnyatā*.

He redefines Buddhist meditation practice. While sitting in quiet meditation, Śāriputra is told that it is not true quiet sitting. True quiet sitting is not the form but the mental attitude. "Not arising out of your samadhi of complete cessation and yet showing yourself in the ceremony of daily life—this is quiet sitting. Not abandoning the principles of the Way and yet showing yourself in the activities of a common mortal—this is quiet sitting. . . . Entering nirvana without having put an end of earthly desires—this is quiet sitting" (37).

Subhūti is an advanced disciple known for his wisdom. When he comes to Vimalakīrti's house begging for food, the latter tells him that he is worthy to receive it only if he meets these conditions: "Subhūti, if you cannot cut yourself off from lewdness, anger, and stupidity and yet not be a part of these; . . . if you can seem to be a perpetrator of the five cardinal sins and yet gain emancipation; . . . if you are willing to join hands with the host of devils and make the defilements your companion; if you can be no different from all these devils and these dusts and defilements; if you can bear hatred toward all living beings, slander the Buddhas, vilify the Law, not be counted among the assembly of monks, and in the end never attain nirvana—if you can do all this, then you will be worthy to receive food" (41–43).

These contrasting and opposing qualities aptly describe Vimalakīrti himself. He is all things to all men, moving freely among the good and the bad, appealing to them on their own familiar terms. He is in the world but not of it. He asks Subhūti to be like him. Upali is the disciple who specializes in monastic discipline. When two monks violate the rules, he explains to them what they must do to make restitution. Vimalakīrti comes by and rebukes Upāli:

> Ah, Upāli, do not make the offense these monks have committed even worse than it is! You should go about wiping out their doubts and remorse at once and not trouble their minds further! Why do I say so? Because their offenses by its nature does not exist either inside them, or outside, or in between. As the Buddha has taught us, when the mind is defiled, the living being will be defiled. When the mind is pure, the living being will be pure. As the mind is, so will be the offense or defilement . . . deluded thoughts are defilement. Where there are no deluded thoughts, that is purity. Topsy-turvy thinking is defilement. Where there is no topsy-turvy thinking, that is purity. (47)

"Topsy-turvy thinking" is a colorful way of describing the deluded mind engaged in dualistic and dichotomous thinking. Failing to know everything is empty, Upāli is bound by the letter of the monastic discipline and discriminates between what acts are allowed and what are not, or between purity and defilement. For Vimalakīrti, however, it is not the act per se but the mind behind it that determines the nature of the act. The mind can only make the correct determination when one sees reality as empty.

He is even more revolutionary in his reinterpretation of renunciation and the meaning of "home leaving." When a person wishes to leave home and join the monastery, he must have his parents' permission. But Vimalakīrti tells the sons of rich men in the audience that if they set their minds on attaining buddhahood, "That is the same as leaving the household, the same as taking monastic vows" (49). If a person wishes to become a monk, he does not have to get permission from his parents before shaving off his hair. It is not the outer form but the inner aspiration for buddhahood that sets a person apart as a true renunciate.

Illness as Metaphor

After all the advanced disciples have declined to visit and inquire about Vimalakīrti's illness, Mañjuśrī, the bodhisattva of wisdom, agrees to go. Chapter 5, "Inquiring about the Illness," is one of the highlights of the sutra. When he enters the house, he sees Vimalakīrti lying alone on a bed in an empty room. Their initial exchanges indicate that both are deeply steeped in the dialectic of the *Perfection of Wisdom* tradition. Vimalakīrti said, "Welcome, Mañjuśrī! You come without the marks of coming, you see me without the marks of seeing me." Mañjuśrī said, "Just so, layman. What has already come can hardly be coming. And what has already departed can hardly be departing. What do I mean? What comes has nowhere to come from, what departs has nowhere to go, and what is seen cannot be further seen" (65). In everyday life, we speak of coming, going, seeing, and being seen. However, in the light of *śūnyatā*, there is neither coming nor going, and neither seeing nor being seen. The two exchange repartee on the level of ultimate truth.

Mañjuśrī then returns to the level of conventional truth and asks about the cause of Vimalakīrti's illness and how long he has been ill. Vimalakīrti answers,

> Because all living beings are sick, therefore I am sick. If all living beings are relieved of sickness, then my sickness will be mended. Why?

Because the bodhisattva for the sake of living beings enters the realm of birth and death, and because he is in the realm of birth and death he suffers illness. If living beings can gain release from illness, then the bodhisattva will no longer be ill. It is like the case of a rich man who has only one child. If the child falls ill, then the father and mother too will be ill, but if the child's illness is cured, the father and mother too will be cured. The bodhisattva is like this, for he loves living beings as though they were his children. If living beings are sick, the bodhisattva will be sick, but if living beings are cured, the bodhisattva too will be cured. You ask what cause this illness arises from—the illness of the bodhisattva arises from the great compassion. (65–66)

Several important messages are revealed here: first, illness is a metaphor for samsara, the realm of life and death. Second, living beings who are caught in samsara are ill. Third, Vimalakīrti is ill because living beings are ill, just as parents are ill if the child is ill. Fourth, Vimalakīrti uses illness as the expedient device. Fifth and finally, he is not only the bodhisattva but the father of living beings. In the *Lotus Sutra,* as we have seen, the Buddha is said to be the father of living beings. It is indeed a bold claim that Vimalakīrti, a layman, plays the same role.

Interestingly, like the Buddha, Vimalakīrti is also the king of physicians. He is ill, but he also has the cure. As a good physician, he first gives the diagnosis, then the etiology, and finally the prescription. This is very much the way that the Buddha formulates the Four Noble Truths in his first sermon. As we recall, the Buddha points out in the first Noble Truth that there is suffering, which is the diagnosis. In the second Noble Truth he says that desire is the cause of suffering, which is the etiology. The third Noble Truth of nirvana being the end of suffering is the prognosis, and the fourth Noble Truth of the Noble Eightfold Path is the prescription. So, according to Vimalakīrti, what is the source of illness? Instead of desire, it is dualistic views that make us ill with suffering. If one hopes to do away with dualistic views, one should do away with the thought of "I" separate from other living beings. The insight of emptiness dissolves dualistic views in regard to all phenomena and enables one to see all things equally. The consequence of viewing things nondually is what a bodhisattva does.

In early Buddhism, samsara and nirvana are sharply opposed, and the call is to forsake one for the other. The new Mahayana teaching of *śūnyatā* does away with this dichotomy. When one engages in dualistic thinking, one will inevitably be mired in liking some things and disliking others. Intellectual discrimination ends with emotional entanglement. Vimalakīrti says about transcending dualistic thinking, "To be in the realm of birth and death without following its tainted ways, to dwell in nirvana while not seeking eternal extinction—such is the practice of the bodhisattva" (72). Anticipating a possible misunderstanding of emptiness, Vimalakīrti makes clear that the insight of emptiness does not lead to inactivity but, on the contrary, to compassionate action. "Though he moves in the realm of emptiness, he plants many roots of virtue—such is the practice of the bodhisattva" (73).

The Bodhisattva

The sutra uses humor and magic to demonstrate how Vimalakīrti the bodhisattva behaves compared with the disciples who represent early Buddhism. In chapter 6, "Beyond Comprehension," the great assembly of disciples and bodhisattvas arrive at Vimalakīrti's room. Śāriputra is worried when he does not see any seat in the empty room. Intuiting what is on his mind, Vimalakīrti asks teasingly, "Did you come here for the sake of the Law, or are you just looking for a place to sit?" Śāriputra says that he came for the Law; Vimalakīrti then says, "Ah Śāriputra, a seeker of the Law doesn't concern himself even about life or limb, much less about a seat!" (75). Using his transcendental powers, he has thirty-two thousand lion seats brought from a buddha land into his room, which becomes broad and spacious enough to hold them all. Śāriputra is bewildered by this miraculous event and asks for an explanation. Vimalakīrti says that this is an example of buddhas' and bodhisattvas' emancipation called "Beyond Comprehension." It is beyond comprehension because both space and time are transformed.

> When a bodhisattva dwells in this emancipation, he can take something as tall and broad as Mount Sumeru and put it inside a mustard seed without enlarging one or shrinking the other and Mount Sumeru, king of mountains, will still have its original shape. . . . This bodhisattva can take the waters of the four great oceans and pour them into the opening that holds a single hair . . . and those great seas will still have their original form. . . . This bodhisattva can stretch seven days into a kalpa, so that to those beings they really seem like a whole kalpa . . . this bodhisattva can squeeze a kalpa into seven days so that to those beings it seems like only seven days. (78–79)

This kind of emancipation is called "Beyond Comprehension" because it defies ordinary logic. Like the previous scene of filling Vimalakīrti's room with huge lion seats, this is a magical display to shock the audience and to compel them to step outside their ordinary dualistic consciousness. It is none other than a display of *upāya*. A bodhisattva who is a master of *upāya* may even appear as a devil if that is what is needed in his work of teaching people. "Among those who play the part of devil kings in the immeasurable asamkhyas of worlds in the ten directions, there are many who in fact are bodhisattvas dwelling in the emancipation Beyond Comprehension. They employ their skill in expedient means to teach and convert living beings by appearing in the guise of devil kings" (81). In this regard, the *Vimalakīrti Sutra* goes further than the *Lotus Sutra* in pushing the limit of *upāya*. In order to break down all dichotomies, be they intellectual, emotional, or moral, the sutra transposes traditional values. According to early Buddhism, desire is the cause of suffering. The most effective way to eliminate desire is to leave home and live the life of a celibate monastic. The new teaching of emptiness breaks down the opposition between living as a layman subject to desire and living as a monk free from the temptation of desire. Such a distinction is a mark of ignorance. In fact, the householder who must deal with desire is capable of attaining buddhahood. In one parable the householder is compared to the lotus that grows in the mud, while the monk is the lotus that fails to grow on the high ground.

> The lotus does not grow on the upland plain; the lotus grows in the mud and mire of a damp low-lying place. . . . It is only when living beings are in the midst of the mire of earthly desire that they can turn to the Buddha Law. . . . You should understand that all the various earthly desires are the seeds of the Thus Come One. If you do not descend into the vast ocean, you can never acquire a priceless pearl. In the same way, if you do not enter the great sea of earthly desires, you can never acquire the treasure of comprehensive wisdom. (95–96)

The householder bodhisattva is best exemplified by Vimalakīrti.

Such a novel interpretation of *upāya* is based on a thorough understanding of *śūnyatā,* the core of Mahayana wisdom. The relationship between the two is set forth in these verses:

Wisdom is the bodhisattva's mother,
expedient means his father;
of those who guide and teach all beings,
there are none not born of these.
Dharma joy is his wife,
pity and compassion of mind are his daughters,
the good mind and sincerity his sons,
final emptiness and tranquility his dwelling. (96–97)

Wisdom and expedient means must go hand in hand. They are the parents who give birth to the bodhisattva. This statement makes it absolutely clear: "Wisdom without expedient means is bondage; wisdom with expedient means is liberation. Expedient means without wisdom is bondage; expedient means with wisdom is liberation" (70). When a bodhisattva achieves the perfect union of wisdom and expedient means, he is fully endowed with compassion and can transform himself into gods, water, fire, medicinal herbs, and food to save living beings.

At times he becomes the sun, the moon, a heavenly being,
an Indra, a Brahma, Lord of the world;
at others he may become earth or water,
or again become wind or fire.
If during the kalpa there is pestilence,
he manifests himself as medicinal herbs;
those who drink potions made from them
will be healed of sickness, cleansed of all poison.
If during the kalpa there is famine,
He manifests his body as food and drink,
First relieving hunger and thirst,
Then telling people of the Law. (100–101)

Similarly, like Vimalakīrti, a bodhisattva can appear as a village headman, a merchant, an official, a servant, a man, or a woman if this will facilitate the work of teaching the Dharma.

Sometimes he shows himself as a woman of pleasure,
Enticing those prone to lechery.
First he catches them with the hook of desire,
Then leads them into the Buddha way. (102)

This is a very significant passage for two reasons. First, instead of eliminating desire, one should welcome it. Why? Because desire serves as fertile ground for spiritual training, just as dirty mud enables a lotus to grow. Desire is used here as *upāya* to lead others to enlightenment. Second and more significantly, here a bodhisattva transforms himself into a woman instead of the Dragon Princess transforming herself into a man as in the *Lotus*. The inversion of values in the sutra discussed so far pales in comparison to this new take on gender. The transgressive challenge to tradition makes this scripture unique in Mahayana Buddhism.

The Goddess

Chapter 7 of the *Vimalakīrti Sutra* tells the celebrated story of the Goddess, who is a female bodhisattva. Since false distinction and "topsy-turvy" thinking cause suffering, when wisdom frees us from engaging in discrimination, all oppositions between self and others, monastic and lay, rich and poor, purity and pollution, nirvana and samsara, male and female should all fall away. But according to Buddhism, a bodhisattva or a buddha must be male because Śākyamuni Buddha was male. He was adorned with thirty-two major marks and eighty minor marks. While all the marks were masculine, one was uniquely so, for it was said that he had a retracted penis. To conform to this particular physiological feature, a woman must first transform herself into a man, as the case of the Dragon Princess demonstrates in the *Lotus Sutra*.

The Goddess is among the assembly gathered in the layman's room. Delighted by the witty and profound exchange between Mañjuśrī and Vimalakīrti, she scatters heavenly flowers over the bodhisattvas and advanced disciples. When the flowers touch the bodies of the bodhisattvas, they immediately fall off, but they stick to the bodies of the disciples even when they try to shake the flowers off with their supernatural powers. This makes Śāriputra very uncomfortable, because being adorned with flowers is contrary to the Buddhist monastic rules. The Goddess tells him, "Don't say these flowers are not in accordance with the Law. Why? Because the flowers make no such distinction. You in your thinking have made up these distinctions, that's all. The flowers do not stick to the bodhisattvas because they have already cut off all thought of distinction" (87). Impressed by her, Śāriputra asks, "Why don't you change out of this female body?" (90). He means this as a compliment, reflecting the conventional view that no female can be so advanced as the Goddess yet still retain her female form. The

Goddess tells him that all things, including the body, have no fixed form; therefore, why does he ask her to change out of her female form?

She uses magic and illusion to teach Śāriputra a lesson by changing him into a goddess like herself, while she takes on Śāriputra's form. She then asks him to change out of this female body. Flustered, he answers, "I don't know why I have suddenly changed and taken on a female body!" The ensuing exchange brings the rhetoric of illusion to center stage, arguing that one's physical appearance is mere illusion. The Goddess says, "Śāriputra, who is not a woman, appears in a woman's body. And the same is true of all women—though they appear in women's bodies, they are not women. Therefore the Buddha teaches that all phenomena are neither male nor female" (91). The Goddess uses her magical powers a second time and restores Śāriputra to his former body. When she asks him, "Where now is the form and shape of your female body?" he answers, "The form and shape of my female body does not exist yet does not not exist." The Goddess gives her approval and says, "All things are just like that—they do not exist, yet do not not exist. And that they do not exist, yet do not not exist, is exactly what the Buddha teaches" (91).

When one must use language to describe the insight of nonduality, one of the favorite ways is to state that it is neither this nor that, as is done here. But are there other methods to express the state of nonduality? Chapter 9, "Entering the Gate of Nondualism," provides some answers.

Entering the Gate of Nondualism

Chapter 9 opens with Vimalakīrti asking the many bodhisattvas how a bodhisattva enters the gate of nondualism. He is not seeking guidance but testing their knowledge, like a teacher asking about what the students know. In most scriptures, the role of the questioner is usually assumed by the Buddha. But here it is Vimalakīrti, the householder. The implication is that this layman is more advanced than all the attending bodhisattvas. This indeed proves to be the case at the end of the chapter, after each bodhisattva presents his answer.

The dualisms mentioned are the ones with which all of us are familiar. They are, among others, samsara and nirvana, I and not I, ignorance and enlightenment, form and emptiness. On the level of conventional truth, they are different because we discriminate between the dualities in each pair. However, illuminated by the insight of *śūnyatā,* we realize that they should not be differentiated and thus, on the level of ultimate truth,

"Vimalakīrti and the Doctrine of Nonduality" by Wang Zhenpeng (ca. 1275–ca. 1330).
China. Dated 1308. Metropolitan Museum of Art

they are not different. By abandoning dualistic views, one enters the gate of nondualism, which is "beyond comprehension" when viewed from the perspective of common sense.

The bodhisattva Good Will says, "The realm of birth and death and that of nirvana form a dualism. But if one sees the true nature of birth and death, one sees that there is no birth or death, no binding, no unbinding, no birth, no extinction. One who understands in this way thereby enters the gate of nondualism." The bodhisattva Universal Guardian says, "'I' and 'non-I' form a dualism. But when one cannot grasp even 'I,' how can one grasp 'non-I'? One who has seen into the true nature of 'I' will no longer give rise to these two concepts, and in this way enter the gate of nondualism." The bodhisattva Lightning God says, "Enlightenment and ignorance form a dualism. But the true nature of ignorance is none other than enlightenment. And enlightenment cannot be seized but is apart from all enumerations. One dwells in the center, in the equality without dualism, and in this way enters the gate of nondualism" (106). The bodhisattva Joyful Seeing says, "Form and the emptiness of form constitute a dualism. But form is none other than emptiness; emptiness does not represent the extinction of form. Form is itself empty by nature. . . . Dwelling in the midst of these concepts and understanding them thoroughly, one may in this way enter the gate of nondualism" (107). This statement is the same as is found in the *Heart Sutra,* a succinct summary of the *Perfection of Wisdom* corpus.

When Mañjuśrī, the bodhisattva foremost in wisdom, is asked the same question, he replies, "To my way of thinking, all dharmas are without words, without explanations, without purport, without cognition, removed from all questions and answers. In this way one may enter the gate of nondualism." For Mañjuśrī, then, the highest spiritual state is beyond language, because all words fail to do justice to it. This is why the sages who composed the Hindu sacred texts called *Upaniṣads* described the ultimate reality as "*neti, neti* (not this, not this)." Medieval Christian mystics preferred using *via negativa* (through negation) to refer to God. The *Daode jing* also begins with the declaration "The Way that can be talked about is not the constant Way." Yet, although Mañjuśrī, like his spiritual companions, knows that language is inadequate, he still uses it to deny the adequacy of language. Is there any other way to transcend the dilemma? Mañjuśrī says to Vimalakīrti, "Each of us has given an explanation. Now, sir, it is your turn to speak. How does the bodhisattva enter the gate of nondualism?" and what happens next is something no one expects: "At that time Vimalakīrti remained silent and did not speak a word." This lion's roar of silence makes Mañjuśrī burst out in praise, "Excellent, excellent. Not a word, not a syllable—this truly is to enter the gate of nondualism" (110–111). This is perhaps another reason the sutra is so beloved by the Chinese, who are familiar with what the *Daode jing* says about the Daoist sage in chapter 56: "One who knows does not speak; one who speaks does not know."

Self-Glorification of the *Vimalakīrti Sutra*

We have examined two Mahayana sutras that have exerted tremendous influence on Chinese Buddhists down the centuries. Although they are different in some respects, they also share many features in common. While the *Lotus Sutra* is preached by the primordial Buddha, the *Vimalakīrti Sutra* is by a layman bodhisattva. While the *Lotus Sutra* uses parables and the emphasis is more on compassion, the *Vimalakīrti Sutra* uses paradoxes and the emphasis is more on wisdom. In terms of reception, the former has more general appeal and the latter is more attractive to literati and monks interested in philosophy.

However, what they share is as important as their differences. Both affirm universal buddhahood and the central importance of *upāya*. Finally, although to a lesser extent, the *Vimalakīrti Sutra* glories itself like the *Lotus Sutra*, encouraging people to "believe, understand, accept, uphold, read, recite, and practice it" (137). When a person does these things, the blessings will be immeasurable. Not just blessing but even more exalted reward is awaiting such a person. "If there are those who believe and understand this sutra, even just one four-line verse of it, and can expound it to others, let it be known that such persons will forthwith receive a prophecy of the attainment of *anuttara-samyak-sanbodhi* [perfect complete enlightenment]" (135). Faith and missionary zeal assure that one will attain buddhahood. This tendency to promote and elevate itself is already seen in the earliest Mahayana scriptures such as the *Perfection of Wisdom in 8,000 Lines.* As some scholars have suggested, this might be a strategy for the survival and spread of the movement. In order to spread the message to more people in faraway places and future times, it is necessary to convince people of its truth. The scriptures must be memorized, recited, and copied, and there also must be preachers who can lecture on them. Indeed, even after Buddhism took deep root in China, the recitation and copying of sutras remained favorite devotional activities, as we have read above. Dharma masters were as much respected and admired as meditators and translators.

As in the *Perfection of Wisdom in 8,000 Lines,* the teaching of emptiness is characteristic of early stage Mahayana scriptures, such as the *Lotus Sutra* and the *Vimalakīrti Sutra.* While this teaching is secondary to those of the eternal Buddha and universal buddhahood in the *Lotus Sutra,* it is central in the *Vimalakīrti Sutra.* The philosophy of emptiness was formalized in the Indian Madhyamaka school.

There are three philosophical schools in Indian Mahayana Buddhism: Madhyamaka, Yogācāra, and Tathāgatagarbha. While the first two enjoyed great popularity and constituted the mainstream traditions in India, Tathāgatagarbha thought did not receive the same attention. It was in China and subsequently East Asia that the latter became the dominant tradition. It is otherwise known as the teaching of Buddha nature. We shall discuss the scriptures central to this tradition. The discussion of the thought of Madhyamaka and Yogācāra and their development in China will be in chapter 5.

Tathāgatagarbha

Tathāgatagarbha thought, the third Buddhist philosophical tradition, is introduced by a short sutra, the *Tathāgatagarbha Sutra,* composed in the middle of the third century. Tathāgata is the epithet of the Buddha favored by the Mahayanists. The Chinese translation, Rulai, means that the Buddha is someone "Who Has Thus Come," implying that the manner of the Buddha's coming into the world is beyond our comprehension. The most common meanings of *garbha* are "womb" and "embryo." The Chinese translated it as "secret store" (*cang*). The message of the sutra is that all sentient beings have the potential to become buddhas. This is because all the excellent virtues of the Buddha are stored within them. However, because these virtues are covered over by the vexations (*kleśas*) of ignorance, greed, anger, and lust, they are hidden. Once the vexations are removed, buddhahood is revealed. This optimistic good news forms the foundation of Buddha nature thought.

The *Tathāgatagarbha Sutra* opens with the Buddha expressing himself in a verse:

> It is like the wilted flowers;
> Before their petals have opened,
> One with supernatural vision can see the unstained body of the
>   Tathāgata.
> After the wilted flowers are removed,
> One sees, without obstacle, the Teacher,
> Who, in order to sever kleśas,
> Triumphantly appears in the world.
> The Buddha sees that all kinds of beings
> Universally possess the tathāgatagarbha.
> It is covered by countless kleśas,
> Just like a tangle of smelly, wilted petals.
> So I, on behalf of all beings,
> Everywhere expound the true Dharma,
> In order to help them remove their kleśas
> And quickly reach the buddha way.
> I see with my buddha eye
> That in the bodies of all beings
> There lies concealed the buddhagarbha,
> So I expound the Dharma in order to reveal it.[11]

The sutra uses eight similes to explain how *tathāgatagarbha* is covered over by *kleśas*. It is like: (1) pure honey in a cave or on a tree, surrounded and protected by a swarm of bees; (2) a kernel of wheat that has not yet had its husk removed; (3) genuine gold that has fallen into a pit of waste and been submerged and not seen for years; (4) a store of treasure hidden beneath an impoverished household; (5) the pit inside a mango that does not decay; (6) a statue of pure gold that is wrapped in worn-out rags; (7) a poor, ugly, despised woman who bears a noble son in her womb; (8) the radiant and dazzling color of a statue of pure gold hidden within a scorched and blackened earthen mold.

While the majority of the similes indicate that buddhahood is already in existence, two of them, that of the pit of the mango and the fetus carried within the womb of a poor and despised woman, indicate that buddhahood is to be realized in the future. This ambiguity is also present in the *Nirvana Sutra,* in which the terms *tathāgatagarbha* and "Buddha nature" both appear and are used synonymously.

The *Nirvana Sutra*

There are two Chinese translations of the *Nirvana Sutra,* one by the famous pilgrim Faxian and Buddhabhadra (359–429) in 418 in the south and one by Dharmarakṣema (385–431) in 421 in the north. The former version contains only the first six volumes; Dharmarakṣema's version contains the complete forty volumes and has become the standard. The scripture was widely circulated and popular during the fifth and sixth centuries.

In the history of Chinese and of East Asian Buddhist thought generally, the *Nirvana Sutra* occupies a unique position. There are three central themes: (1) the Buddha is eternal; (2) nirvana has four characteristics: permanency, bliss, self, and purity; and (3) all sentient beings have Buddha nature and thus can achieve buddhahood.

The *Lotus Sutra* also proclaims that the Buddha has always existed and that all can become buddhas. However, it downplays nirvana in contrast to buddhahood by comparing it to one day's wages versus the inheritance of the entire estate. The *Nirvana Sutra,* however, treats it as equivalent to buddhahood, the supreme goal of the religious endeavor. What is even more astonishing is how nirvana is reimagined. In early Buddhism, nirvana is compared to the blowing out of a flame (karma). No positive terms are used to describe it. But nirvana is here described in very positive terms, in contrast to samsara. Whereas everything in this world is impermanent, suffering, no self, and impure, nirvana is exactly the opposite. If reality is emptiness in the literature of the *Perfection of Wisdom,* in the *Nirvana Sutra,* reality is nonemptiness. This positive understanding about reality is a distinctive feature of a group of scriptures representing Tathāgatagarbha thought. The *Nirvana Sutra* presents itself as the core of the Dharma because of its central teaching of Buddha nature.

The teaching that all sentient beings possess Buddha nature has received much scholarly attention concerning two issues. Does it mean that, regardless of immoral behaviors, all people have Buddha nature and will become buddhas? Does it mean that all people already possess Buddha nature, or is it something that all can potentially attain? This is similar to the ambiguity seen earlier in the similes of the *Tathāgatagarbha Sutra*.

The first issue concerns whether the *icchantikas*—evil people who commit murder, theft, fornication, and lying or, more specifically, those who kill their parents, kill arhats, or cause the Buddha to bleed and destroy the harmony of the monastic community—have Buddha nature and can become buddhas. The *Nirvana Sutra* mentions these people but holds contradictory views about them. One view is that the *icchantikas* do not have Buddha nature and are unable to give rise to the thought for enlightenment. They are compared to a burned-out seed that cannot germinate, a muddied pearl that cannot be cleaned, or a terminally ill patient whom no physician can heal. In contrast, another view affirms that even the *icchantikas* have Buddha nature, because there is a difference between Buddha nature and the root of goodness. Human beings have either the root of goodness or the root of evil. Although the *icchantikas* are devoid of the root of goodness, their Buddha nature is not cut off. Listening to the Dharma plays a crucial role. Hearing the Dharma can awaken the Buddha nature of those who presently do not possess the root of goodness.

Daosheng (d. 434) was a great admirer of the sutra. When he read the statement about *icchantikas*' lack of Buddha nature in the incomplete translation by Faxian, he boldly claimed that this was incorrect. This caused a big scandal, and he was almost expelled from the monastic order. But he was vindicated when he found statements affirming the *icchantikas*' possessing Buddha nature in the complete translation by Dharmarakṣema. The Chinese Buddhist tradition has concurred with Daosheng. The belief that all sentient beings possess Buddha nature has been the foundation of the Buddhist schools created in the Sui and Tang dynasties during the sixth to tenth centuries.

The second issue, whether Buddha nature is fully present or is in a latent state, also gave rise to vigorous debate. This is a crucial question because it is existentially important. It asks whether we are already enlightened and are buddhas even though we live in the world of samsara, or whether we will achieve enlightenment and become buddhas only in the future. The sutra provides an answer by explaining what is meant by "having Buddha nature."

There are three ways of having: first, to have in the future, secondly, to have at present, and thirdly, to have in the past. All sentient beings will have in future ages the most perfect enlightenment, namely, the buddha-nature. All sentient beings have at present defilements, and so do not now possess the thirty-two marks and eighty noble characteristics of the Buddha. All sentient beings had in the past ages performed deeds leading to the elimination of defilements and so can now perceive the buddha-nature as their future goal. For such reasons, I always proclaim that all sentient beings have the buddha-nature. . . . Good sons! It is just like a man who has coagulated milk at home. If someone asks him, "Do you have butter?" he will reply, "I have." Butter is not milk. However, by using the proper methods, one will definitely obtain butter from milk, so the man answers that he has butter even though all he has is milk. The same is true of sentient beings, all of whom are endowed with a mind. Since they are all endowed with a mind, they will definitely attain the most perfect enlightenment. I always proclaim that sentient beings have the buddha-nature.[12]

The analogy of milk and butter with sentient beings and buddhahood is reminiscent of the two similes in the *Tathāgatagarbha Sutra:* the pit of the mango fruit and the noble fetus carried in the womb of the poor woman. To say that we have Buddha nature, therefore, clearly does not mean that we are already buddhas. It is a promise to be fulfilled in the future. The potentiality of buddhahood is actualized through religious practice and discipline. The sutra uses similes to stress both the necessity of religious discipline and the affirmation of Buddha nature. In addition to the necessity of religious practice by following the Buddhist path, the sutra points out the critical role played by a "good friend" who serves as a spiritual guide. This is because people are oblivious of their Buddha nature, which is covered over by their ignorance and vexations. A spiritual guide enables them to uncover the hidden treasure and come to know who they really are. Like the *Tathāgatagarbha Sutra,* the *Nirvana Sutra* compares Buddha nature to buried gold. One story, for instance, says that behind the house of a poor woman there is gold buried underground and no one in her family knows about it. She finds out only when she is told by a stranger. Another story is about a strongman who is born with a pearl between his eyebrows. One day he gets into a fight with someone and the pearl sinks under his skin and develops into a boil. When he seeks help from a physician, he is told that the boil is caused by the pearl under the skin. He does not believe it at first, but when the physician holds up a mirror to show his face to him, the strongman sees the concealed pearl. Both stories illustrate the point that Buddha nature is covered over by defilement, just as the gold is covered by dirt and the pearl is hidden within the boil. In the case of the strongman, the story is striking in another aspect. Because the pearl is originally a part of him, the implication is that Buddha nature is intrinsic to us. Even though we cannot perceive it now because we are in a state of ignorance, we can be sure that our destiny is buddhahood because we are endowed with Buddha nature at birth. This optimistic message of the *Nirvana Sutra* forms the foundation of the *Awakening of Faith,* a treatise that has influenced Chinese Buddhist thought as much as, if not even more than, the sutra discussed above.

The *Awakening of Faith in Mahayana*

Traditionally this treatise was attributed to Ashvaghosha of the second century and translated by Paramartha in 550, but scholars now believe that it was a Chinese composition. One measure of its importance is that it has had more than 170 commentaries written about it over the centuries. In one sense this was a Chinese synthesis of Madhyamaka, Yogācāra, and Tathāgatagarbha thought. It in turn laid the theoretical foundation of both Huayan and Chan, two major schools of Chinese Buddhism to be discussed in chapters 5 and 6.

As explained by Yoshito Hakeda, the translator of the treatise, the faith to be awakened in the title is not faith in Mahayana Buddhism in contrast to Hinayana Buddhism, but rather faith in the Mahayana, which is defined as the Absolute, or Suchness. There is only one reality, which is the One Mind. It is the totality of everything. The One Mind has two aspects: Suchness and ignorance. It is possessed by both buddhas and sentient beings. Within this One Mind, the Absolute and the phenomenal, enlightenment and unenlightenment, nirvana and samsara coexist. They are mutually inclusive. They are nondual, not two—the inconceivable state "beyond comprehension" mentioned in the *Vimalakīrti Sutra*. According to Hakeda, "The Absolute order, therefore, does not exist apart from the relative order; rather, they differ epistemologically but not ontologically. Man is presented as being located at the intersection of these opposing orders. The state of man, who belongs intrinsically to the Absolute order and yet in actuality remains in the phenomenal, finite, and profane order, is expressed in terms of the *Tathāgatagarbha*."[13] The *Nirvana Sutra* also refers to reality as Suchness. The treatise provides a helpful explanation:

> That which is called "the essential nature of the Mind" is unborn and is imperishable. It is only through illusions that all things come to be differentiated. If one is freed from illusions, then to him there will be no appearances (*lakṣaṇa*) of objects [regarded as absolutely independent existences]; therefore all things from the beginning transcend all forms of verbalization, description, and conceptualization and are, in the final analysis, undifferentiated, free from alternation and indestructible. They are only of the One Mind; hence the name Suchness. All explanations by words are provisional and without validity, for they are merely used in accordance with illusions and are incapable [of denoting Suchness]. The term Suchness is, so to speak, the limit of verbalization wherein a word is used to put a stop to words. But the essence of Suchness itself cannot be put an end to, for all things [in their Absolute aspect] are real; nor is there anything which needs to be pointed out as real, for all things are equally in the state of Suchness. It should be understood that all things are incapable of being verbally explained or thought of; hence, the name Suchness.[14]

Just as the *Nirvana Sutra* declares that we have Buddha nature, the *Awakening of Faith* says that we are originally enlightened. The treatise raises three existential questions: (1) If we are originally enlightened, why do we not know it? (2) What is the cause of our fall from the state of enlightenment? (3) How can we recover from the state of unenlightenment? The answer to both of the first two questions is ignorance. Because we are under the influence of ignorance, we are in samsara. Appearing as the first link of the twelve-link chain of dependent origination, ignorance has always been the Buddhist diagnosis of the human condition. What is revolutionary about this treatise is its insight that ignorance does not exist separately from enlightenment. True to the Buddhist antimetaphysical tradition, the treatise does not ask the origin of ignorance. Instead, it provides a mythical explanation: ignorance is the state when a deluded thought suddenly arises. Since it coexists with Suchness, ignorance cannot be destroyed. The water in the ocean, the wind, and the waves are used to illustrate the relationship between Suchness and ignorance. The nature of water is wetness (Suchness). It is originally tranquil, but when it is disturbed by the wind of ignorance, waves (phenomena) appear. However, even when the originally tranquil ocean becomes agitated with surging waves, its nature of wetness never disappears. Once the wind of ignorance ceases, the state of tranquility or Suchness reemerges. "Water and wind are inseparable; but water is not mobile by nature, and if the wind stops, the movement ceases. But the wet nature remains undestroyed. Likewise, man's Mind, pure in its own nature, is stirred by the wind of ignorance. Both Mind and ignorance have no particular forms of their own, and they are inseparable. Yet Mind is not mobile by nature, and if ignorance ceases, then the continuity [of deluded activities] ceases. But the essential nature of wisdom [i.e., the essence of Mind, like the wet nature of the water] remains undestroyed."[15]

While ignorance has no beginning but has an end, the One Mind, Suchness, or enlightenment has no beginning and no end. The text uses permeation or perfuming to describe how ignorance and Suchness work. When we are permeated by ignorance, we remain in samsara. But when we are permeated by Suchness, we achieve buddhahood. The impetus for enlightenment is found within us. This is original enlightenment. As with Buddha nature in the *Nirvana Sutra,* original enlightenment must be actualized by religious practice carried out under a spiritual guide. This is called the process of actualization of enlightenment. This process is illustrated in Hakeda's elegant diagram:

> nirvana > samsara > nirvana; potential > unawareness of potential + partial awareness > actualization of the potential; or Absolute order > phenomenal order > Absolute order. The process is flight of Suchness to Suchness; nirvana to nirvana; Buddha to Buddha.[16]

The text mentions five types of religious practice: charity, precept, patience, zeal, and cessation and clear observation. While the first four practices correspond to the first four of the six perfections, the last one corresponds to both meditation and wisdom.

The great popularity of the *Awakening of Faith* and its profound influence on Chinese Buddhism since the sixth century are not hard to understand. The belief in our intrinsic Buddha nature known as original enlightenment resonates with the faith in the innate goodness of human nature advocated by Mencius. The emphasis on religious practice in order to actualize the original enlightenment echoes that found in both the Confucian and the Daoist traditions. Just like the Confucian *Great Learning* and the *Daode jing*, the treatise provides a road map, enabling us to return to our true nature and become truly ourselves.

In this chapter we have discussed four Mahayana sutras and one treatise that are central to Chinese Buddhism. Before closing, I must also mention Tantric or esoteric Buddhism. During the Tang dynasty (618–907), a large body of new scriptures was introduced into China by three tantric masters: Śubhakarasimha, Vajrabodhi, and Amoghavajra. Tantric Buddhism is said to be the third and final teaching of the Buddha. It appeared in the seventh century and is called Vajrayana or Tantrayana, coming after Hinayana and Mahayana. Because this is the Buddhism practiced in Tibet, it has become synonymous nowadays with Tibetan Buddhism. It is called Tantrayana because it is based on the tantras instead of sutras. Unlike sutras, tantras contain secret teachings accessible only when one is initiated through a consecration ritual. For this reason, while sutras are exoteric, tantras are esoteric. Tantric Buddhism is usually referred to as esoteric Buddhism.

Like Mahayana, esoteric Buddhism believes that everyone can become enlightened. However, it believes that enlightenment is possible in our present life with our human body if we carry out the esoteric practice properly under a guru. By achieving coordination between our speech, body, and mind and those of buddhas and bodhisattvas, we become the same as they. Mantras or *dharanis* (spells) enable our speech to correspond with divine speech, *mudras* (hand gestures) enable our body to correspond with the divine body, and visualizations of mandalas (cosmographs) enable our mind to correspond to the divine mind. The practitioner is made divine by the threefold coordination. Because the guru who initiates one into this path is indispensable, one takes refuge not in the traditional three treasures but in four: Buddha, Dharma, Sangha, Guru.

Esoteric Buddhism enjoyed royal patronage in the Tang. It was favored by the Mongol rulers of the Yuan because they followed Tibetan Buddhism and also received patronage from some emperors in the Ming and Qing. It did not exist as a separate school like Tiantai or Chan. Nor did it become a part of mainstream Chinese Buddhism. However, as we will read in chapter 3, esoteric elements are important components of some rituals. Some popular forms of Guanyin, such as the Thousand-Handed and Eleven-Headed Guanyin, are derived from esoteric scriptures. Moreover, during the last two decades, many people in China and Taiwan have become fascinated with Tibetan Buddhism.

Discussion Questions

1. What are the most important differences between the *Lotus Sutra* and the *Vimalakīrti Sutra?*
2. Which parable in the *Lotus Sutra* do you find most instructive? Why?
3. How do you understand the concept of expedient means (*upāya*)?
4. How do you understand *śūnyatā,* the central idea of the *Perfection of Wisdom* scriptures?
5. What is the significance of the *Awakening of Faith?* Why is it so important for Chinese Buddhists?

Further Reading

Benn, James A. *Burning for the Buddha: Self-Immolation in Chinese Buddhism.* Honolulu: University of Hawai'i Press, 2007.

Hakeda, Yoshito S., trans. *The Awakening of Faith.* New York: Columbia University Press, 2006.

Teiser, Stephen F., and Jacqueline I. Stone, eds. *Readings of the Lotus Sutra.* New York: Columbia University Press, 2009.

Watson, Burton, trans. *The Lotus Sutra.* New York: Columbia University Press, 1993.

Watson, Burton, trans. *The Vimalakirti Sutra.* New York: Columbia University Press, 1997.

Notes

1   Edward Conze, I. B. Horner, David Snellgrove, and Arthur Waley, eds., *Buddhist Texts through the Ages* (New York: Harper and Row, 1964), 152.

2   Conze et al., *Buddhist Texts through the Ages,* 52.

3   Donald S. Lopez Jr., ed., *Buddhist Scriptures* (New York: Penguin, 2004), 455.

4   Lopez, *Buddhist Scriptures,* 458.

5   Conze et al., *Buddhist Texts through the Ages,* 161.

6   Edward Conze, *The Prajñāpāramitā Literature* (The Hague: Mouton, 1960), 15.

7   Watson, *The Lotus Sutra,* 24. Subsequent page references in this section are to this work.

8   Daniel B. Stevenson, "Tales of the Lotus Sūtra," in *Buddhism in Practice,* ed. Donald S. Lopez Jr. (Princeton, NJ: Princeton University Press, 1995), 434.

9   Kathryn Ann Tsai, *Lives of the Nuns: Biographies of Chinese Buddhist Nuns from the Fourth to the Sixth Centuries* (Honolulu: University of Hawai'i Press, 1994), 132, 144, 130.

10 Watson, *The Vimalakirti Sutra,* 29. Subsequent page references in this section are to this work.

11 William H. Grosnick, "The Tathāgatagarbha Sūtra," in *Buddhism in Practice,* edited by Donald S. Lopez Jr. (Princeton, NJ: Princeton University Press, 1995), 96.

12 *Da Banniepanj Jing* (Mahanirvana Sutra). *Taishō shinshū daizokyō* (T.) vol. 12, no. 374: 511. My translation.

13 Hakeda, *The Awakening of Faith,* 8.

14 Hakeda, *The Awakening of Faith,* 39–40.

15 Hakeda, *The Awakening of Faith,* 47.

16 Hakeda, *The Awakening of Faith,* 71–72.

CHAPTER 2

Cults of Buddhas and Bodhisattvas

Throughout its two-thousand-year history, the scriptures discussed in the last chapter served as an important medium for some people, such as monks, scholars, poets, and other Chinese of the upper classes, to know Buddhism. But most people in premodern times came into contact with Buddhism by listening to stories about buddhas and bodhisattvas, seeing their sculpted and painted images, and participating in rituals and festivals worshiping and commemorating them. It was through the cults of buddhas and bodhisattvas that Buddhism touched people's hearts and minds and took deep root in China. We will discuss some of the most popular and enduring cults—Śākyamuni, Maitreya, Amitāyus (Measureless Life) or Amitābha (Measureless Light), Guanyin, and the Medicine Buddha—in this chapter and some major rituals and festivals in the next chapter.

The word *cult*, used in the title of this chapter, has unfortunately acquired a derogatory connotation in contemporary usage. To many people it now means, according to *Webster's New Universal Unabridged Dictionary*, "a religion or sect considered to be false, unorthodox or extremist, with members often living outside of conventional society under the direction of a charismatic leader." This is definitely not what I mean here. I use the original meaning of the word as defined by the *Oxford English Dictionary*: "worship, reverential homage" and "devotion or homage . . . esp. paid by a body of professed adherents or admirers." Furthermore, I agree with Robert Campany, who cites the definitions and then says, "I here propose to revive the term to designate any or all of the ways—ritual, yes, but also verbal, gestural, graphic, plastic, personal, collective, narrative, poetic, musical, mythological, associative, symbolic, theological, and so forth—in order to *present* a deity, spirit, or saint."[1]

People in China worship buddhas and bodhisattvas in rituals, write poems and novels about them, praise them in songs and hymns, and tell stories and stage plays about them. And above all else, they worship the images of these holy beings. Such worship is central to Buddhism, resulting in its being called the religion of images. Buddhas and bodhisattvas are represented by three-dimensional images, frescos, and paintings.

Buddhist art, like all religious art, is intimately connected with the spiritual lives of the faithful. When we go to museums, we are moved by the beauty of the image of the Madonna or Guanyin. But we should remember that these images were originally worshiped in a church or a temple. They are first and foremost icons, although they can, of course, be appreciated as objects of art. At first, images of buddhas and bodhisattvas were sculpted by artisans following Indian and Central Asian models. As time went on, their appearance became more Chinese. Donors who commissioned the images sometimes had their names inscribed on the back or the lower edge together with a short dedication. When the images were completed, they would be ritually consecrated and installed in temples. The Buddhist faithful had a close personal relationship with these icons, which were regarded as alive. There are stories about images that could walk, talk, emit light, or shed tears. They appeared in the visions and dreams of the worshiper to predict future events and indicate what they wanted. They could answer people's prayers and intervene physically to save people from danger. In one miracle story about a Guanyin statue discussed later, the image even bore the executor's knife on behalf of its devotee.

Some devotees had their own personal icons. There is a moving story about Wang Yen, a Buddhist devotee, and a votive icon of Guanyin first given to him by the master under whom he took refuge to become a Buddhist when he was living in present-day Vietnam as a child. Although he was very young, he and his younger brother diligently worshiped it. Later the family home had to be renovated, and there was no proper place to keep the image. It was taken to a temple for temporary safekeeping. At that time, however, many gilt bronze statues were stolen and melted down to make coins. Several months after the icon was sent to the temple, Wang was sleeping during the daytime and had a dream in which he saw the icon by his side. Curious about the dream, he decided to go to the temple and bring the icon home, although it was getting dark. The same evening, more than ten other images were forcibly removed from the temple by robbers. After that the icon shone brightly at night, illuminating the ground around it. This happened in the fall of 463.

The story did not end there. In 471 Wang Yen moved to present-day Anhui and befriended a monk from the Monastery of Many Treasures located in the capital. He asked the monk to keep the icon in that temple temporarily. Several years went by, and he did not think of the image. But in 478 he met the monk again and was reminded that the image was still in the temple. When he went to the capital, he visited the abbot of the temple and asked for it. But the abbot told him that no such image was there. He was very disappointed and felt great sadness at losing the icon. That same night he had a dream in which a man told him that the icon was still there but the abbot had forgotten about it. Still in a dream, the man took him back to the temple and opened the door to the main hall. He saw clearly the image belonging to him nestled among many small images in the eastern section of the hall. Early the next morning he went back to the temple and told the abbot about his dream. When the abbot led him to the hall and opened it, they indeed found the icon in the eastern section of the hall.

This story helps us appreciate the intimate relationship between a devotee and his personal icon. Twice he found a safe home for it in a temple so that it would not be disturbed by the rebuilding of his home or the uncertainties of travel. From the matter-of-fact way Wang Yen relates the story, Buddhist images were apparently either donated to temples or put there for temporary residence by the faithful in the fifth century, just as some are today. The image sent him warnings or directions through dreams. He regarded it as the living embodiment of Guanyin.

Images made of wood and metal are installed in monasteries. We have a detailed description of how an image was made and ritually consecrated during the time the Tiantai master Zunshi was the abbot of Paoyun Monastery in present-day Ningpo. In 999 he hired an artisan from Hangzhou to make an image of Guanyin for the monastery. After an unblemished block of white sandalwood was chosen, the material, the craftsmen, and the area where the image was to be carved were purified with incantation of spells and holy water. This image was therefore carved at a ritually sanctified setting. When the carving was completed, the image became ritually potent with the dotting of the eyes with paint and the insertion of *dharani* scrolls written in gold letters in its torso. Zunshi invited over a hundred monks to participate in the consecration ceremony when the image was installed in the Dharma Hall. Finally, he read a commemorative essay written for this occasion to complete its empowerment. The essay contained three vows requesting that "the statue would inspire conversion and offer protection from calamity to all who encounter it."[2]

Śākyamuni

In India, by the third century before the Common Era, the belief in the seven buddhas already existed, Śākyamuni being the last of the seven. Early Buddhism and Mahayana Buddhism share the belief in a future buddha, Maitreya. However, unlike early Buddhism, Mahayana teaches that there

Standing Buddha. India. Gupta Period. Late sixth–early seventh century. Metropolitan Museum of Art

are many other buddhas in addition to Śākyamuni. They carry out the work of teaching the Dharma in their buddha fields, which exist in the ten directions outside of our world system. Buddha Amitāyus or Amitābha and his Pure Land in the west, commonly known as the Western Paradise, became most popular in China.

The Buddha was represented by three-dimensional statues made of gilt bronze and images chiseled on rock faces. The statues depicted the Buddha either standing or seated. The earliest surviving gilt bronze image of a seated Buddha is 15.5 inches in height and dated 338. But some statues are giant standing ones. For instance, the five standing buddhas carved in the Yungang Caves are over seventy feet tall. They were made in 454 by the Northern Wei ruler to represent his five predecessors, who were regarded as buddhas. Influenced by the models of India and Central Asia, Buddhists in the north carved grottoes along mountain ranges. The most famous ones are Dunhuang, Yungang, and Longmen, which are all adorned with statues of buddhas and bodhisattvas as well as wall frescos depicting the life of the Buddha and scenes from Buddhist scriptures. All three have been named World Heritage sites by UNESCO and draw tens of thousands of visitors from all over the world.

Dunhuang Caves. Photo by Yao Chongxin

The caves in Dunhuang are grottoes carved into the face of rocky hills. Situated at the intersection where the northern and southern Silk Roads converged, Dunhuang played a seminal role in the introduction of Buddhism. The Dunhuang Caves are called the Thousand Buddha Caves, highlighting the great number, although there are now actually 492. The earliest ones were carved in 366 and served as monks' cells as well as the place where they practiced meditation and worshiped. In the richness and variety of its Buddhist art, Dunhuang is unparalleled. Clay statues, murals, paintings on silk, and manuscripts all attest to the enormous devotion of the faithful over the centuries. The Yungang Caves are located in Datong, Shanxi, which was the capital of the Northern Wei. There are some 252 grottos housing 51,000 statues. When the capital was moved to Luoyang in 494, the work at Yungang came to a stop. But the construction of the Longmen Caves, located near Luoyang, had already begun in 493 and continued in later periods, receiving special support from Empress Wu (624–705) of the Tang. Scholars tell us that there are 100,000 statues, ranging from one inch to fifty-seven feet in height. The cult of Śākyamuni was actively promoted by the Northern Wei dynasty (386–534), which was founded by the Toba, people who are said to be Turkic. Being foreigners, they saw Buddhism, a religion also of foreign origin, as a unifying force in ruling their Han subjects.

Longmen Caves. Photo by Yao Chongxin

Other buddhas and bodhisattvas were also enshrined in these three sites. The construction of Yungang and Longmen required enormous financial resources and manpower, which were provided by the court. But the statues adorning the caves were donated by individuals, including royal family members, aristocrats, monks, nuns, and ordinary people. Religious societies would sometimes pool their resources to have a statue carved. For instance, there is an inscription in Yungang Cave 11, dated 483, explaining why fifty-three people formed such a society. They hoped that by carving statues of the Buddha, they might create religious merit for themselves as well as others. The group had three specific objectives:

> First, they prayed for the peace and prosperity for the realm, also prosperity, honor, and longevity for the ruling house. May its power be like that of the universal monarch, may it spread the three jewels to all corners of the empire, and may no shortcomings ever befall the ruling house. Second, the group prayed that their deceased ancestors and their teachers and all their relatives might be reborn in the Pure Land and live there without blemish and be nurtured by the lotus. If these ancestors or teachers should be reborn again, may they become a deity or a human being with all their needs fulfilled. If they should meet with misfortune and be reborn in the evil modes of existence, then may they be freed from the torments of misery. Third, the group prayed that all people in the village might from that time on be faithful and sincere in their devotion to the Buddha, that they might be more diligent in spreading the religion and that they might practice the career of the bodhisattva, thus to convert all sentient beings.[3]

Although this inscription is much longer and more detailed than some others, it is not atypical. With the merit generated by the creation of the Buddha statues, the donors hoped to benefit the ruling house, their dead and living family members, and all other sentient beings. The inscription tells us much about the state of knowledge about Buddhism among the common people in the fifth century. They knew about the mutual interdependence between Buddhism and the state. Buddhism provided a blessing to the ruling house, which in turn offered patronage. The patrons hoped their ancestors (and themselves) would be reborn in the Pure Land after death or, failing that, be reborn as deities or humans, but never in the other three evil paths. They were also familiar with the ideal of the bodhisattva and the need to share the meritorious karma with their neighbors as well as sentient beings in general. Most likely they learned this by listening to the sermons given by monks when they attended Buddhist rituals.

The Buddha's birthday on the eighth day of the fourth lunar month was celebrated as early as the second century of the Common Era, soon after the entry of Buddhism into China. As in India, the ritual for his birthday took two forms: the bathing of the image of the Buddha and the "walking the image of the Buddha." "Bathing the image" meant worshipers would pour scented water over the image; "walking the image" meant it would be carried by worshipers on a float and paraded on the street. Since the sixth century, bathing the Buddha has remained an important festival, while the ritual of carrying the Buddha's image in a parade is no longer practiced. Nowadays, it is usually a small bronze image of the infant Buddha that is bathed at the ceremony. Worshipers line up and take turns pouring water over its head.

Another occasion for the common people to learn about Buddhism was by participating in a fast. This tradition originated in early Buddhism. Lay believers were encouraged to attend fasting ceremonies six days a month, which were held on the eighth, fourteenth, fifteenth, twenty-third, twenty-ninth, and thirtieth. In addition, there were also three long fasting months, which were the first fifteen days of the first, fifth, and ninth months. Participants had to confess their faults, observe the fast and seven other abstinences for "one day and one night," and listen to Buddhist scriptures recited and commented upon by monks. The goal was to become purified physically, morally, and spiritually. This practice was based on the belief that the four heavenly kings, their sons, or messengers would come down to earth to inspect human beings' deeds on every fasting day and make a report to Śakra, the supreme god in the world of desire. Humans who did good deeds would be rewarded with rebirth among the gods, and those who did bad deeds would be condemned to be reborn in hell. During the Sui and Tang dynasties, these fast days were not only observed by pious believers but also enforced by the court, which prohibited the killing of animals and the execution of criminals.

While the birth of the Buddha was celebrated by believers with rituals of bathing the Buddha, his death or nirvana was commemorated with religious structures known as stupas in India and pagodas in China. According to the Buddhist tradition, after the Buddha was cremated, some remnants of his teeth and bones were found among the ashes. They were relics or *śarīra.* They were described as being "like jasmine buds, washed pearls, and nuggets of gold and as coming in various sizes (as big as mustard seeds, broken grains of rice, and split peas)."[4] The ashes and the relics were distributed among eight kingdoms and buried in stupas. Buddhists made pilgrimages to circumambulate the stupas as acts of devotion in order to create merit. The Buddhist emperor Aśoka promoted the cult of relics. He redistributed the Buddha's relics and had 84,000 stupas built in his empire to house them. He was said to have had stupas built not only in India but also in other countries. This legend gave rise to the belief that as many as nineteen Aśokan stupas were located in China.

The stupa was a dome-shaped mound in India, but in China it was transformed into a several-tiered tower known as a pagoda. Although it was claimed that some contained relics, most did not. Nevertheless, because of the close association with the Buddha, early monasteries were built around pagodas. Some of the Buddhist caves, such as Yungang, also have a central pillar representing the stupa so that resident monks or pilgrims can circumambulate it. Although many centuries have passed, pagodas remain an indispensable part of Chinese monastic structure, and even freestanding pagodas dot the Chinese landscape today. Whenever one sees a pagoda or a statue of the Buddha, one remembers Śākyamuni.

Maitreya

Maitreya is the future Buddha. His name is derived from *mitra,* meaning friend or friendliness. Just like Śākyamuni before his birth, Maitreya is now living in Tushita Heaven, the sixth and highest heaven in the world of desire, waiting to descend to Earth; and like Śākyamuni before him, he will be born as a prince, leave home, and become enlightened.

Buddhism teaches impermanence. Like everything else in the universe, the Buddhist teaching itself, the Dharma, will not last forever. According to a common Buddhist belief, after the death of the Buddha, the next five hundred years were the Age of True Dharma. During this period, Buddhism flourished. People had strong faith in Buddhism and followed its teachings. They supported the monastic order, and it was easy to achieve enlightenment. This was followed by the Age of Counterfeit Dharma, which lasted one thousand years. During this period, Buddhism underwent inner decay, although its external form remained in place. Monastics did not practice the religion, and ordinary people did not support the monastic order as strongly as before. It was very hard to achieve enlightenment.

Finally, the Age of Decline of Dharma will see the disappearance of Buddhism. Over the course of these ten thousand years, Buddhism will decline not only in its inner spirit but also in its external form. Eventually, no monastics or monasteries will exist. All images of buddhas and bodhisattvas, all Buddhist scriptures, and all relics will disappear from the face of the Earth, leaving no trace of Buddhism. At the same time, there will be natural disasters accompanied by political and social chaos. When the world finally comes to the end, Maitreya will appear and renew Buddhism. When that happens, the world will also be renewed. People will live in peace and prosperity once more.

Daoan was a devotee of Maitreya, and he hoped to be reborn in Tushita Heaven to meet Maitreya and listen to his teaching. But many people also hoped to be reborn as humans when Maitreya comes down to Earth. According to the *Scripture of Maitreya Becoming a Buddha* and the *Scripture of Maitreya Descending to Be Born,* after 5.6 billion years in Tushita Heaven, Maitreya will become a buddha beneath a dragon-flower tree and preach the Four Noble Truths and Law of Dependent Origination to an assembly of men and gods. He will hold three assemblies, and all who attend will achieve enlightenment.

Images of Maitreya are very distinctive, showing him seated with legs crossed. He is also depicted in a pensive posture, one hand touching his chin while that arm rests on the right leg, which is raised over the left knee. In the inscriptions, donors of Maitreya images vow "to hear the words of the Dharma at the three assemblies of the dragon-flower tree when Maitreya descends and is born." While people from all social classes were donors of Maitreya images, there were more officials, monks, and nuns than commoners.

In the centuries after the Tang, the cult of Maitreya was overshadowed by other cults of buddhas and bodhisattvas, such as those of Amitāyus/Amitābha, the Healing Buddha, and Guanyin. Because the coming of the future Buddha was connected with the dawning of a new world order, it inspired millenarian expectations. Since the twelfth century, movements led by rebels claiming to be the messengers of Maitreya or even Maitreya himself arose from time to time despite persecution by the court. Various sectarian religions with different names but sharing the same beliefs continued to challenge the central authority throughout late imperial China.

At the same time, Maitreya also exerted much influence in popular culture. During the thirteenth century, people regarded a monk with supernatural abilities as the incarnated Maitreya. Known as the Cloth-Bagged Monk because he always carried a cloth bag on his shoulders, he did not live in a temple but wandered freely and mingled with the common people. He dispensed gifts to children and helped people in need. This legend gave rise to the image of the Laughing Buddha. With an exposed potbelly and broad grin, he symbolizes prosperity and good luck. He was depicted with a potbelly instead of a normal girth as in earlier periods, following the Indian model. This is because prior to modern times, Chinese regarded having enough to eat so as to become somewhat overweight as a sign of prosperity. In fact, as late as the early twentieth century, when a guest came to visit, the first greeting of the host was "Have you eaten?" It was then followed by "You look well. It is wonderful that you have gained weight!"

The laughing Maitreya is the first statue one sees in the hall after entering a Buddhist temple and before ascending to the main Buddha Hall. This is also the image often found in Chinese restaurants and gift shops. Instead of a pensive meditator, he is an auspicious symbol welcoming visitors to monasteries and customers to businesses.

Amitābha

The cult of this buddha is based on the Pure Land sutras, in which he appears under two different names. He is called Amitāyus (Measureless Life) in the *Amitāyus Sutra* translated by Sanghavarman about 252 CE. He is called Amitābha (Measureless Light) in the shorter *Amitābha Sutra* translated by Kumārajīva about 402 CE. Just as this buddha has two names, his land has three names. It is known as Sukhāvatī, the Land of Supreme Bliss, for there is no suffering. Because it is located to the west of our world system, it is also known as the Western Paradise. Unlike in our world system, no evil paths of rebirth as animals, hungry ghosts, and hells are found, and it is a land of great beauty. The third name is the Pure Land. This marvelous land contains otherworldly wonders: multicolored trees of the seven precious jewels (gold, silver, beryl, crystal, coral, red pearl, and emerald), great rivers flowing with fragrant water, and huge lotus flowers radiating brilliant rays of light.

The Pure Land is level everywhere, without mountains or hills. The ground is perfectly even and paved with gold. The kinds of suffering humankind experiences in our world no longer exist because desire ceases. One is never hungry. Nor is one troubled by sexual or other kinds of

physical desires, because there are no women in the Pure Land. It is difficult to reconcile the Buddha's compassion with the exclusion of women
from his Pure Land. This problem is related to the greater issue of Budh-
hism and gender, which we will discuss in chapter 8.

Freedom from suffering is, of course, very attractive. But an even
greater attraction is the prospect of attaining enlightenment in the Pure
Land instead of here on Earth. This is because one can listen to the teachings of Amitābha and his two attending bodhisattvas, Guanyin and
Dashizhi. Even the celestial music created by the flowing water and bloom-
ing flowers is a constant reminder of the Buddhist teaching of impermanence, suffering, and no self. Although the land is devoid of animals, the
melodious voices of magically transformed birds join in the spiritual choir.
Once in the Pure Land, one is delivered from the cycle of rebirth. However,
emulating the compassionate bodhisattva, one is encouraged to make vows
to return to the world in order to help others.

Based on the inscriptions on the images donated by the faithful, they
envisioned the Pure Land very much like a paradise. Perhaps for this reason, this buddha was always addressed as Amitāyus instead of Amitābha in
the early period of his cult. "Measureless Life" resonated with immortality,
which was a goal of the Daoists in their cult of immortals. It was only later,
during the Tang, when his cult became more popular than that of Maitreya, that this buddha became known universally as Amitābha.

The Pure Land cult is often described as following an easy practice
because the only requirement is to have faith in Amitābha by calling his
name. This is because many eons ago, Amitābha Buddha, living then as the
monk Dharmakara, made vows to save those who do. One is saved from the
cycle of rebirth through faith, not by effort. For this reason, this is referred
to as a religion of "other power" in contrast to the "self power" of early Buddhism. Of the new doctrinal innovations of Mahayana, this is perhaps the
most striking one, seemingly contradicting the strict law of karma that the-
oretically does not allow the intervention of grace. This can be reconciled
because of the Mahayana doctrine of transfer of merit. Buddhas and bodhisattvas become enlightened after they have accumulated enormous
amounts of merit through their spiritual practice carried out over many lifetimes. They themselves have no use for this merit. Because they are compassionate, they will transfer their merit to sentient beings who need it. When
one is sincerely mindful of Amitābha and invokes his name by chanting
"Namo Omituofo (Adoration of Amitābha Buddha)," the devotee is able to

be born in the Pure Land after he dies. When he is near death, he will have a vision of Amitābha and his chief attendant, the bodhisattva Guanyin, who will lead him to the Land of Bliss. As faith in Amitābha developed in China, in addition to statues of Amitābha and Guanyin, depictions of the Pure Land became favorite themes in murals and paintings.

Guanyin

Guanyin (Perceiver of Sounds) or Guanshiyin (Perceiver of the World's Sounds) is the Chinese name for Avalokiteśvara, the bodhisattva of compassion, whose cult has attracted the greatest number of followers in China. Bodhisattvas are beings dedicated to the salvation of everyone. In carrying out this noble task, they choose to become buddhas instead of seeking personal nirvana as arhats do. Thus they became new cultic objects for Mahayana Buddhists, while the early Buddhists worship only the historical Buddha and use the term "bodhisattva" to refer only to the Buddha's previous lives before his final enlightenment. Indeed, Hinayana Buddhists believe in a very limited number of bodhisattvas, namely Śākyamuni Buddha in his previous lives and Maitreya, the future Buddha. The Mahayana belief in many bodhisattvas and the corresponding call for all people to give rise to the thought for enlightenment are two of the most significant differences between the two Buddhist traditions.

A Chinese saying aptly describes the great popularity of this savior bodhisattva: "Everybody knows how to chant Omituofo, and every household worships Guanyin." Guanyin is closely connected with Amitābha Buddha as not only Amitābha's chief attendant but also his successor. Of all the bodhisattvas, only Guanyin carries a small buddha image on his crown in all the statues and paintings. This unique and distinctive iconographic feature indicates their special relationship as that between a monarch and heir apparent or a father and son. Although Guanyin, like all buddhas and bodhisattvas, was originally presented as a masculine deity (like Śākyamuni or Maitreya) in scriptures and depicted thus in art, he alone underwent a sexual transformation in China and became a feminine deity.

There are many Buddhist scriptures connected with Guanyin. The bodhisattva appears in more than eighty sutras. His roles vary widely in these scriptures, from a walk-on bit player in the entourage surrounding Śākyamuni Buddha to the star of his own grand dramas of universal salvation. The face of the bodhisattva in canonical scriptures, just as in art and other media, is thus highly multivocal, multivalent, and multifaceted. At least three separate and distinct cults can be identified: that of a compassionate savior not bound to a specific place as represented by the *Lotus Sutra;* that of the chief helper of Amitābha Buddha, as found in the Pure Land sutras; and that of a sage connected with the holy island Potalaka, as seen in the *Huayan* or *Flower Garland Sutra.*

Prior to the translation of the *Lotus Sutra* in the third century, there was no Chinese deity comparable to Guanyin, who was not only a universal and compassionate savior but also easily accessible. Chapter 25 of the *Lotus Sutra* translated by Kumārajīva in 406 is titled "Universal Gateway" and devoted to Guanyin. It preaches a new and democratic way of salvation. To be saved, one does not need to become a scholar learned in scripture, a paragon of virtue, or a master proficient in meditation. One does not have to follow a special way of life, take up a vegetarian diet, or practice any ritual. The only requirement is to call Guanyin's name with a sincere and believing heart. This was a new deity who would help anyone in difficulty, with no discrimination on the basis of status or gender. And the benefits of worshiping him are both spiritual and worldly. He delivers people from life-threatening perils; the three poisons of lust, hatred, and ignorance; and grants children to infertile women. The sutra declares this good news: "If they hear of this bodhisattva, Perceiver of the World's Sounds and single-mindedly call his name, then at once he will perceive the sound of their voices and they all gain deliverance from their trials."[5] This chapter began to be circulated very early independently from the *Lotus Sutra* and has remained one of the most popular scriptures among Chinese Buddhists.

Indigenous sutras also helped to promote and disseminate the belief in Guanyin in China, as did the translated sutras, miracle stories, new images, pilgrimage, and rituals devoted to the bodhisattva, each in a different way.

Indigenous sutras are closely connected with miracle stories. *King Kao's Guanshiyin Sutra,* first mentioned in 664, was supposed to have resulted from a miracle. In the most popular version of the origin myth, the hero was Sun Jingde, a common soldier who was wrongly condemned to death. Sun worshiped an icon of Guanyin that he kept in his room. When he managed to finish chanting the sutra that a monk revealed to him in a dream one thousand times prior to his beheading, the executioner's knife broke into three sections. Although the executioner changed the knife three times, the same thing happened. This was reported to the ruler, who was moved and pardoned Sun. When Sun returned to his room, he saw three cuts made by a knife on the neck of the Guanyin image. The implication is clearly that the

Guanyin. Dazu, Beishan. Niche 235. Southern Song. (1127–1279). Institute of Dazu Stone Sculptures

icon bore the blows of the knife, thus sparing Sun. This was supposed to have happened between 534 and 537 CE. Other stories relate similar events. Instead of going to a temple to worship Guanyin, early devotees carried icons on their bodies as talismans. Since they were worn in the hair or on top of the crown, they must have been small and light. Indeed, a number of tiny gilt bronze images of Guanyin, some measuring only an inch or so, have survived and can be seen in museums. When we view them in the light of such miracle tales, we might speculate that they were small because they were intended to be used as personal talismans. Icons were also sometimes created for such devotional use after miraculous deliverances.

Compilation of miracle stories began in the fourth century, not long after the first translation of the *Lotus Sutra* by Dharmaraksha in 286. Miracle tales about Guanyin are an important and enduring genre in Chinese Buddhism. They have been collected down the ages and are still being produced and collected today. Miracle tales served as a powerful medium for transforming and domesticating Guanyin. Because the stories relate real people's encounters with the bodhisattva at specific times and places and under critical circumstances, Guanyin was no longer the mythical figure mentioned in the sutras but became a "real presence." Miracles happen to vouch for Guanyin's efficacy (*ling*). They work because there is the relationship of sympathetic resonance (*ganying*) between the sincere devotee and the bodhisattva. Both concepts have deep cultural roots in China.

Many miracle tales mention images of Guanyin. There is a close relationship between the devotees and the icons of Guanyin revealed in some early tales. New forms of Guanyin appearing in devotees' visions of the bodhisattva, as contained in some later miracle tales, served as effective media for the sexual transformation of this bodhisattva. While most early miracle tales refer to Guanyin as a monk when he appears in the dreams or visions of the devotee, the bodhisattva gradually appears as either a "person in white," indicating perhaps his lay status, or a "woman in white," indicating her female gender. Changing visions of Guanyin led to new artistic representations of the bodhisattva. But conversely, Guanyin depicted with a new iconography could also predispose the devotees to see him/her in a new way in their visions and dreams.

The intimate and dialectical relationship of visions, media, and iconography highlights the role art has played in the cult of Guanyin. Art has been one of the most powerful and effective media through which the Chinese people have come to know the bodhisattva. It is also through art that one can most clearly detect the gradual yet undeniable sexual transformation. Buddhist scriptures always present the bodhisattva as either masculine or asexual. The statues of Guanyin in Yungang, Longmen, and Dunhuang, as well as Guanyin images painted on the murals and banners of Dunhuang, like those of the buddhas and bodhisattvas, appear masculine, sometimes with a thin moustache that clearly indicates his gender.

But the deity underwent a profound and startling transformation beginning sometime during the tenth century, and by the sixteenth century, Guanyin had become not only completely Chinese but also the most beloved Goddess of Mercy, a nickname coined by Jesuit missionaries, who were much impressed by the similarities between her iconography and that of the Madonna. Of all the imported Buddhist deities, Guanyin is the only one who has become a genuine Chinese goddess—so much so that many Chinese, if they are not familiar with Buddhism, are not even aware of her Buddhist origin.

Chinese created indigenous forms of Guanyin, just as they composed indigenous sutras. In time, several distinctive Chinese forms emerged from the tenth century onward. They are the Water Moon Guanyin, White-Robed Guanyin, Child-Giving Guanyin, Guanyin of the South Sea, Fish Basket Guanyin, and Old Mother Guanyin. The creation of new iconographies might be connected with the regional character of Chinese Buddhism and Buddhist art. The new icons were also closely connected with Buddhist theology, ritual, and devotion. The Water Moon Guanyin was an indigenous icon that appeared before the White-Robed Guanyin and served as a prototype for it. The White-Robed Guanyin gave rise to a cult of fertility in the late imperial period. With her own indigenous scriptures, rituals, and miracle stories, she came to be known colloquially as the Child-Giving Guanyin. The appearance of feminine forms of Guanyin in China was thus inseparable from the domestication and regionalization of the bodhisattva. The appearance of the Guanyin of the South Sea (Nanhai Guanyin) coincided with the construction of Putuo Island as the Chinese Potolaka, the sacred island home of the bodhisattva described in the *Flower Garland Sutra* and other esoteric sutras.

Many Chinese people are familiar with the story of Princess Miaoshan (Wonderful Goodness), who is believed to be an incarnation of Guanyin. The story is as follows. Miaoshan (Wonderful Goodness) was the third daughter of King Miaozhuang (Wonderful Adornment). She was by nature drawn to Buddhism, keeping a vegetarian diet, reading scriptures by day, and meditating at night from an early age. The king had no sons and hoped to choose an heir from among his sons-in-law. When Miaoshan reached marriageable age, however, she refused to get married, unlike her two elder sisters, who had both obediently married the men chosen by their father. The father was greatly angered by Miaoshan's refusal and punished her harshly in different ways. She was first confined to the back garden and made to do hard labor. When, with the aid of gods, she completed the tasks, she was allowed to go to the White Sparrow Nunnery to undergo further trials in the hope of discouraging her from pursuing the religious path. She persevered, and the king burned down the nunnery, killed the five hundred nuns, and had Miaoshan executed for her unfilial behavior. While her body was safeguarded by a mountain spirit, Miaoshan's soul toured hell and saved beings there by preaching to them. She returned to the world, went to Fragrant Mountain, meditated for nine years, and achieved enlightenment. By this time, the king had become seriously ill with a mysterious disease that resisted all medical treatment. Miaoshan, disguised as a mendicant monk, came to the palace and told the dying king that there was only one remedy that could save him: a medicine concocted with the eyes and hands of someone who had never felt anger. She further told the astonished king where to find such a person. When the king's messenger arrived, Miaoshan willingly offered her eyes and hands. The father recovered after taking the medicine and came to Fragrant Mountain with the royal party on a pilgrimage to offer thanks to his savior. He recognized the eyeless and handless ascetic as none other than his own daughter. Overwhelmed with remorse, he and the rest of the royal family all converted to Buddhism. Miaoshan was transformed into her true form, that of the esoteric Thousand-Eyed and Thousand-Handed Guanyin. After the apotheosis, Miaoshan passed away and a pagoda was erected to house her relics.

This legend reconciles the Confucian demand of filial piety with Buddhist aspiration. Miaoshan, a most unfilial rebel in defying her father's order to get married, became a most filial daughter by willingly sacrificing herself to save him. It is not hard to understand why this legend became so popular. We do not know how early it began, but the first written record of it was dated 1100, a "life" of Princess Miaoshan written by an official and carved on a stele at the request of the abbot of a temple in Honan, a pilgrimage center for Guanyin worship. The bodhisattva was provided with not only a name, a birth date, and a family but also a biography; none of these is found in Buddhist scriptures. Her birthday, the nineteenth day of the second month, has become the most important holy day for the faithful, who celebrate it in temples, just as they do the birthdays of all other Chinese gods and goddesses. Clearly, this transformation fits the Chinese model of divinity. Since the Chinese religion does not posit a sharp distinction between the transcendent and the immanent, human beings can become gods and gods can appear on earth as human beings. Laozi, for instance, was already deified in the second century and was believed to have transformed himself many times to teach people about the Dao. Stories about Daoist immortals, those fabulous beings who straddle the boundary between the human and the divine, serve as another rich resource for such imagination. The legend of Miaoshan anchored Guanyin to China by making her conform to the Chinese model of divinity. It also provides a charter for marriage resistance. Some Buddhist women could and did follow Miaoshan's example in refusing to get married and pursuing their religious lives, either at home or by joining the monastic order.

The Joint Worship of Guanyin and Dizang

The creation of images of Guanyin unauthorized by scriptures is not a unique phenomenon. In temples and cave sculptures made after the eleventh century, Guanyin is often paired with Dizang, another important bodhisattva in China.

Guanyin and Dizang. Dazu, Beishan. Niche 253. Northern Song (960–1126). Photo by Yao Chongxin

This pairing is also not attested to by any scripture. The canonical basis of Dizang worship is the *Great Extended Scripture on the Ten Wheels*, which depicts Dizang, like Guanyin, as very much concerned with saving people from all kinds of problems in life.

Dizang became exclusively identified as the savior of beings in hell when the *Scripture of Dizang's Original Vow*, an indigenous sutra, superseded the *Scripture on the Ten Wheels* in popularity. The pairing of the two is therefore due to the new role Dizang came to play. The *Scripture of Dizang's Original Vow* calls upon its reader to recite it for the dying to relieve their suffering and help them secure a better rebirth. But a number of esoteric sutras introduced into China several centuries earlier already attribute to Guanyin the power to cure illnesses, to enable a person to die a good death, and to save beings from hell when one recites the *dharanis* revealed by her. In this instance, indigenous sutras overshadowed the esoteric sutras, making Dizang instead of Guanyin the savior of beings in hell.

One of the earliest such scriptures centering on Guanyin as the universal savior is the *Sutra of Evocating Guanyin* (Qing Guanyin jing), translated between 317 and 420. The chanting of the *dharani* revealed therein will save a person from all manner of disasters. If one is faithful and dedicated in chanting, he will be able to have a vision of Guanyin while alive and, having been freed from all sins, will not suffer rebirth in the four woeful realms of hell, hungry ghosts, animals, and asuras. Because Guanyin playfully travels in all realms of rebirth, even if a person is so unfortunate as to be born in hell or as a hungry ghost, Guanyin is right there to help him. The bodhisattva is said to suffer in hell in place of the sinner, and by bestowing sweet milk, which issues from his fingertips, he satisfies the hunger and thirst of hungry ghosts.

The pairing of the two bodhisattvas appears in the illustrated copies of the *Scripture on the Ten Kings*, another indigenous sutra recovered from Dunhuang, and they were evoked together in Buddhist mortuary rituals for the benefit of dead ancestors. These ritual texts were created from the Song to the Ming (eleventh to the seventeenth centuries). For instance, in the ritual text *Compassionate Precious Penance Formulated by Emperor Wu of Liang*, dated to the twelfth century, the presiding priest asks both Dizang and Guanyin to descend to the consecrated space three times. An even more important mortuary ritual created in the tenth century (which has remained popular down the ages) is that of feeding hungry ghosts, to be discussed in the next chapter. Guanyin and Dizang collaborate in this ritual.

The two bodhisattvas thus join in helping people both in life and in death. When and how did Guanyin and Dizang come to specialize in only one sphere? The clue can be found in art and temple architecture. Based on surviving examples of floor plans of temples dated to the Liao and Jin (eleventh and twelfth centuries), four separate halls were built for worshiping the four bodhisattvas: Mañjuśrī (Wenshu), Samantabhadra (Puxian), Guanyin, and Dizang. The floor plan of Shanhua Monastery in Datong, Shanxi, shows Wenshu Hall (no longer standing) facing Puxian Hall, while Dizang Hall faces Guanyin Hall. But Guangsheng Monastery, built in the sixteenth century, retained only the two halls dedicated to Dizang and Guanyin, still facing each other. This arrangement has remained until now. In many temples, Guanyin Hall is across from Dizang Hall. The Ten Kings and scenes of hellish punishments would be depicted in Dizang Hall, while images of goddesses known as Niangniang (Ladies) would be found in Guanyin Hall. With a setup like this, it is clear that worshipers pray to Dizang as the savior of people who are in hell and to Guanyin as the granter of health, fertility, and long life. As Dizang became the sole guardian of beings in hell, Guanyin became the chief protector of people in life. The relationship between the pair underwent changes through time. Although there is no scriptural basis for worshiping Guanyin and Dizang together, there is nevertheless a logic grounded in the existential needs of the faithful.

Guanyin, the Goddess of Mercy

Although there were goddesses in China before the appearance of Guanyin, none of them seems to have enjoyed a lasting and continuously active cult. There was thus a religious vacuum that Guanyin could conveniently and comfortably fill. Buddhism thus supplied the necessary symbols and ideals to the host country. As people adapted it to the different religious and cultural traditions in China, they developed new and different forms of Buddhism. The creation of the Tiantai, Huayan, Chan, and Pure Land schools (discussed in chapters 5, 6, and 7) is a prominent example. Although the Chinese based their main teachings and practices on some scriptures translated from Indic languages, the specific emphases and formulations reflected the native modes of thought and cultural values. This process of domestication created diversity in the pan-Asian Buddhist tradition. Guanyin's transformation into the compassionate Goddess of Mercy in China is an example. Since this bodhisattva became a feminine deity only in China and, furthermore, since this happened only after the Tang (618–907), it is necessary to offer some hypothetical explanations in the context of new developments in Chinese religions including Buddhism since the Song (960–1279). The emergence of the feminine Guanyin must also be studied in the context of new cults of other goddesses, which, not coincidentally, also happened after the Song. The feminine Guanyin in indigenous sutras, art, miracle stories, and the legend of Miaoshan appeared in the tenth to the twelfth centuries.

At that time, Neo-Confucianism was established as the official ideology, functioning very much like a state religion. This was not by coincidence; it had been the hegemonic discourse and ruling ideology of China during the preceding one thousand years. Neo-Confucianism was a philosophy and a system of political thought, but it was also an ideology sustaining the lineage and family system. It was very male-oriented, patriarchal, and hierarchical and did not recognize the presence of goddesses or provide much support for the intellectual and spiritual strivings of real women. It did not encourage or promote devotionalism. It did not appreciate religious enthusiasm or emotional fervor. Organized Buddhism and Daoism did not fare much better. The Chan rhetoric of nonduality and the Daoist elevation of the feminine principle did not translate into actual institutional support for women or provide the same opportunities for women practitioners as they did for men. We cannot name many women who became prominent Chan masters or Daoist priestesses. In one sense, then, the new goddess cults can be seen as similar responses to this totalistic system of belief and praxis, but in another way, the feminine Guanyin might be viewed as the model and inspiration for the other goddesses.

It is often assumed that when a religion provides goddesses to worship, it can empower women. When Avalokiteśvara was transformed into Guanyin, the Goddess of Mercy, new forms and expressions of religiosity became available to women and men in China. But as long as the traditional stereotypical views about women's pollution or inferiority remained unchallenged, the feminine images of Guanyin had to be either more or less than real women. They were not and could not be endowed with a real woman's characteristics. For this reason, the White-Robed Guanyin, though a fertility goddess, is devoid of sexuality. Real women, in the meantime, together with their male countrymen, worshiped the Child-Giving Guanyin, who saw to it that the family religion would never be disrupted by the lack of a male heir. The cult of Guanyin did indeed come to serve

Confucian family values. As a common saying familiar to many Chinese people goes, "Guanyin is enshrined in every household." The bodhisattva did indeed find a home in China.

The Medicine Buddha

The cult of the Medicine Buddha is important, although not as prominent as the ones discussed above. Śākyamuni Buddha is called the Supreme Physician and his teachings are called the King of Medicine.[6] When we analyze the Four Noble Truths, they can be understood as diagnosis, prognosis, and prescription. The first and second Noble Truths point out that we are ill with suffering and that the cause of the illness is desire. This is the diagnosis. The third Noble Truth of nirvana is the prognosis, and the fourth noble truth, the Noble Eightfold Path, is the prescription. When we cultivate ourselves morally and spiritually, we will be free from the suffering that is the cycle of rebirth. Nirvana is the state of complete well-being.

The Medicine Buddha's full title is the Lapis Lazuli Radiance Buddha, Master of Healing. The main scripture, *Sutra on the Merits of the Fundamental Vows of the Master of Healing, the Lapis Lazuli Radiance Tathāgata,* was translated by Xuanzang in 650. Instead of light or flames issuing from the body of the Buddha as in the *Lotus Sutra* and other Mahayana scriptures, he is described as radiating a lapis lazuli light from his body. There are no early images of the Medicine Buddha in India. None of the Chinese pilgrims mentioned his worship in India. Based on these factors, scholars suggest that the cult started in Central Asia, not India.

Medicine was one of the requisites monks were allowed to own. In order to carry out their religious vocation, they had to be healthy. Healing was one of the skills monks learned in order to treat their fellow monastics and laypeople. As we read in chapter 1, one of the famous parables found in chapter 16 of the *Lotus Sutra* is about a physician who provides medicine to cure his sons. The physician is the father, the sons are us, and the medicine is the Dharma.

As Amitābha Buddha makes forty-eight vows, the Medicine Buddha makes twelve vows. These are the conditions for his enlightenment. Also, like Amitābha, who welcomes sentient beings to his Pure Land west of our world system, the Medicine Buddha welcomes sentient beings to his Lapis Lazuli Pure Land in the east. The twelve great vows cover a wide range of physical and spiritual benefits that he bestows on sentient beings who have faith in him. Chief among them are the following:

Sixth Great Vow: "I vow that when I attain enlightenment in a future age, if there are sentient beings whose bodies are inferior, whose sense organs are impaired, who are ugly, stupid, deaf, blind, mute, bent and lame, hunchbacked, leprous, convulsive, insane, or who have all sorts of diseases and sufferings—such beings when they hear my name shall obtain proper appearances and practical intelligence. All their senses will become perfect and they shall have neither sickness nor suffering."

Seventh Great Vow: "I vow that when I attain enlightenment in a future age, if there are any sentient beings who are ill and oppressed, who have nowhere to go and nothing to return to, who have neither doctor nor medicine, neither relatives nor immediate family, who are destitute and whose sufferings are acute—as soon as my name passes through their ears they will be cured of all their diseases and they will be peaceful and joyous in body and mind. They will have plentiful families and property, and they will personally experience the supreme enlightenment."[7]

The Medicine Buddha has a special message for women. The Eighth Great Vow is addressed to them:

I vow that when I attain enlightenment in a future age, if there are any women who suffer from any of the hundred woes that befall women, who are wearied at the end of their lives and wish to abandon their female form—when these women hear my name, they all will obtain transformation in rebirth from female into male physical forms. They all will personally experience the supreme enlightenment.[8]

Buddhism, like all religions, reflects contemporary historical and social realities. In ancient India, women were not the equals of men. It was believed that to be born a woman was the result of bad karma. Indeed, women's lives had unique hardships because of pregnancy and childbirth. That is why the Medicine Buddha enables a faithful woman to be born a man in her next life. This is also the reason Amitābha's Pure Land is devoid of women. Moreover, according to some Mahayana sutras, such as the *Lotus Sutra* and this one, women can achieve enlightenment only after they have been transformed into men. The reasoning goes that since Śākyamuni Buddha was a man with a number of specific male features, only a person with a man's body could achieve enlightenment. Yet, although this sutra upholds a biased view about women, the Medicine Buddha cares for and protects women and their sons.

> If there is a woman about to give birth who suffers from acute pain, if she is able to praise the name and form and reverently worship that Tathāgata with utmost sincerity, then all her pain will be relieved and her child will be born without bodily defect. The appearance of her child will be perfect, and all who see him will exclaim with joy. The child will be endowed with keen sense organs, intelligence, and tranquility. He will seldom become ill, and non-human beings will never snatch away his vital spirit.[9]

We find many similarities between this sutra and the Pure Land sutras as well as the *Lotus Sutra*. For instance, like the Pure Land of Amitābha, the Medicine Buddha's Lapis Lazuli Pure Land is splendid. "The ground is made of lapis lazuli, and roads are marked with gold. The walls and gates, palaces and pavilions, balconies and windows, draperies and curtains are all made of the seven precious substances. It is similar to the Joyous Realm of the West; its merits and adornments are no different."[10] Just as Amitābha is attended by the two great bodhisattvas, Guanyin and Dashizhi, the Medicine Buddha is attended by two bodhisattvas, All-Pervading Solar Radiance and All-Pervading Lunar Radiance. Like Guanyin in the *Lotus Sutra,* the Medicine Buddha saves people from mortal dangers such as being burned by fire, drowned in water, imprisoned, or executed. The most distinctive commonality among the three cults of Amitābha, Guanyin, and the Medicine Buddha is their emphasis on faith as expressed by the calling of their names. When one hears the name, she or he must keep it in mind, hold it with sincere faith, and constantly invoke it.

Although many buddhas and bodhisattvas were introduced into China, only some enjoyed a cultic following. The Chinese Buddhists chose their favorites, just as they did with the many Mahayana sutras. In making these choices, they also created new pantheons not based on scriptures. We have discussed how the pairing of Guanyin and Dizang is not based on any scripture. During the Tang dynasty (618–907), around the eighth century, new Buddhist triads appeared in sculptures. Both Amitābha and the Medicine Buddha were attended by Guanyin and Dizang instead of by Guanyin and Dashizhi in the former case and All-Pervading Solar Radiance and

All-Pervading Lunar Radiance in the latter case. This is a good example of how Buddhism, an originally foreign religion, became Chinese Buddhism. It was a two-way, dialectical process. The Chinese people received the new religion. They also modified it through the creative choices they made. In the history of how Indian Buddhism became Chinese Buddhism, the cults of buddhas and bodhisattvas played an essential role.

Discussion Questions

1. How are Buddhist images viewed by believers? What roles do they play in their lives?
2. Describe some of the ways the Buddha is worshiped.
3. Why is Guanyin the most beloved bodhisattva?
4. Who is Maitreya, the future Buddha? Does he play a role similar to any figure you know in other religions?
5. What is the most distinctive difference between the Pure Land of the Medicine Buddha and that of Amitābha Buddha?

Further Reading

Birnbaum, Raoul. *The Healing Buddha.* Boulder, CO: Shambhala, 1979.

Campany, Robert F. "The Real Presence." *History of Religion* 32 (1993): 233–272.

Kuan-yin Pilgrimage. DVD. Written and directed by Chün-fang Yü, 1987. Distributed by Columbia University Press.

Sponberg, Alan, and Helen Hardacre. *Maitreya, the Future Buddha.* Cambridge: Cambridge University Press, 1988.

Yü, Chün-fang. *Kuan-yin: The Chinese Transformation of Avalokiteśvara.* New York: Columbia University Press, 2001.

Zhiru. *The Making of a Savior Bodhisattva: Dizang in Medieval China.* Honolulu: University of Hawai'i Press, 2007.

Notes

1 Campany, "The Real Presence," 262–263.

2 Daniel B. Stevenson, "Protocols of Power: Tz'u-yun Tsun-shih (964–1032) and T'ian-t'ai Lay Buddhist Rituals in the Sung," in *Buddhism in the Sung,* ed. Peter N. Gregory and Daniel A. Getz Jr. (Honolulu: University of Hawai'i Press, 1999), 345–346.

3 Kenneth K. S. Ch'en, *Buddhism in China: A Historical Survey* (Princeton, NJ: Princeton University Press, 1964), 168.

4 John S. Strong, *The Buddha: A Short Biography* (Oxford: Oneworld Publications, 2001), 145.

5   Burton Watson, trans., *The Lotus Sutra* (New York: Columbia University Press, 1993), 298–299.

6   Birnbaum, *The Healing Buddha,* 3.

7   Birnbaum, *The Healing Buddha,* 153–154.

8   Birnbaum, *The Healing Buddha,* 154.

9   Birnbaum, *The Healing Buddha,* 163.

10   Birnbaum, *The Healing Buddha,* 155.

CHAPTER 3

Buddhist Festivals and Rituals

There are many ways a person is introduced to Buddhism and becomes so interested that she becomes a believer. She may by chance meet a monk or nun whose dignified bearing attracts her admiration. He may accidentally pick up a Buddhist sutra and be impressed by its ideas. But in China, most people come into contact with Buddhism and monastics by attending festivals and participating in rituals. This was the case historically in China and is still the case today. These are also the most effective media through which Buddhism came to be disseminated among all levels of Chinese society.

Buddhist Festivals

The birthday of the Buddha, on the eighth day of the fourth lunar month, is the most important festival in the liturgical calendar. As early as the fifth century, bathing the image of the Buddha was the focal point of the ritual. Buddha's awakening on the fifteenth day of the twelfth lunar month and his nirvana or death on the fifteenth day of the second lunar month were also celebrated, although less prominently these days. Interestingly, although neither other buddhas, such as the future Buddha Maitreya, Amitābha, and the Medicine Buddha, nor the great bodhisattvas such as Guanyin, Wenshu (Mañjuśrī), Puxian (Samathabhadra), and Dizang, were historical personages, all of them were provided with birthdays and celebrated by the Ming dynasty (1368–1662). This followed the model of indigenous Chinese deities, on whose birthdays the most important annual public worship takes place.

There is no sharp demarcation between gods and humans in Chinese religion; mythical figures such as the Yellow Emperor were turned into historical cultural heroes who were venerated as the founding fathers of

Chinese civilization. In contrast, popular gods and goddesses, such as Lord Guan and Mazu, also known as the Queen of Heaven, were originally real people. Unlike in ancient Greece, where human heroes were turned into Olympian gods, in China, gods were thought to be real human beings.

The transformation of mythical buddhas and bodhisattvas can be illustrated with the case of Guanyin. Guanyin had to become Princess Miaoshan, a living woman, before she could be worshiped as a Chinese goddess. The legend of Princess Miaoshan provides a biography. The nineteenth day of the second lunar month, the day Princess Miaoshan was born, became known as Guanyin's birthday. The celebration of Guanyin's birthday was first listed in the monthly calendar section of the *Pure Rules of Huanzhu,* the monastic code created by the Chan master Mingben in 1317 for his own temple, Huanzhu (Illusory Abode). He stipulated that offerings of flowers, candles, incense, tea, fruit, and delicacies should be made and prayers be read aloud, just as on the day commemorating the Buddha's nirvana. Like the birthdays of other Chinese deities, this has become the most important festival for devotees. Subsequently, reflecting the three holy days in the cult of the Buddha, celebrations were also held on the day she attained enlightenment, the nineteenth day of the sixth lunar month, and the day of her apotheosis, the nineteenth day of the ninth lunar month.

People in China also went on pilgrimage to the sacred sites where the bodhisattvas were believed to have manifested themselves. Pious pilgrims regarded these holy sites as the bodhisattvas' homes. By journeying there, they hoped to receive blessings and, if they were lucky, have a divine vision of the deity. The phrase "Four Famous Mountains" refers to Mount Wutai in Shansi, the home of Wenshu; Mount Omei in Sichuan, the home of Puxian; Mount Putuo in Zhejiang, the home of Guanyin; and Mount Jiuhua in Anhui, the home of Dizang. While the *Flower Garland Sutra* provided legitimacy for connecting the bodhisattvas to mountains, the mountains in the scripture were not real places, just as the bodhisattvas were not historical personages. This is another example of how Buddhism was made Chinese by identifying real mountains located in specific places in China as the mythical mountains mentioned in the scriptures.

Pilgrimage sites came to be regarded as the places where the bodhisattvas resided. Visiting them was modeled upon the pilgrimage to sites where the historical Buddha left his traces, which started early in the history of Chinese Buddhism. For those who could not make such a difficult journey, the Buddha's relics came to be the focus of his cult. During the Tang dynasty, several temples in the capital, Chang'an, claimed to possess the Buddha's teeth, which were put on display for public viewing each year for a week. People would make many kinds of offerings, including food, medicine, cash, incense, flowers, fruit, and so on. The finger bone enshrined in Famen Temple outside the capital became famous because Han Yu, the Confucian scholar and archcritic of Buddhism, wrote a memorial in 819 remonstrating against its veneration by the emperor in the palace. Several times the finger bone was carried to the palace in a procession with worshipers lining the streets along the way. One witness's account describes such an event:

> On the eighth day of the fourth month of 873, the bone of the Buddha was welcomed into Ch'ang-an. Starting from the An-fu Building at the K'ai-yüan gate, all along the way on both sides, cries of invocation to the Buddha shook the earth. Men and women watched the procession of the relic respectfully, while monks and nuns followed in its wake. The emperor went to the An-fu Temple, and as he personally paid his respects, tears dropped down to moisten his breast. . . . The prominent families of Ch'ang-an all vied with one another in ornamenting their riding carriages for this occasion. Streets in every direction were filled with people supporting the old and assisting the young. Those who came to see the spectacle all fasted beforehand in order that they might receive the blessings of the Buddha. At that time, a soldier cut off his left arm in front of the Buddha's relic, and while holding it with his hand, he reverenced the relic each time he took a step, his blood sprinkling the ground all the while. As for those who walked on their elbows and knees, biting off their fingers or cutting off their hair, their numbers could not be counted. There was also a monk who covered his head with artemisia, a practice known as disciplining the head. When the pile of artemisia was ignited, the pain caused the monk to shake his head and to cry out, but young men in the market held him tight so that he could not move. When the pain beame unbearable, he cried out and fell prostrate on the ground.[1]

In an effort spearheaded by the Taiwanese Buddhist master Xingyun, the finger bone from Famen Temple was welcomed to Taiwan in 2002. Accompanied by Chinese religious and political dignitaries, it toured all the major temples on the island for over a month and was venerated by three to four million people. However, no such extreme behavior inspired by religious zeal as described above was reported.

Important seasonal festivals also marked the Buddhist liturgical calendar. Traditional China was an agrarian society, and the yearly festivals followed the agrarian cycle. The year was divided into two halves, corresponding to yin and yang, and Buddhist festivals meshed well with the existing seasonal celebrations. The Chinese New Year and the Lantern Festival on the first and fifteenth day of the first lunar month celebrated the change from winter to spring and the increasing strength of yang, whereas the Ghost Festival of the fifteenth day of the seventh lunar month marked the change from summer to winter and the increasing strength of yin. While the former was the time of planting, the latter was the time of harvest. On the three major celebrations—Chinese New Year, the Lantern Festival, and the Ghost Festival—monasteries held Dharma assemblies with sutra chanting, prayers, and merit-making rituals.

The Lantern Festival and the Ghost Festival have close associations with the Buddhist tradition. On the night of the first full moon of the new year, the fifteenth day of the first month, all the monasteries vied with each other by displaying lanterns of many colors and shapes. People would carry brightly lit torches and wander the streets all night. It was a time of merrymaking. In traditional China, upper-class women were confined to the inner chambers and not allowed to go out of doors. But on this night they could be seen out viewing the lantern display, mingling with common people and the opposite sex. The Buddhist version of how this festival started reflects its perennial rivalry with Daoism as well as the desire for imperial legitimacy. According to the Buddhist version, its origin went back to Emperor Ming (r. 58–75 CE) and the time when Buddhism was first introduced into China. Because Daoist priests challenged the truth claims of Buddhist scriptures, the emperor ordered that both Buddhist and Daoist scriptures be set on fire to test their authenticity. When the fire touched the sutras, instead of being consumed, the leaves glowed brightly. Emperor Ming decreed that lanterns should be lighted each year on the fifteenth day of the first month to commemorate this miraculous event.

The Ghost Festival was also known as the Ullambana Festival. It is the only time when the hungry ghosts will return to earth and enjoy offerings. Hungry ghosts are the unfortunate creatures who suffer perpetual hunger and thirst. But on this occasion, their suffering can be assuaged by the food offerings made by filial descendants, delivered according to ritual. The festival was based on two Buddhist scriptures about the monk Mulian saving his mother in hell. According to Stephen Teiser, who studied the Ghost Festival and translated the *Yulanpen Sutra* and the *Sutra on Offering Bowls to Repay Kindness,* the origin of these scriptures is not clear. They might have been composed in India or Central Asia around the year 400 and translated into Chinese; another possibility is that they were compiled in China in the early sixth century.[2]

Mulian was a monk with great spiritual powers. He wished to repay the kindness of his parents for nursing and feeding him. With his divine eye he saw his mother reborn among the hungry ghosts because of her extreme bad karma. She had nothing to eat or drink, and her "skin hung off her bones." Mulian felt great pity and offered his mother a bowl filled with rice. But when she tried to eat the rice, it turned into flaming coals even before reaching her mouth. Mulian was overcome with sorrow and wept bitterly. He ran to the Buddha and asked for help. The Buddha explained that the mother's sin was too grave for Mulian to save her by himself. He must rely on the collective spiritual power of the sangha to deliver her. The spiritual power of the monks was greatest when they finished the three-month-long rain retreat, stipulated by the Vinaya or monastic rules. In order not to harm living creatures during the monsoon season, monks were not to travel but stay in one place and engage in meditation and study. At the end of the rain retreat, lay believers offered them new robes, and the monks celebrated the occasion by venting any grievances against fellow monks and confessing their own mistakes. This was known as "releasing oneself." By releasing themselves, the monks also released hungry ghosts from suffering with this ritual. The Buddha told Mulian:

> On the fifteenth day of the seventh month, when the assembled monks of the ten directions release themselves, for the sake of seven generations of ancestors, your current parents, and those in distress, you should gather food of the one hundred flavors and five kinds of fruit, a basin for washing and rinsing, incense, oil lamps and candles, and mattresses and bedding; take the sweetest, prettiest things in the world and place them in a bowl and offer it to the assembled monks, those of great virtue of the ten directions. . . . When you make offerings to these kinds of monks as they release themselves, then your current parents, seven generations of ancestors, and six kinds of relatives will obtain release from suffering in

the three evil paths of rebirth; at that moment they will be liberated and clothed and fed naturally. If one's parents are living, they will have one hundred years of joy and happiness. If they are deceased, then seven generations of ancestors will be reborn in the heavens.[3]

The origin story of Mulian saving his mother was disseminated through many media. Traveling monks propagated the message by giving lectures on the Buddhist sutras. This in turn gave rise to the genre of transformation texts; the earliest one about Mulian appeared about 800.[4] In time, the story of Mulian also became a favorite subject in plays and precious volumes, a new genre of popular religious literature that appeared in the sixteenth century. One can understand why the Ghost Festival has been so popular down the ages. The filial son Mulian, just like his counterpart, the filial daughter Miaoshan, proved that celibate monastics were in fact exemplars of filial piety. At the same time, the story demonstrates the indispensable role monks and monasteries came to play for the welfare of the Chinese family. Traditional ancestor worship must be carried out by making offerings to monks and monasteries, for only through them could both the living parents and the dead ancestors going back to seven generations achieve a good rebirth.

New Year and the Lantern Festival have gradually lost their Buddhist associations and become secularized. In contrast, the Ghost Festival and the birthdays of the Buddha and Guanyin have kept their religious significance and are still observed. However, despite their fame and popularity, these festivals take place only once a year. Other types of Buddhist rituals can take place anytime throughout the year. They exert more impact on the lives of the people. We will now discuss three kinds of rituals: releasing life (*fangsheng*), mortuary rituals of feeding hungry ghosts (*shishi*) and the Water-Land Assembly (*shuilu*), and the Great Compassion Repentance (*Dabeichan*).

Buddhist Rituals

Releasing Life

"Releasing life" refers to saving the lives of captured creatures by buying them from vendors and setting them free. They are usually small creatures such as shrimp, fish, turtles, and birds, which one buys and then sets free in water or air. People are encouraged to bring aquatic creatures to set free in a large "pond for releasing life" dug on monastic grounds. But sometimes, though rarely, large animals such as sheep, pigs, and cows are also saved and kept in a barnyard behind the monastery. Although nonkilling is a basic precept observed by all Buddhists everywhere, vegetarianism and releasing life are uniquely emphasized in Chinese Buddhism. The precept of not killing does not necessarily lead to the latter two practices, for there is not an obvious connection linking the three. That is why Buddhists in other countries tend not to be vegetarians. Nor is releasing life practiced universally. However, if we cannot bear to kill a creature, the same compassionate feeling toward the creature may make us loath to eat it. A further extension of this compassion is to save it from becoming somebody else's food. Releasing life should therefore be the perfection of nonkilling.

Both the court and leading Buddhist masters promoted nonkilling and releasing life throughout Chinese history. During the Sui dynasty, in 583, it was legally stipulated that in the first, fifth, and ninth months of the year, as well as on the "six fast days" (eighth, fourteenth, fifteenth, twenty-fourth, twenty-ninth, and thirtieth) of every month, no one should kill any living beings. The choice of these particular dates was based on the rules set down in the *Sutra of Brahma's Net,* which contains fifty-eight bodhisattva precepts. As the basic precepts of Mahayana Buddhism primarily addressed to lay believers, these have always enjoyed great popularity as well as authority in China. The sutra says that during those same three months and on those six days of every month a lay devotee should keep eight specific precepts, which include the prohibitions against killing and theft and the rule of not eating after the noon meal. On the six fast days, the four Heavenly Kings will descend to earth to make inspection, observe the good and evil deeds of men, and make a record of them. Therefore, a person should be especially cautious on these days.

A decree was issued in 619, during the Tang dynasty, forbidding the slaughter of animals as well as fishing and hunting during the first, fifth, and ninth months of every year. This decree apparently met with varying degrees of success until the Huichang persecution in 845. The ritual of releasing life was institutionalized with the establishment of ponds for releasing life very early on. The earliest reference to ponds for releasing life dated back to the reign of Emperor Yuan of the Liang dynasty (552–555), when a pavilion was constructed for this purpose, although we do not know the date of its construction or any details concerning its use. During the Tang, Emperor Suzong issued a decree in 759, setting up eighty-one ponds for releasing life.

The gradual popularity of the practice of releasing life was due mainly to the successful evangelism of outstanding monks. Yongming Yanshou (904–975), the great synthesizer of all Buddhist schools, was a strong advocate of the joint practice of Chan and Pure Land. When he was in charge of taxes for the king of Wuyue (before he became a monk), he used government money to buy fish and shrimp and set them free. Zunshi (963–1032), a Tiantai master who also advocated Pure Land practice, persuaded many fishermen to change their profession. It is said that when he was lecturing at Kaiyuan Monastery, people stopped drinking wine and butchers lost their business. He was also instrumental in setting up new ponds for releasing life. In 1017 Emperor Zhenzong issued a decree calling for the establishment of ponds along the rivers Huai and Zhe as well as in Hunan and Hubei, where fishing was prohibited.

Zunshi also promoted the organization of "meetings for releasing life." He sent a memorial to the throne in 1018 requesting that the emperor's birthday be celebrated by having the West Lake, the famous scenic site in Hangzhou, established as a pond for releasing life. From then on, "meetings for releasing life" were organized every year on Buddha's birthday, the eighth day of the fourth month, and participation became very fashionable. The "meetings for releasing life" were a new type of Buddhist lay association that flourished during the Song dynasty. Buddhist lay associations could be traced back to Huiyuan's Lotus Society and to the many organizations whose traces were found at Dunhuang. However, these new meetings were quite different. Whereas the earlier associations were organized for the purposes of erecting statues of the Buddha, building caves to store Buddhist treasures, copying and making sutras, reciting sutras, or organizing Buddhist feasts and religious festivals, the Song associations were focused on only one activity: releasing living creatures. Zunshi wrote manuals directing how the rite should be carried out. As Daniel Stevenson says, "the releasing living creatures ceremony takes the form of a kind of conversion liturgy. Beings are first freed of their gross physical and mental impediments through offerings and incantation, then brought to the Buddhist path through preaching of the dharma and administering of the Three Refuges."[5]

It was also during the Song that tracts exhorting people to refrain from killing animals for food and to keep a vegetarian diet started to appear in great numbers. The Ming Buddhist master Zhuhong (1535–1615) continued this trend by writing two essays, "On Refraining from

Killing" and "On Releasing Sentient Beings," which were reprinted and distributed widely. They had lasting influence during his time and down the ages. They were received with such enthusiasm and became so famous that the mother of the emperor sent a special emissary to seek further instruction from Zhuhong. They also started the vogue among lay circles of organizing "societies for releasing life," which raised funds to build ponds for releasing life and held regular meetings to set free captured birds, fish, and other domesticated animals (which they usually bought from fishermen or at the marketplace).

In "On Releasing Sentient Beings," Zhuhong uses many examples drawn from historical records, legends, contemporary reports, and personal experiences to illustrate the efficacy of releasing life. More powerful than rational and doctrinal persuasion, these stories helped to convince not only his contemporaries but also later readers of the reality of karma, which ensures that a good deed is always rewarded. By stressing how the numinous worked in the miraculous, the magical, and the uncommon, he struck a responsive chord.

Two anecdotes Zhuhong tells in this essay give a good idea of the type of story he used. Both happened in his own day: one to himself, the other to someone in his native Hangzhou. The first took place in 1570. While he was staying at a small temple during his travels after he became a monk, he saw that someone had captured several centipedes and was fastening their heads and tails together with a bamboo bow. Zhuhong bought the centipedes and set them free. Only one was still alive and got away; the rest were dead. Later on, one night while he was sitting with a friend, he suddenly caught a glimpse of a centipede on the wall. After he had tried to drive it away but failed, he said to the centipede, "Are you the one I set free before? Have you come here to thank me? If so, I shall teach the Dharma to you." He then continued, "All sentient beings evolve from the mind. The ones with violent minds are transformed into tigers and wolves, and the ones with poisonous minds are transformed into snakes and scorpions. If you give up your poisonous heart, you can cast off this form. Listen carefully and do not move." After he finished talking, the centipede slowly crept out the window without having to be driven away. The friend was greatly amazed.

The second anecdote happened in 1581, to a family named Gan living near Hangzhou. A neighbor was robbed, and Gan's daughter presented the neighbor's mother with ten eels when she went to commiserate.

The eels were put away in a big jar and then forgotten. One night the mother dreamed that ten men dressed in yellow gowns and wearing pointed hats knelt before her and begged for their lives. Upon waking, she consulted a fortune-teller, who told her that some creatures were begging to be released from captivity. She searched all over the house and finally found the jar containing the eels. They had grown to enormous size by then and numbered exactly ten. She was utterly astonished and set them free right away.[6]

In the words of Zhuhong, these and other stories were meant to prove that "of the persons who set creatures free, some are spared from disasters, some recover from mental illnesses, some achieve rebirth in heaven, and some attain enlightenment in the Way. There is clear evidence that as he releases life, he assuredly receives a reward."[7] The same essay offers concrete guidelines about releasing life. First, everyone is enjoined to buy animals whenever the opportunity presents itself. One should not begrudge the money spent, for money does not last, whereas the merit created by saving animals lasts forever. If a person does not have money, he will still accumulate merit so long as he has a compassionate heart and persuades others to buy animals, and so long as he takes delight in such actions by others.

Second, it is the deed of releasing, not the size or quantity of the animals released, that counts most. The rich man who saves the lives of many animals and the poor man who saves only one insect are equally praiseworthy. What is most important is that it be done as often as possible—continuously. There are people who do not understand this principle. They buy a great number of creatures who are small in size in the hope of gaining more merit. This is no more than calculated greed; it is certainly not compassion for sentient beings.

Third, in releasing life, one is enjoined to try whenever possible to perform a religious ceremony in which sutras are read and Amitābha Buddha's name is recited. For one should save not only the creature's physical body but also its spiritual life. However, if this cannot be conveniently arranged, one should be flexible. Where there is not time for sutra recitation, calling the Buddha's name alone is enough. If for the sake of the religious ceremony one keeps the animals overnight and allows some of them to perish, the consequences surely will negate the intention.

Vegetarianism and releasing life have remained distinctive features of Chinese lay Buddhist piety. Ponds for releasing life are found in all large monasteries in China. A book titled *Drawings to Protect Life* by Feng Zikai

(1898–1975), a famous writer, painter, and cartoonist, generated great interest in vegetarianism and releasing life among the elites. The book contains fifty drawings that promote vegetarianism and release of animals captured for food. The ritual of releasing life is still being performed in China, Taiwan, and Hong Kong and among overseas Chinese communities. Groups of Buddhist faithful carry large numbers of fish, crabs, shrimp, or turtles in plastic bags or containers and drop them into the ocean, lakes, or rivers. They are not concerned with the ecological consequences of doing so. Under the influence of Humanistic Buddhism, Buddhist teachers in Taiwan have urged a new way to express compassion. They advise people to use their resources and energy to protect the environment and to save domestic pets from abuse and abandonment.

Mortuary Rituals

There are three major Buddhist mortuary rituals being performed today for the benefit of one's ancestors and family members as well as for all sentient beings: the Ghost Festival, feeding hungry ghosts, and the Water-Land Assembly. We have discussed the Ghost Festival already and will concentrate here on the latter two. Once again, the Tiantai master Zunshi was responsible for first codifying them. Manuals for these rituals continued to be written from the Song to the Ming (eleventh–seventeenth centuries). Of the three, the ritual of feeding hungry ghosts is performed most often and thus best known. This is because it can be performed anytime and is not limited to the seventh lunar month as is the Ghost Festival. And unlike the Water-Land Assembly, which requires seven days, the ritual of feeding hungry ghosts can be completed in a few hours.

As noted in the introduction, the cult of ancestor worship, remembering and honoring one's dead ancestors, was a Chinese tradition from the beginning of history. This was done by offering them food and wine. In the Song, people continued the traditional practice by offering the dead uncooked meat and wine. Paper money and clothing made of papier-mâché were also burned for them to enjoy in their afterlife. This is still done today. If the descendents do not maintain this ritual, or if the dead have no descendents, they become so-called vengeful ghosts. However, according to Buddhism, one is reborn in one of the six realms of rebirth after an interval of forty-nine days, or alternatively, one can be reborn in the Pure Land if one is a pious believer of Amitābha Buddha. Although these three different postmortem destinies are clearly in conflict, people were not troubled by it.

However, since a person is always reborn in another state, according to Buddhist doctrines, she or he really cannot receive any benefit from the things offered by the living. Strictly speaking, Buddhist rituals cannot be called mortuary rituals for this reason. Rather, they are performed for the benefit of sentient beings out of compassion. Buddhist masters became interested in creating rituals for the dead in the Song because new beliefs not found in either Chinese religion or Buddhism appeared during the tenth century. After death, people are judged in the courts of the ten kings in what Stephen Teiser calls the Chinese "purgatory."[8] They receive different punishments in accordance with the kind of sin committed while alive. For instance, if one commits evil speech, one's tongue will be torn out. Only after one completes this series of juridical trials and punishments is one reborn in the six realms by the order of King Yama. People with too much negative karma become hungry ghosts and perpetually suffer from hunger and thirst. Only food and drink offered by monks at properly performed rituals can relieve their suffering. This belief was conveniently combined with the traditional Chinese belief in ghosts bereft of offerings and resulted in the transformation of the rituals of universal compassion into Buddhist mortuary rituals. Although no one wants to believe that his dead family members have become hungry ghosts, this is always a possibility. Even if it is not, sponsoring such rites will unfailingly generate a great deal of merit, which can be transferred to dead relatives to help them achieve a good rebirth. It can also bring blessings to oneself in the present life in the form of health, wealth, and long life. Therefore, these rites have always been very popular in China.

The Tiantai master Zunshi campaigned against the use of blood sacrifice and wine in the rite for the dead ancestors. He created the ritual of feeding hungry ghosts based on the *Sutra on the Dhāraṇī for the Deliverance of the Flaming-Mouth Hungry Ghost,* an esoteric sutra translated by Amoghavajra (705–774). Ānanda is visited by a hungry ghost named Flaming Face, who tells Ānanda that in three days, the latter will die and be reborn as a hungry ghost. Greatly alarmed, Ānanda goes to the Buddha the next morning for help and is taught the method of feeding hungry ghosts. When food is ritually offered, it becomes a magical nectar that will transform those who consume it into buddhas. Zunshi advocated daily performance of a shortened version of this rite and chanting the spell from the sutra to deliver ancestors who might have been reborn as hungry ghosts as well as ghosts unknown to oneself. Although the ritual claims this scriptural pedigree and was first formulated by Zunshi in the eleventh century, its performance nowadays is based on a manual written by Zhuhong in 1606. The ritual is believed to be the most effective means of delivering one's dead relatives from hell. It has enjoyed great popularity.

Zhuhong's manual provides directions to the ritual master in carrying out the threefold ritual activities. The ritual is a coordination of body, speech, and mind, the "three mysteries," which are represented by forming mudras, chanting *dharanis*, and meditative visualization.

The two bodhisattvas, Guanyin and Dizang, appear at critical junctures of the ritual procedure. The high point is reached when the presiding ritual master becomes identified with Guanyin through meditative visualization. The manual used by monks today is a simplified version of that by Zhuhong, made a hundred years after his time. The ritual procedure is complicated and demands great concentration.

At the beginning, a picture of the hungry ghost Flaming Face is placed on the altar facing the assembled monks. The Great Compassion *Dharanis* and a hymn praising Guanyin are chanted before the altar. After the ritual master "fixes the area of the five directions," accompanied by an invocation to five different buddhas, Guanyin is invoked directly. The presiding monk makes a mudra called Guanyin meditation mudra, through which the ritual master enters into the Guanyin samadhi. The main action of the ritual is performed by Guanyin in the person of the ritual master. The highlight of the ritual is when he makes the mudra of opening up the gate of hell. He visualizes three red rays emitting from his mouth, hands, and chest, which open the gates. The rays represent three powers that can destroy the three categories of sins of the body, speech, and mind committed by beings in hell. At this point, Dizang is invoked to help the dead come forth to accept the offerings. This is accomplished by several mudras. After the invited ghosts are helped to repent by the mudra of repentance, the presiding monk transforms water into nectar by performing the mudra of sweet dew. He then enables them to drink it by performing the mudra of opening up the throat. He visualizes a green lotus held in his left hand, from which "sweet dew" flows out for the ghosts to drink.

The Water-Land Assembly is another major mortuary ritual performed widely today. It consists of chanting sutras and doing penance, and the service ends with offering food to the dead. The performance of these two rituals brought income to the temples, a major source of support for the monks in the twentieth century. Of all the Buddhist mortuary rites, the

Water-Land Assembly is the most elaborate, lasting for seven days. In 1934, a prominent Buddhist monk, Fafang (1904–1951), commented sadly on the prominence of ritualism in Chinese monasteries: "In every temple of China, although the placard on the main gate says it is such-and-such Meditation Hall, inside the Meditation Hall one realizes that it has been changed into the Hall for Chanting Sutras and Reciting Penances or the Inner Altar of the Water-Land. As for the monks living there, even though they call themselves Chan monks, they are simply monks specializing in chanting sutras and reciting penances."[9] Many Buddhist leaders were critical of the commercialization of such rituals. To change people's perception that Buddhism was only concerned with death, Taixu (1890–1947) coined the term "Buddhism for Human Life" to emphasize that it was concerned with human beings living in this human realm, one of the Buddhist six realms of rebirth. Contemporary Humanistic Buddhism originated in Taixu's reevaluation of mortuary rituals.

The ritual manual used today for the Water-Land Assembly was composed by Zhuhong, based on his revision of the text used in his time. The ritual is not based on a sutra but is traced to a founding myth. According to Zhuhong, the original ritual text was created by Emperor Wu of Liang (r. 502–549), the pious Buddhist ruler. General Bai Qi of the Chin once buried four hundred thousand people alive in the third century BCE. Because of the enormity of his sin, he was consigned to hell for eternity with no hope of relief. He visited Emperor Wu in a dream and asked for help. The emperor consulted Master Baozhi (425–514) for a way to save the general. Baozhi compiled a ritual text based on relevant scriptures in the Buddhist canon. After the text was completed, the emperor prayed for a sign. The whole hall lit up brilliantly, and he took this to mean that the text met with divine approval. This is how the ritual came to be handed down.

Despite the hoary mythical origin, the ritual probably dates from the late Tang and became popular during the Song, when it was performed for the imperial ancestors. It was conducted for the ruling families of the Yuan and the Ming. By Zhuhong's time, it had become so popular that he felt the need to codify the ritual text. The Water-Land is an elaborate and all-inclusive banquet to which the souls of all dead sentient beings are invited. The list of invited "guests" provides an excellent picture of the Chinese vision of the other world. Not only buddhas and bodhisattvas but also Daoist gods, popular deities of mountains and rivers, the god of Mount Tai, gods of the infernal courts, as well as gods of earth, grains, wind, and rain are included. The invited souls from the realm of the dead represent all social classes: emperors, ministers, Confucian scholars, merchants, farmers, artisans, soldiers, and Buddhist and Daoist clergy. As the name of the ritual indicates, all people who have died on land and in water will receive spiritual succor and material sustenance. Even suicides, women who died in childbirth, and aborted fetuses are invited to attend. Scrolls called Water-Land paintings that depict the invited spirits mentioned in the manual were made and hung along the temple walls when the ritual was performed.

The Great Compassion Repentance

The Buddhist ritual performed most often nowadays in all temples is without question the Great Compassion Repentance. The Great Compassionate One refers to the Thousand-Handed and Thousand-Eyed Guanyin, the form featured in an esoteric sutra bearing the same name, and the ritual is connected with this bodhisattva. The performance of this ritual is an indispensable segment of the liturgy celebrating Guanyin's "birthdays," carried out on the three holy days (the nineteenth day of the second, sixth, and ninth lunar months). Most temples also perform it regularly throughout the year.

Repentance was a very important part of religious life for Buddhists. From as early as the time when the Vinaya or monastic discipline was compiled in India, the *posadha* or precept recitation ritual was performed. Twice monthly, on the days of the full moon and half moon, monks gathered to listen to the recitation of the *prātimokṣa* (the 250 precepts for a *bhikshu* or ordained monk). Any monk who committed an offense while the rules were being read aloud had to confess in front of the assembly. He would then receive either absolution or punishment, depending on the nature and severity of the offense. Confession and repentance were also carried out at the end of the rain retreat. The *posadha* ritual was also observed in China, although according to Zhuhong, that was no longer the case in the sixteenth century. He reinstated it for his monastery. While he used the Indian model, Zhuong expanded it to include the precepts for lay Buddhists, novices, and bodhisattvas in addition to the precepts for monks. At the ceremony, the five precepts, the ten precepts, the complete set of 250 precepts for a monk, and finally the ten grave and forty-eight light precepts for a bodhisttva were recited in front of an assembly of all the monks of the temple. Offenses were then to be confessed and the precepts received anew.

This was still the the practice later in China. Although the *posadha* was not continuously performed in monasteries prior to Zhuhong's time, it probably served as the inspiration for the creation of many new repentance rituals appearing in China in the fifth and sixth centuries. They differ from the Indian model on two accounts. First, the ritual texts were not derived from the Vinaya but written by laypeople, the most famous being the one composed by Emperor Wu of Liang. *Emperor Liang's Confession* is often performed today, particularly in the seventh lunar month in connection with the Ghost Festival. The second difference is the content of the ritual text. Instead of confessing specific offenses, one repents for one's sins in general. Beverley Foulk McGuire writes, "Most confessions are formulaic and prearranged, beginning by lamenting one's karmic obstacles, then stating a general list of sins, and finally confessing that one has committed sins; variation comes only when practitioners insert their names at certain parts."[10] This also characterizes the Great Compassion Repentance.

The Great Compassion Repentance is performed in a monastery by lay believers under the direction of monks. They confess their sins and seek Guanyin's protection. The Tiantai master Zhili (960–1028) in the early Song wrote the first manual formulating the procedure. The model he used was the ritualized meditation regimens created by Zhiyi (538–597), the founder of the Tiantai school, to be discussed in chapter 5. For these thinkers, meditation must be preceded by confession. Moral purity is a prerequisite of spiritual enlightenment. According to Daniel Stevenson, Zhiyi's four forms of samadhi, meditation programs believed to have the power to remove karmic obstacles and induce enlightenment, were based on the repentance rituals and meditative practices in the first half of the fifth century, and they led to devotional practices beginning in the sixth century. The Tiantai rituals served several purposes. They could be integrated into daily worship in the monastery at six intervals during the day: morning, noon, late afternoon, early night, midnight, and late night. They could be practiced by serious and advanced meditators for a specific period of time and in a specially sanctified arena to achieve a religious goal. More important, they could be performed as public ceremonies for the benefit of many people, providing them with material protection and spiritual succor. While the first two modes of practice serve monastics, the third serves ordinary people.[11]

The four forms of samadhi are differentiated by the sutras recited, the length of the meditation, and the different body postures and movements of the meditator. The meditator is to sit constantly, walk constantly, sit half the time and walk half of the time, or neither sit nor walk but be at ease. Of the four, the most famous is the Lotus Repentance. It requires the meditator to chant the *Lotus Sutra* while practicing sitting meditation half of the time and walking meditation the other half of the time. It lasts twenty-one days. Zhili used the Lotus Repentance as the model to create the Great Compassion Repentance.

Like his contemporary Zunshi, Zhili was a fervent practitioner of Tiantai repentance rituals. Both men were ready to undergo physical suffering in practicing repentance rituals. Zunshi pledged to devote himself until death to regularly practicing the four forms of samadhi on the day commemorating the death of Zhiyi. He sealed the vow by scorching the crown of his head.[12] In 1016, when Zhili was fifty-seven, he made a vow to perform the Lotus Repentance for three years and then immolate himself as an offering to the wonderful sutra and in the hope of going to the Pure Land. Early the following year he made a pact with ten fellow monks to carry out this three-year project. But when his plan to commit suicide became known, many people, including Zunshi, the governor, and the imperial son-in-law, begged him to desist. Eventually, he and the ten monks agreed. When they finished the Lotus Repentance, they performed the Great Compassion Repentance for three years instead of immolating themselves as originally planned. Even though Zhili was prevented from carrying out his vow, he is said to have burned off three fingers as an offering to the Buddha.

The Great Compassion Repentance is performed at Nongchan Temple, the home temple of Chan master Shengyan in Taipei, twice each month. When I asked Shengyan why this ritual is performed so often, he answered, "It is because the Chinese people have an affinity with Guanyin." Temples in China, Taiwan, Hong Kong, and overseas Chinese communities also perform it regularly and often.

I attended a Great Compassion Repentance ceremony held at Nongchan Temple in 1996. The ceremony lasted about two hours. Led by an officiating monk known as "master of repentance" and his assistants, the congregation recited selected passages from the *Dharani Sutra of the Great Compassionate Heart Taught by the Thousand-Handed and Thousand-Eyed One*, an esoteric sutra translated by Bhagavadharma in 650–660. The service was a well-choreographed and moving experience. Sonorous chanting was interspersed with singing in lilting cadences. There were constant and vigorous bodily movements for the entire two hours. The congregation stood, bowed, prostrated, and knelt for periods sometimes up to ten minutes each. The highlight was the recitation of the *dharani* known as the Great Compassion Dharani twenty-one times, and the confession of sins.

The ritual as performed in Taiwan and elsewhere follows a text dating to the Qing (1644–1912), which is a simplified version of the original by the Song master Zhili. The ritual sequence roughly follows that formulated by Zhili, which consists of ten parts: (1) sanctifying the place of practice; (2) purifying the three activities of body, speech, and mind; (3) creating a ritual space; (4) making offerings; (5) inviting the Three Treasures and various gods; (6) offering praise and prayer; (7) doing prostrations; (8) making vows and chanting the *dharani;* (9) making confession and repentance; and (10) practicing discernment. Zhili used the Lotus Repentance as the model but substituted circumambulation and recitation of the *Lotus Sutra* with prostration, making vows, and chanting the *dharani.*

The ritual begins with three invocations of the Great Compassion Bodhisattva Guanyin, followed by the hymn of incense offering. The congregation then reads a passage explaining the reason for performing the ritual. This is followed by prostrations to Śākyamuni Buddha, Amitābha Buddha, the Great Compassion Dharani, The Thousand-Handed and Thousand-Eyed Guanyin, Dashizhi (Mahātsthāmaprāpta), Maitreya, Wenshu (Mañjuśrī), Puxian (Samanthabhadra), and many other bodhisattvas. The congregation kneels and prostrates after each title is called out. The name of Zhili is invoked, just before prostrations are made to the Four Heavenly Kings; the gods of oceans, rivers, ponds, swamps, trees, and herbs; the earth; the mountains; palaces; houses; and so on. After the prostrations, key passages of the *Dharani Sutra* are recited aloud:

> If a monk, nun, layman, laywoman, young man, or young girl wants to keep and recite the *dharani,* you must give rise to the heart of compassion toward all sentient beings and make the following vows after me.
>
> Namah Guanyin of Great Compassion, may I quickly learn everything about the Dharma.
>
> Namah Guanyin of Great Compassion, may I speedily obtain the eyes of wisdom.
>
> Namah Guanyin of Great Compassion, may I quickly save all sentient beings.
>
> Namah Guanyin of Great Compassion, may I speedily obtain expedient means.

Namah Guanyin of Great Compassion, may I quickly sail on the boat of wisdom.

Namah Guanyin of Great Compassion, may I speedily cross over the ocean of suffering.

Namah Guanyin of Great Compassion, may I quickly obtain the way of discipline and meditation.

Namah Guanyin of Great Compassion, may I speedily ascend the nirvana mountain.

Namah Guanyin of Great Compassion, may I quickly enter the house of nonaction.

Namah Guanyin of Great Compassion, may I speedily achieve the Dharma body.

If I face a mountain of knives, may it naturally crumble; if I face a roaring fire, may it naturally burn out; if I face hell, may it naturally disappear; if I face a hungry ghost, may it naturally be satiated; if I face an asura, may its evil heart naturally become tame; and if I face an animal, may it naturally obtain great wisdom.

The congregation calls the name of Guanyin ten times and that of Amitābha Buddha ten times. This is followed by another sutra passage in which Guanyin declares to the Buddha: "If anyone recites the *dharani*, should he fall into the three evil realms of rebirth, or not be born into one of the buddha lands, or not attain unlimited samadhi and eloquence, or not get all his wishes and desires in the present life, I will not achieve complete, perfect enlightenment. If one does not obtain all that one wishes for in the present life, the *dharani* is not called the Great Compassionate Heart Dharani." This is then followed by collective chanting of the *dharani* twenty-one times.

Then the congregation kneels and makes the following confession, reading aloud part of the text originally composed by Zhili. Zhili first sets forth the Tiantai credo of the One Mind that is originally pure and shared by both buddhas and sentient beings. However, under the influence of ignorance, people develop wrong views and attachment. He next tells us to confess all possible sins we might have committed both in our past lives and the present life. He then explains the wondrous power of the Great Compassion Dharani, which can destroy all the obstructions created by the sins. He further teaches us to ask for the protection of the Thousand-Handed and Thousand-Eyed, who is the giver of the *dharani*. Finally, he exhorts us to seek rebirth in Amitābha's Pure Land.

Disciple So-and-So makes confession with a mind of utmost sincerity. . . . I have committed all possible sins in many existences. I have done the ten evil deeds [of killing, stealing, adultery, lying, double-tongue (speaking falsely), coarse language, filthy language, covetousness, anger, and perverted views] and five deadly sins [of patricide, matricide, killing an arhat, shedding the blood of a buddha, and destroying the harmony of the sangha]. I have slandered the Dharma and other people, broken the precepts and fasts, destroyed stupas and temples, stolen monks' possessions, polluted the pure life of a monk, and embezzled food and property belonging to the sangha. . . . Now I have encountered the perfect and divine Great Compassionate Dharani, which can quickly destroy all these sinful obstructions; that is why I today recite it with utmost sincerity and take refuge in Guanshiyin Bodhisattva and the great masters of the ten directions, give rise to the thought for enlightenment, and practice the action of the True Word [the Great Compassionate Dharani]. . . . I beseech the Great Compassionate Guanshiyin Bodhisattva to protect us with his thousand hands and illuminate us with his thousand eyes so that both internal and external obstructions will be extinguished, vows benefiting the self and others can be fulfilled, original knowledge will be revealed, demons and heretics will be subdued, and the threefold karmas [of body, speech, and mind] can be diligently advanced. By cultivating the cause of rebirth in the Pure Land, I am determined to be reborn in Amitābha Buddha's world of Supreme Bliss when I give up my present body and will not go to any other realm of rebirth.

After making the confession, the congregation takes refuge in the Three Treasures. The rite concludes with giving praise to Śākyamuni Buddha, Amitābha Buddha, the Great Compassionate Dharani, Thousand-Handed and Thousand-Eyed Guanshiyin Bodhisattva, Dashizhi Bodhisattva, and Dharani King Bodhisattva.

In the ritual I attended, the language of the confessional was elegant and the chanting was beautiful, a deeply moving experience. It was no wonder that some were moved to tears while reciting the confessional. At the same time, there were displays of popular piety. I saw a great number of containers filled with water lined up along the wall behind the altar. They were plastic bottles of various sizes brought there by participants who would take them home after the service. I was told that the water, thus charged with the luminous power of the service, became "Great Compassion water" and would have curative effects. Such a belief can be traced back to the tenth century and even earlier. Since the Qing (seventeenth century), the chanting of the Great Compassion Dharani, together with the *Heart Sutra,* has been a part of the morning and evening services in Chinese temples. Most lay Buddhists have memorized the Great Compassion Dharani and are proficient in chanting it, which they make part of their daily practice.

In this chapter, we have examined the various ways people worship the buddhas and bodhisattvas. People pray to their images, honor them in festivals, and seek their protection and blessings through rituals. The cult of buddhas and bodhisattvas is built on the personal relationship between the devotee and the divine. Such a relationship is possible because of the Chinese belief in *ganying* ("stimulus and response" or "sympathetic resonance"). The prayer of the devotee is the initiating stimulus or trigger that, when sincere enough, is answered by the response from the buddha or bodhisattva. The theory of *ganying* is rooted in the Chinese view of the universe prior to the introduction of Buddhism. As discussed in the introduction, all living and nonliving things in the universe are constituted of qi, or life force. Qi refers to yin and yang and the five phases of wood, fire, earth, metal, and water, which evolve from the interaction of the two. This is the worldview shared by all Chinese religions. Because humans are of the same substance as the rest of the universe, there is the possibility for communication between us and our environment. This belief is implied by the concept of stimulus and response, which became an article of faith during the first and second centuries of the Common Era, the same time period when Buddhism entered China.

The indigenous belief in *ganying* was quickly applied to the workings of buddhas and bodhisattvas. According to Jizang, the Three Treatises master (to be discussed in chapter 5), the bodhisattva both affects and responds. The Tiantai school uses the image of water and moon to describe the "wonder of affect and response," one of the thirty wonders associated with calling the buddha's name. According to Mahayana Buddhism, all sentient beings are endowed with Buddha nature. There is no essential difference separating buddhas and bodhisattvas from ordinary people, except that buddhas and bodhisattvas are enlightened, whereas ordinary people have not achieved the same realization about the nature of reality. In this regard, there is congruence between Buddhist ontology and indigenous

Chinese belief. Just as humankind can form a trinity with Heaven and Earth, they can also become buddhas through the experience of enlightenment. Sincerity and good karma are thereby equally emphasized and skillfully harmonized by the cults of buddhas and bodhisattvas. Worship enables the devotee to achieve salvation as well as gain worldly benefits. Miracle stories were compiled to testify to the efficacy of not only praying to buddhas and bodhisattvas but also chanting the *Diamond Sutra, Lotus Sutra,* and *Flower Garland Sutra.* The faith in savior figures and saving texts enabled Buddhism to take root in China.

According to Daniel Stevenson, by the Southern Song most large monasteries had halls for worship of Guanyin and Amitābha, and special areas for the performance of the Water-Land Assembly as well as the ritual of feeding hungry ghosts. Monastic codes listed a liturgical cycle of rituals often corresponding to the traditional Chinese calendar of monthly ordinances and festivals that the public could celebrate in those halls. These included the Great Compassion Repentance and releasing life.[13] When the cults of buddhas and bodhisattvas were institutionalized, their rituals became part of people's lives.

Discussion Questions

1. Why are nonkilling and releasing living creatures encouraged in Chinese Buddhism?
2. How are Buddhist mortuary rituals connected with Chinese ancestor worship?
3. Who is Mulian? How is he connected with the Ghost Festival?
4. What is "stimulus and response"? How is this concept used to argue for the efficacy of Buddhist rituals?
5. What role does confession play in the life of a Buddhist? Why is the Great Compassion Repentance the most popular ritual performed today?

Further Reading

Getz, Daniel A., Jr. "T'ien-t'ai Pure Land Societies and the Creation of the Pure Land Patriarchate." In *Buddhism in the Sung,* edited by Peter N. Gregory and Daniel A. Getz Jr., 477–523. Honolulu: University of Hawai'i Press, 1999.

Stevenson, Daniel B. "Protocols of Power: Tz'u-yün Tsun-shih (964–1032) and T'ian-t'ai Lay Buddhist Ritual in the Sung." In *Buddhism in the Sung,* edited by Peter N. Gregory and Daniel A. Getz Jr., 340–408. Honolulu: University of Hawai'i Press, 1999.

Teiser, Stephen F. *The Ghost Festival in Medieval China*. Princeton, NJ: Princeton University Press, 1988.

————. *The Scripture on the Ten Kings and the Making of Purgatory in Medieval Chinese Buddhism*. Honolulu: University of Hawai'i Press, 1994.

Yü, Chün-fang. *The Renewal of Buddhism in China: Chu-hung and the Late Ming Synthesis*. New York: Columbia University Press, 1981.

Notes

1   Kenneth K. S. Ch'en, *Buddhism in China: A Historical Survey* (Princeton, NJ: Princeton University Press, 1964), 281.

2   Teiser, *The Ghost Festival in Medieval China*, 48.

3   Teiser, *The Ghost Festival in Medieval China*, 50–52.

4   Teiser, *The Ghost Festival in Medieval China*, 87.

5   Teiser, *The Ghost Festival in Medieval China*, 368.

6   Yü, *The Renewal of Buddhism in China*, 79.

7   Yü, *The Renewal of Buddhism in China*, 80.

8   Teiser, *The Scripture on the Ten Kings*.

9   Yü, *The Renewal of Buddhism in China*, 149.

10   Beverley Foulk McGuire, *Living Karma: The Religious Pratices of Ouyi Zhixu* (New York: Columbia University Press, 2014), 58.

11   Daniel B. Stevenson, "The T'ien-t'ai Four Forms of Samadhi and Late North-South Dynasties, Sui, and Early T'ang Buddhist Devotionalism," PhD diss., Columbia University, 1987, 350–354.

12   Stevenson, "Protocols of Power," 344.

13   Stevenson, "Protocols of Power," 390.

CHAPTER 4

The Monastic Order

Prior to the coming of Buddhism, every man and woman in China was expected to get married and have children. Not to do so would end the family line and deprive ancestors of continuous sacrifice from their descendents. That was why Mencius said that of all the things an unfilial son might do, not producing an heir was the most grievous. The Buddhist monastic order of celibate monks and nuns was therefore a truly revolutionary institution. It challenged and disrupted the traditional social order. No wonder it was looked upon by its critics with suspicion. For this reason, throughout history, both the monasteries and their residents were regulated and controlled by the state. This was in sharp contrast to the situation in India. Although we do not know the details about monastic life in India, according to the Vinaya or monastic rules, entering the sangha was an individual matter and the state was not involved. Each monastery was also governed by its members and not subject to secular jurisdiction.

Buddhism was introduced to China by foreign missionaries. For the first two hundred years the monastic order consisted mostly of foreign monks and a small number of their Chinese disciples. Because Buddhism was regarded as a foreign religion, the sangha was at first put under the control of the Office of Foreign Affairs. The Chinese word for monastery, *si,* meaning "office," might have been derived from this term. The layout of monasteries did not follow the Indian model but was distinctively Chinese in style. This might be because early monasteries were often converted private residences. But when newly constructed, they were modeled upon secular official buildings.

Chinese monasteries were built with wood, which was subject to fire. At present the oldest surviving structure is Foguang Temple located at

Nanhua Monastery, Guangzhou. Photo by Yao Chongxin

Mount Wutai. The main hall was rebuilt in 857. The majority of monasteries we see today date to more recent centuries. Due to historical and regional variations, there is no standard Buddhist monastery. However, it is possible to provide a general picture. The most important structures are the stupa and the Buddha Hall. As we read earlier, stupas enshrine the relics of the Buddha, objects of veneration. In China, stupas are multileveled structures called pagodas.

Many pagodas display images of buddhas and bodhisattvas on their façades, making what one scholar calls "iconographic architecture."[1] Located in the central courtyard of the monastery or near the monastic compound, they mark the sites as hallowed ground. The Buddha Hall usually houses three large seated images. Śākyamuni Buddha is always in the center with the buddhas of the past and the future on either side. He may also be accopanied by Amitābha Buddha and the Medicine Buddha on either side. Other arrangements may have Amitābha Buddha flanked by two bodhisattvas, Guanyin (Avalokiteśvara) and Daishizhi (Mahāsthāmaprāta), or Vairocana Buddha flanked by Wenshu (Mañjuśrī) and Puxian (Samathabhadra). The former is called the "Three Holy Ones of the West" and the latter the "Three Holy Ones of Huayan." In addition, there might be separate halls dedicated to important bodhisattvas such as Guanyin, Mañjuśrī, or Dizang. All the halls are called *dian,* the same term used to refer to the halls in a palace or an official building.

By the fourth century Buddhism had found a home in China. It offered a new cosmology and worldview. It introduced impressive new deities and efficacious rituals. It provided a new lifestyle and way of religious cultivation. Monasteries and small temples had been established in the capitals and countryside. Monks and nuns with shaven heads and wearing dark-colored robes mingled with the people. Buddhism attracted believers from all levels of society. However, along with its success, it met resistance and persecution. Buddhists had to defend their religion against criticism from Confucian officials. Moreover, since both Buddhists and Daoists relied upon the patronage of the state, vigorous debates between the opposing parties formed a distinctive genre of apologetical literature. Criticisms and counterarguments started as early as the fourth and fifth centuries. Such debates never disappeared altogether but resurfaced from time to time in later centuries.

There were four types of anti-Buddhist arguments:

1. Political arguments. The activities of the monastics are contrary to social convention and are harmful to the stability and prosperity of the state.
2. Economic arguments. Monastics do not engage in farming and weaving. They are unproductive and useless to society. In fact, since they do not pay taxes and are exempt from conscripted labor, they are a burden on the state.
3. Moral arguments. By leading celibate lives apart from society, monastics violate the five Confucian fundamental human relationships: the virtues of loyalty to the ruler, filial piety to parents, conjugal harmony between husband and wife, fraternity among brothers, and trustworthiness among friends. Of the five relationships, critics focus on that between parents and sons. Because monks are celibate, they are therefore unfilial.
4. Chauvinistic arguments. The Buddha is a "barbarian" and Buddhism is a foreign religion. Buddhism was not mentioned by ancient sages. It may be suitable for uncivilized foreigners, but not for Chinese.

The Buddhist counterarguments:

1. The monastic order provides lasting peace and prosperity to the state. Individual monks might engage in wrong activities, but the entire sangha should not bear the blame.
2. Monastics are not useless, though their usefulness is not of this world.
3. There is no fundamental difference between Buddhism and Confucianism. The five precepts are comparable to the five cardinal virtues of humaneness, righteousness, propriety, wisdom, and trustworthiness. The Buddha was not unfilial because he converted his father after he achieved enlightenment.
4. Buddhism has been known in China since the time of Emperor Aśoka. Therefore one cannot say that it was only for barbarians.

Much ink was spilled on account of the last counterargument. Buddhist apologists used the myth of the eighty-four thousand Aśokan stupas to prove that Buddhism was already known in the third century BCE. On the other hand, some writers turned the charge that Buddhism was a foreign religion on its head, claiming that Buddhism was in fact the Indian version of Laozi's teaching. This led to the legend of Laozi going to India to convert the barbarians. As we read in the introduction, it also gave rise to the polemical *Sutra of Laozi's Conversion of Barbarians,* written by a Daoist around 300 CE. Daoists used it in their debates with Buddhists. Although edicts prohibiting the circulation of the text were issued several times in the Tang and Yuan dynasties, not until 1285, during the Yuan dynasty under the rule of the Mongols, were all the woodblocks used to print the text finally destroyed.

Although criticisms based on political and economic grounds were often used against Buddhism, the charge of unfiliality was by far the most serious. Buddhist apologists therefore devoted most of their energy to a defense on this issue. Huiyuan was the first true defender of the faith. He argued that there were two kinds of Buddhists: lay and monastic. While the former should observe loyalty and filial piety, for the latter it was different. He argued that "the monk who has left the household is a stranger dwelling outside the world of human relations. . . . Having altered the common practice they cannot share the rites imposed by secular codes."[2] Based on the same reasoning, citing the custom in India, Huiyuan wrote a famous essay arguing that monks need not bow down to the ruler. But due to the different cultural and historical traditions, this Indian monastic model could not be translated into Chinese reality. The sangha never existed independently from the state in China.

A different line of defense against the charge of unfiliality came from Sun Cho (c. 300–380), a contemporary of Huiyan, who argued that Buddhists practiced "a higher form of filial piety."[3] Because father and son shared the same qi energy, if the son should achieve buddhahood, the father would enjoy the benefits, and that was the highest way to be filial. Most defenders in later generations combined the two lines of argument. They would first distinguish what filial piety entailed for householders and for monks, then argue that the Buddhist way of being filial was higher and better. They contrasted the Confucian understanding of filial piety as physical caring and biological reproduction with the Buddhist one of merit making and spiritual enlightenment. In the essay "Admonition on Filial Piety," the Chan master Mingben (1263–1323) elaborated on these arguments and concluded that a Buddhist monk was in fact a truly filial son.

> All parents of this world nurture and love their children. Sages and worthies therefore teach us to be filial to our parents. Filiality means imitation. Children imitate parental nurturing and repay their parents with nurturing. Children imitate parental love and repay their parents with love. . . . However, there are two ways of nurturing and love. To serve parents with grain and meat, to clothe them with fur and linen is to nourish their physical body. To discipline oneself with purity and restraint and to cultivate blessedness and goodness for them is to nourish their dharma nature. The nourishment of their physical body follows human relationship, but the nourishment of their dharma nature conforms to heavenly principle. Even sages and worthies cannot perform both. That is because there is a difference between being a householder and being a monk. If one is a householder but fails to nourish the physical body of his parents, he is unfilial. If one is a monk but fails to nourish the dharma nature of his parents, he is also unfilial. This is what I mean by the two ways of filiality. To inquire after one's parents morning and evening and dare not leave them for any length of time is what I call love with form. To engage in meditation effort whether walking or sitting, to vow to realize the Way within the span of this life and, with this, to repay the kindness of parents is what I call formless love. . . . Thus the Way is no other than filial piety and filial piety is no other than the Way.[4]

In addition to the writings of prominent Buddhist masters, several indigenous sutras composed during the Tang also argue the case. They celebrate the filial acts of the Buddha in his previous and most recent lives and describe his extraordinary devotion and self-sacrifice to his parents. The *Sutra on the Buddha's Repaying Parental Kindness* and *Sutra on the Weight of a Father's and Mother's Kindness* were widely circulated. Some scenes from the sutras were also carved in Buddhist cave temples and at pilgrimage sites such as Mount Peak of Treasure in Sichuan.

Anti-Buddhist rhetoric was a constant undercurrent in the history of Chinese Buddhism. From time to time it erupted as active campaigns against the monastic order. This was the case with the three persecutions in 446 under Emperor Wu of Northern Wei, 574–577 under Emperor Wu of Northern Zhou, and 845 under Emperor Wu of Tang. The state began to regulate the sangha early on. It controlled the types and numbers of monasteries and the qualifications and numbers of monastics. Throughout history, the relationship between Buddhism and the state in China has always been close but ambivalent. The state relied upon the blessings of the sangha yet regulated and controlled it. The sangha relied on the patronage of the state while being subject to its supervision.

State Control of Monasteries

Buddhist monasteries varied greatly. Some were located in the cities, some were in the countryside, while others were in the mountains. Some were very large, had lands and orchards, and housed hundreds or even thousands of monks. Others were small, did not own property, and were maintained by just a few monastics. There were several ways a monastery could be established. The most prestigious ones were built with funding from the imperial house, the nobility, and wealthy families. They were often started by monks with support from the faithful. Local villagers might also raise funds to build a temple for a monk who offered religious benediction and ritual services. No matter the size, the location, or who initiated their founding, monasteries were distinguished according to three categories. The first was based on whether the monastery had an imperial plaque, the second on whether it was public or private, and the third on its main activities and functions. These categories have been in place since the Song (960–1279).

The imperial plaque is a plaque with the name of the monastery written on it by the emperor. This testifies to its prestige and legitimacy. Such monasteries not only enjoyed state patronage but also were spared during times of persecution. Abbots eagerly sought such favor with the help of their patrons among the local officials and literati.

Monasteries were divided into two types: public and private. The criterion for naming a monastery public in contrast to private was the manner in which the abbot was chosen. A public monastery was called "forest of ten directions" because it did not belong to one tonsure family. A tonsure family referred to all the monks who received their tonsure (had their hair shaved) by the same master. A private monastery was modeled upon the family structure. The monk who was tonsured by his master called the latter "master father." He called the master's master "master grandfather" and his fellow monks who received the tonsure from the same master "master brothers." Just as in a family, property was passed from father to son and remained in the same family. The property of a private monastery stayed in the tonsure family, and the position of abbot was passed from the master to his tonsure disciple.

In contrast, the property of a public monastery belonged to the entire community. None of the resident monks received tonsure from the abbot. If he wished to accept a layperson as a member of the community, he would send him away to another monastery to receive tonsure. In other words, all members of a public monastery were tonsured elsewhere, not by their own abbot. Most significantly, the position of the abbot had to be occupied by a senior monk noted for his leadership and good reputation and chosen through community consensus. When a vacancy occurred, local officials, literati, and abbots of neighboring public monasteries would recommend qualified candidates. It was usually the governor or prefect who selected the final candidate and made the appointment.

Finally, there were three categories of public monasteries based on their specialization: meditation (*chan*), doctrinal teaching (*jiao*), and discipline (*lü*). Chan Buddhism reached the height of its development in the Song, and therefore the most famous monasteries were Chan. Monasteries focusing on Tiantai and Huayan teachings were *jiao*. Although those specializing in Vinaya were called *lü*, they did not exist as such for long but were turned into Chan. During the Ming (1368–1662), the founding emperor, Taizu (r. 1368–1398), dropped the classification of temples specializing in discipline and replaced it with a classification for those specializing in religious rituals. The revised categories are now *chan*, or meditation; *jiang*, or doctrine; and *jiao*, or practical instruction. The *jiang* was the same as the *jiao* of the Song and referred to temples that stressed doctrinal study. The term *jiao* was no longer applied to monasteries specializing in doctrinal study but was used to refer to a new and different type of temple that specialized in ritual performance, which then constituted the third category. Sometimes these temples were also called yoga or *yujia*. They focused on chanting sutras and reciting penances. Besides performing the rituals in the temple, these monks also went to the homes of devotees to conduct funeral services as well as rites of seeking long life, speedy recovery from disease, and so on. Buddhist reformers in the modern period blamed the decline of the moral and spiritual discipline of monastics on the commercialization of these activities.

Taizu's decree apparently was not enforced, for most monasteries styled themselves as Chan. But this did not mean that only meditation was practiced. Unlike in Japan, sectarianism was never a distinctive feature of Chinese Buddhism. The saying "Tiantai and Huayan for doctrine, Chan and Pure Land for practice" accurately describes the situation. One might study Tiantai or Huayan but practice Chan meditation or the invocation of the Buddha's name (*nianfo*). Meditation and doctrinal study could be combined, and Chan and Pure Land were similarly harmonized, as will be discussed in chapter 7. There could be a Chan meditation hall coexisting with a hall for calling the Buddha's name in the same monastery.

How many monasteries were there in traditional China? There were sporadic counts. For instance, according to the *Record of Buddhist Monasteries in Luoyang* (compiled in 547), in the early fourth century, there were 42 monasteries during the Jin (265–420). That number swelled to 1,367 during the Northern Wei (386–534). These figures refer to large monasteries only; the Tang monk Falin (572–640) provided a more detailed account. He distinguished the monasteries according to their funding sources, which also indicated their different sizes and functions. He wrote that under the Northern Wei, there were 47 grand monasteries of the state, 839 monasteries of the princes and eminent families, and 30,000 monasteries of the common people.[5] It is clear that small temples built by the common people and located in villages far exceeded those sponsored by the court and noble families and located in the capital and cities. Regardless of the size and the number of residents, any building inhabited by monks was called *si,* which can be translated as monastery, temple, shrine, or hermitage.

The fortune of Buddhism was closely tied to the personal interests of emperors and changing state policies. When emperors and members of the royal family showed favor to Buddhism, the numbers of monasteries and the population of monastics increased. But both decreased when Buddhism was persecuted. At those times, it was mostly the small temples housing very few residents that suffered. This is evident from the record of what happened during the persecution of 845. "More than 4,600 monasteries are being destroyed throughout the empire; more than 260,500 monks and nuns are being returned to lay life and being subject to the double tax; more than 40,000 temples and shrines are being destroyed."[6] Since the census showed that most of the monks who returned to lay life lived in the 40,000 small temples, there were probably only two or three monks in each one.

Using data from various censuses, Jacques Gernet provides statistics of the number of monasteries and monastics from the fourth century to 1291. He states, "The total number of great and minor Buddhist establishments remained almost constant across widely separated periods: between 30,000 and 40,000 in the middle of the sixth century, 44,600 in 845, and much later in 1291, 42,318."[7] He concludes that up to the thirteenth century, the number of both great and small monasteries remained quite constant, with the great monasteries reaching four to five thousand and the small temples thirty to forty thousand. Although great monasteries housed several thousand monks, "the ordinary monastery had no more than twenty to fifty religious at most." Because the majority were small establishments, it would be easy for Buddhism to be integrated in the daily lives of the common people. But precisely because of its impact on society, the state had always been interested in regulating it.

The Monastic Community

The monastic community was made up of eight types of people: laymen, laywomen, male and female postulants, male and female novices, monks, and nuns. While the first two types got married and led secular lives, the latter six "left home" and lived celibate lives communally. The state did not involve itself in a person's decision to become a lay Buddhist. However, according to Buddhist regulation, they must take refuge in the Three Treasures of Buddha, Dharma, and Sangha and receive the five precepts of abstention from killing, stealing, lying, sexual misconduct, and consumption of alcohol. But the six kinds of monastics had to also meet certain requirements set by the state. In order to become a postulant, parental permission was necessary. The applicant would be turned down if a boy was under nineteen or a girl under fourteen years of age, if he or she had joined before and then returned to the laity, if he or she had committed some crime, if he or she was an escapee from justice, or if there were no adult sons or grandsons in the family.

A male or female postulant lived in a monastery but did not shave off their hair. Postulants would study the scriptures and perform tasks in the monastery, but they were not exempt from paying taxes and performing conscripted labor. That privilege was enjoyed only by ordained novices, monks, and nuns. In order to advance to the status of a monastic, a postulant had to be ordained and obtain an ordination certificate, which served as an ID card. The state controlled the number of monastics through the number of certificates granted. There were three ways to receive ordination: by passing an examination, through imperial favor, or by the purchase of a certificate. Examinations took different forms in different dynasties. During the Tang (618–907), a male postulant had to be able to recite 150 leaves from a sutra such as the *Lotus Sutra*, and a female had to recite 100 leaves. During the Five Dynasties (907–960), they must pass five tests: lecture on the scriptures, practice meditation, memorize a text, compose a piece of literature, and comment on a passage.

During the Song (960–1279), the examination format changed again. A male postulant had to recite 100 leaves and read 500 leaves; a female had to recite 70 and read 300. Interestingly, the examination was conducted by government officials in a government office and not by the monks in a monastery.[8]

Instead of taking the examination, a postulant could obtain an ordination certificate through imperial favor or purchase. The emperor could grant ordination on the occasion of his birthday, on an imperial visit to a new monastery, or when an imperial plaque was bestowed on a monastery. Sale of ordination certificates by the state was carried out at first to meet the fiscal need to put down the An Lushan rebellion in 755–763, but it was increasingly resorted to routinely after the Song.

When a postulant was ordained, he or she became a novice and had their hair shaven by a monk or nun, the tonsure master. Aside from the five precepts, novices must observe five additional rules: not using perfume or decorating oneself with flowers, not occupying high beds, not singing and dancing, not possessing wealth, and not eating after the noon hour. While some novices went on to receive full ordination as monks or nuns, most remained novices. All abbots, scholar monks, and Chan masters were without exception fully ordained monks. Ordained monastics would receive even more precepts. For monks it was 250 and for nuns 350. There was another difference between monks and nuns. While a male novice was ordained by ten qualified monks, a female novice had to undergo a dual ordination that required her to be ordained by ten qualified nuns and then further ordained by ten monks.

The state at times limited the number of monasteries by prohibiting the construction or restoration of those without an imperial plaque. During the time of persecution, monasteries were destroyed outright. Because monks and nuns were exempted from paying taxes and providing labor, decrees to limit their numbers were based on economic grounds. Another measure of state control of the monastic order was instituting monk officials, monks appointed by the state to supervise the sangha. This is the clearest example of the bureaucratization of the sangha by the secular state. The institution of the monk officials had a long history. Traditionally, Yao Xing of the Later Qin dynasty (384–417) was credited with its establishment. Before the Tang dynasty, the degree of bureaucratization was comparatively low, and the Buddhist sangha enjoyed a certain amount of autonomy. Except for grave crimes such as murder, monks were subject only to the judgment of monk officials, who used monastic laws, not state statutes, in passing sentences. There was a major change in the Tang: the sangha was now supervised by monk officials appointed by the state, not by abbots of monasteries. The institution of monk officials was primarily designed to facilitate bureaucratic control. Monks were segregated from the population at large and especially barred from any contact with government officials. If this system functioned as its creator intended, the monk officials would serve as administrators governing the total monastic population. The government could keep a watchful eye on all monks simply by holding the monk officials responsible. At the same time, government officials with orthodox Confucian views could be protected from the possible undesirable influence of frequent exposure to monks in general.

The institution of monk officials continued in later dynasties, although there were changes in their number, title, and function. Despite the increasing incursion of the civil authority, paradoxically, monk officials did not have real administrative power. Just as there were sales of ordination certificates, the title could be bought. Abbots of famous monasteries were often far more powerful and prestigious than monk officials. However, local civil officials, such as the governor, regional commander, or prefect, exerted much influence in the selection of abbots and running of monastic affairs.

With the end of the Qing dynasty in the early twentieth century, the traditional measures of control discussed above were no longer in effect. However, state surveillance of the sangha continues. Both the Republic of China in Taiwan and the People's Republic of China on the Chinese mainland have laws to regulate sangha affairs. But despite the many measures of the government to regulate and control the monastic order, it could not be confined in a separate sphere, for it had already become an integral part of the greater society.

On Entering the Sangha and Becoming a Monk

Why does a person decide to become a monk? What training does he undergo? What is ordination like? We are fortunate to have an eyewitness account by a contemporary monk based on his own experience.[9] Zhenhua was born in 1922 to the Liu family in Honan province. Before he was born, the family fortune had started to decline. Born on the day the Buddha entered nirvana, Zhenhua was the youngest of six children, coming after four brothers and one sister. A blind fortune-teller predicted that the baby was destined to die of hunger. In order to avert this terrible fate, the grandmother went on a pilgrimage to the Temple of Mount Tai to offer incense, make vows, and pray for his safety. She also spent quite a lot of money and asked the fortune-teller to alter the bad fortune. But even though he did not end up dying of hunger, the Liu family soon encountered inexplicably one tragedy after another.

When he was four, within one year, he lost eight of his loved ones. His grandfather and his uncle died within one month of each other. His four brothers and one sister, ranging from six to fifteen years old, followed. Finally, his mother hanged herself. His father left home to join the army, leaving the young boy in the care of the grandmother. Zhenhua lived with the grandmother in poverty until he was fourteen, when he lost her as well. With the death of the grandmother, he had no family left. A kind woman whom he called Auntie Chen came to his rescue. A midwife by occupation, she was friendly with monks at the Temple of Mount Tai. She suggested that it would be best for him to become the disciple of a monk there, emphasizing the good life he would enjoy. So, wearing a new suit of clothing made by Auntie Chen and carrying a huge watermelon weighing more than twenty pounds as an offering, he went to the temple with her in the year 1936.

Becoming a disciple to a monk, in this case, was clearly a way of making a living for poor children who had no families. It was also clear that no one, including his master, seemed to be conscious of the spiritual significance of taking the tonsure. Without ceremony or delay, his head was shaved clean. He was not asked to take the Three Refuges or given the ten precepts, the normal requirements for becoming a postulant. Zhenhua called the Temple of Mount Tai a "small temple," meaning it was a private temple with few resident monks. In contrast to the ideal picture presented by hagiographies and Buddhist chronicles, his story provides a description of monastic career on the ground. Both in the past and in the modern period, there were probably always people who, like Zhenhua, entered the monastic order not because of religious conviction but as a last resort for survival. The monastic order was indeed the refuge. Because of this, the monastic population could be a mixture of good and bad, pure and impure elements. A common saying, which Zhenhua liked to quote, describes the situation well: "A monastery is a place where snakes mingle with dragons." However, as Zhenhua himself testified most eloquently, he was profoundly transformed by his monastic training and became a passionate spokesman for Buddhism. Though perhaps more dramatic than others, Zhenhua's case was not an isolated one.

Although Zhenhua's master did not know much about Buddhism, he made arrangements for Zhenhua to receive training in public monasteries and to be ordained as a monk. While "leaving home" and receiving tonsure is a simple matter, ordination is a solemn ritual. Although one can choose to have one's head shaved at a small temple, one must go to specific public monasteries, all in southern China, to receive ordination. Mount Baohua was the most renowned. In traditional China, before 1911, the frequency of ordination and the number of people to be ordained were decided by the government. Only those who had been properly ordained could receive ordination certificates, which, like diplomas or identification cards, conferred both prestige and privileges to the holders. An ordained monk was traditionally granted exemptions from serving in the army, paying taxes, and working as a conscripted laborer. He could also take up residence at any monastery after presenting his ordination certificate to the guest prefect.

Baohua Monastery was famous for both the length of its ordination session and the severity of its training. The purpose of holding the ordination session was to train the monks in liturgy and deportment, to instill in them the proper knowledge about monastic precepts and how to behave in a dignified manner befitting their new status. In the Chinese Buddhist tradition, ordination consisted of three parts. A person first received the ten precepts for a novice (*sramanera*), then the 250 precepts for a monk (*bhikshu*), and lastly, the fifty-eight precepts for a bodhisattva. Holmes Welch interviewed monks of Zhenhua's generation and provided a detailed description of the entire course of this training at Baohua. One can get a sense of the enormousness of the task by reading what they had to learn just during the first two weeks of their enrollment. "During the first two weeks, those who were becoming monks and nuns—the clerical ordinands—studied how to eat, how to dress, how to lie when sleeping, how to make their beds, how to pack their belongings for a journey, how to stand and walk, how to enter the great shrine-hall, how to hand over the duty (as a duty monk in the meditation hall, for example), and so on."[10]

Zhenhua talked about the hardships of morning devotions and the long hours of kneeling on the stone pavement to receive precepts. He characterized the three stages of receiving the precepts with this saying, "*Sramanera* are made to kneel, *bhikshu*s are beaten, and *bodhisattva*s have scars burned on their heads." The scars refer to the small, round white scars burned into the scalp of the ordinand by moxa after he has received the entire set of precepts. They are called ordination scars or incense scars. They vary in number, from three or nine to twelve, and form vertical lines on the scalp. The practice did not exist in India but started in China only after the Song dynasty. According to one of Welch's informants, it began as an offering to the Buddha, comparable to the burning of fingers.[11] It has now become an indispensable part of the ordination. Although the burning ordination was very painful, for Zhenhua, it paled when compared to kneeling.

> Judging from my own personal experiences of "kneeling, beating, and burning," the most difficult to endure is kneeling rather than burning and beating. Why is this? Because burning and beating lasted only a short time. Also, burning happened only once, and one was not beaten every day. Kneeling, however, was a common exercise. Readers who think I am contradicting myself might ask: "After saying that *sramanera* are made to kneel, how can you turn around and say that kneeling was a common exercise?" Actually, when we took our *bhikshu* and *bodhisattva* precepts, we kneeled just at we had before. Just imagine! In the freezing winter cold of a north wind that pierced like a knife, we knelt on the

coarse-grained flagstones in the courtyard of the great shrine hall for at least two hours each time and waited for the end of the ceremony.[12]

After spending different periods of his life as a wandering pilgrim, meditator, and monastic officer of one type or another, Zhenhua finally became the director of a Buddhist seminary for nuns in Taiwan in his later years. Although he became a monk out of necessity, he ended his life as a renowned teacher. This serves as a case study of a monastic career.

The Sangha and Society

As stated earlier, lay Buddhists were members of the sangha. But monks and nuns did not have a close relationship only with lay Buddhists. They had contact with people from all levels of society, from emperors to the common men and women. Both parties engaged in reciprocal giving. Monks gave people the gift of Buddhist teachings and the people gave the sangha gifts of material offerings. The driving power behind the exchange is the concept of making merit. People were inspired to support the sangha because they believed in merit making. In theory, by performing any pious deeds, such as feeding a beggar or helping a sick person, one created merit that would produce blessings. In reality, however, it was mainly by making donations to the sangha, holding a vegetarian feast, contributing to the building fund of the temple, or casting an image that one would most assuredly accumulate merit. Merit can be thought of as a kind of spiritual currency that would confer blessings on oneself and one's parents in this life and future lives as well as on one's dead ancestors. Monks were called "field of merit" because they were like fertile fields that would produce the desired blessing without fail on account of their presumed moral purity.

The nature and function of the sangha in China underwent changes from the Indian model. Unlike in India, monks in China did not beg for food because there had never been such a religious tradition. For this reason, the sangha relied on lay support, which included not only food, robes, and other necessities of daily life but also temple building, image casting, and land donation. Although the Vinaya prohibited monastics from farming because it involved harming insects, monks in China did engage in farming. Monastic estates developed on land granted by the emperor or donated by the great families. From early on, common people formed religious associations and combined their resources in erecting stupas and making statues and casting images of buddhas and bodhisattvas.

The sangha was not a passive recipient of lay support. In addition to the contribution Buddhism made to the spiritual life of the Chinese people, both monasteries and monastics have played important roles in the economic and social lives of the people. As we have seen in the previous chapter, Buddhist rituals have direct impact on the religious life of the people. We will now look at the economic and social activities of the sangha.

Economic Activities

Based on eyewitness accounts of Japanese pilgrim monks and documents discovered in the library cave of Dunhuang, we have information about the various commercial activities of the sangha during the Tang.[13] These activities included the operation of water-powered mills and oil presses; making monastic buildings available as hostels, pawnshops, storage facilities, and banks; and managing temple lands as landlord. The mills, oil presses, monasteries, and temple lands were either donated by the faithful or purchased with the funds provided by them and were owned by the sangha collectively. By making productive use of these installations and real estate, the sangha generated income that supported its activities.

Water-powered mills to separate husks from grain and oil presses to press hemp seeds into oil were essential in the daily life of all people. The sangha rented out the equipment to households, who did the actual work, but it was responsible for their maintenance and repair. The mills and presses supplied grain and oil to the sangha for its own use. But because common people rented these machines by paying a fee, they provided the sangha with considerable income.

In the Tang dynasty, monasteries instituted the Inexhaustible Treasury, which served as warehouse, pawnshop, and bank. Such storerooms had existed in China since the fifth century. They were originally used to store ritual implements, manuscripts, food, gifts, and donations to the monastery by the faithful. Operating the mills and presses and holding large landed estates in the Tang, monasteries had more material goods than they needed. According to the Vinaya, the sangha was allowed to sell the surplus for profit and use the income to construct or repair temples and stupas. Because such surplus goods were called inexhaustible wealth, the storage area was named Inexhaustible Treasury. The function of these Inexhaustible Treasuries gradually broadened with time. They served as safe deposit vaults in which people from outside the sangha could place their valuable articles for safekeeping. They served as pawnshops where people could pawn their valuables for money. According to the documents recovered from Dunhuang, monasteries loaned money, cloth, or grain with interest to both members of the upper class and peasants. Depending on the borrower's social status and his relationship with the monastery, his treatment differed. For upper-class borrowers, "the loans were usually in money or fabrics, made for a long term, with some sort of security and payment of interest required. In the case of transactions with peasants not connected with the monastery, the loans were usually in grain, made for a short period, with a rate of interest sometimes as high as fifty percent annually, to be paid in kind. However, if the peasants were attached to the monastery, then they enjoyed special treatment and were permitted to borrow grain without any payment of interest."[14] Making loans and charging interest, monasteries worked almost like a modern bank. The monastery used the donated money and land as capital, further gaining interest from loans and rentals. With its productive use of capital and the accumulation of interest, some scholars claim that such economic activities of the sangha foreshadowed modern capitalism.

Because many monasteries were located on mountains or far from urban centers, they served as hostels for travelers who were monks, pilgrims, officials reporting to assigned posts for duty, traveling merchants, and young scholars on their way to take civil exams. Literati, officials, and local gentry visited temples for the peace and serenity of the surroundings. Women from good families, who were generally cloistered, could enjoy outings when they came to worship. The monastery was one of very few public places accessible to all members of society. People who were normally segregated by gender and class might have the opportunity to meet.

A number of literary works have the monastery as their setting. The *Romance of the Western Chamber,* one of the most famous plays written by the Yuan playwright Wang Shifu (1260–1336), was set in the Tang and took place in a temple. It is about a young couple who meet by chance in a temple and fall in love. The hero is a young scholar staying in the temple to prepare for the civil exam. The heroine is the daughter of a chief minister who recently died. On their way to escort the father's coffin to their native home, she and the mother stop at the temple to rest. When the young man sees the girl in the Buddha hall worshiping, he is immediately struck by her beauty. The girl returns the affection when she hears him recite a love poem behind the wall of the western chamber where she is living. Because the girl is constantly watched by the mother, they can only pine for each other. After suffering many disappointments, with the help of the clever maid, the two lovers succeed in meeting secretly. When the mother discovers the affair, she agrees to have them formally married, on the condition that he must pass the highest civil examination held in the capital. After he passes the examination and is appointed to a high official position, they finally get married and the story ends on a happy note. The lovers' secret meeting at night has always fascinated Chinese readers, but it also scandalized those who regarded themselves as guardians of sexual propriety. Although other novels and plays featured temples, the fame of the *Romance of the Western Chamber* probably contributed to a common bias that associated temples with illicit sexual activities.

Social Functions

Traditional China was a patriarchal society with a strict social hierarchy. Education was a privilege not available to poor children of the lower classes. Monasteries were places where they could receive an education. Although many monks were educated in Confucian classics and Daoist works before entering the order, a far greater number probably had little or no prior education. While a person was supposed to be able to read and recite scripture before being allowed to join, it is hard to say whether these requirements were always followed in reality (many anecdotal accounts suggest otherwise). Like the Catholic Church, the monastic order was perceived as a place where young men and women of poor families could find security and advancement. The modern-day Chan master Shengyan (1931–2009) described in his autobiography how he was sent to a local temple at the age of ten because his parents were poor and there were too many children to feed and clothe. After he was taught how to read, his master sent him to other monasteries of greater renown for further education and training. This conformed to traditional practice. Monks were encouraged to travel extensively to different monasteries in order to study under different teachers. Just as success in officialdom was achieved by passing a series of civil examinations, an illustrious monastic career required vigorous training by many masters in famous monasteries. The sangha not only provided educational opportunities to its own members but also served the general population through preaching and popular lectures based on Buddhist scriptures such as the *Lotus Sutra*. Ideas about karma, rebirth, and reward and punishment in accordance with one's moral actions became commonly shared values.

The monastic order offered a place for men and women who chose not to get married. This was an option they had never had before the coming of Buddhism. It was particularly relevant for women. In traditional China, women were known as daughters, wives, and mothers of men. There was no place for unmarried women because they were simply out of place and could not be accommodated. The legend of Miaoshan has therefore served as a model for marriage resistance for women. Becoming a nun was an unprecedented opportunity for those who did not wish to follow the traditional life trajectory. But this was also why more women than men suffered social sanctions when choosing to join the sangha.

In the long history of Chinese Buddhism, many monks and nuns have made contributions in various capacities. Biographies of monks have been collected by generations of monk scholars. The most famous are three compiled before the tenth century. Huijiao (497–554) compiled the first lives of 257 monks in the *Biographies of Eminent Monks*. Daoxuan (596–667) and Zanning (919–1001) wrote two sequels, *Continued Biographies of Eminent Monks* and *Song Biographies of Eminent Monks;* these works cover monks who had lived since Huijiao's time and contain 485 and more than 500 biographies, respectively. Biographies of even more monks were compiled in later periods, amounting to several thousand. Compared to these rich sources, only two modest collections of nuns' lives exist. The first, *The Lives of Nuns,* written by the monk Baochang in or about 516, begins with Zhu Jingnian, who lived around 292–361. Not until the twentieth century was a sequel written, by another monk, Zhenhua (1908–1947), who compiled the *Continued Lives of Nuns.*

The Buddhist tradition credits the founding of the order of nuns to Mahāprajāpatī, maternal aunt and foster mother of the Buddha. According to conventional accounts, as a result of her three repeated requests and intercession by Ānanda, the Buddha's favorite disciple, the Buddha agreed to allow women into the sangha despite his initial reluctance. However, the Buddha did not grant this permission without reservation, for he was supposed to have predicted that the True Dharma would last only five hundred years instead of a thousand years because of this. Moreover, he imposed the so-called Eight Rules of Respect on the nuns, subordinating them institutionally to the monks. These rules vary slightly according to different schools. However, they generally include the following:

1. A nun shall honor every monk as her senior, even if she has been ordained for a hundred years, and he one day.
2. During the rainy season retreat, she shall not reside in a district where there are no monks.
3. The nuns shall schedule their Observance Day in line with the monks.
4. A nun shall invite criticism at the end of the rainy season retreat from both the nuns' and the monks' assemblies.
5. She shall undergo penance (temporary probation) for a serious offense before both assemblies.
6. A female postulant must undergo a two-year novitiate and seek ordination from both assemblies.
7. A nun shall not verbally abuse a monk.
8. Whereas monks are allowed formally to reprove nuns, nuns may not reprove monks.[15]

The order of nuns was never introduced into Tibet. Although it once existed in India and other Buddhist countries, with the disappearance of Buddhism in India in the thirteenth century, the order of nuns also disappeared. It disappeared even earlier in Sri Lanka, around the end of the tenth century. According to the Vinaya, a woman, unlike a man, must receive dual ordination: first from ten fully ordained nuns and then from ten fully ordained monks. But because the order of nuns ceased to exist in Theravada Buddhism, no woman was able to formally become a nun in those countries. The nuns' order in China, in contrast, has fared much better. Although there were some difficulties in ordination at the very beginning, since the order was established, there has been an unbroken lineage from the fifth century onward: Chinese nuns have been receiving the dual ordination ever since 434. Because of their close cultural relationship with China, nuns in Japan, Korea, and Vietnam enjoy the same distinction.

The three collections of monks' lives follow a similar format: the biographies are grouped into ten distinct categories: translators, exegetes, meditators, elucidators of the Vinaya, defenders of the Dharma, thaumaturges, those who sacrifice themselves, chanters of scripture, benefactors, and those with miscellaneous talents. This organizing principle is somewhat arbitrary, for oftentimes a monk could be classified under more than one category. In contrast, *Lives of Nuns* does not classify its subjects this way. There are two other notable differences between the lives of monks and nuns. The first concerns the reasons women decided to become nuns. Unlike for the monks, their motivations were often related to their marital status: they left home either because of widowhood or because they did not want to get married. The second is that no nun is identified as a translator, although several are famed for their ability to lecture and chant sutras. This was no doubt due to the lack of opportunities. Although most nuns were literate and had both the abilities and the qualifications, they were not invited to participate in translation projects. The nuns whose lives were described so long ago come across even today as exceptional and exemplary. Many of them were admired by emperors, nobles, officials, and men of letters. They were patronized by royal families and local gentry. One nun gave advice to the emperor about the appointment of a new governor, and two were asked to accompany governors to new posts as their advisors. These nuns were clearly regarded with respect and admiration. What qualities constituted their unique sanctity?

Like the lives of saints in Christianity, the lives of monks and nuns are more hagiographies than biographies. However, as John Kieschnick points out, the biographies represent "not only reflections of shared perceptions of the monk, they were also an attempt to shape opinions, to instill a particular set of monastic ideals."[16] If we want to find out what the faith community considered to be a great monk or nun, this literature is the place to begin. Kieschnick singles out three "ideal types": the ascetic, the thaumaturge, and the scholar. He suggests that it was through the creation of these three that the Buddhist sangha carried out the "image war" in order to lay claim to the hearts and minds of the people.[17] The same ideal types are found among the nuns. In addition, filial piety, observation of Vinaya rules, proficiency in meditation, and devotion to the Buddhist sutras by marathon chanting were also highly lauded virtues. Many nuns in the *Lives* studied the Vinaya. While some became experts, others were noted for their scrupulous observance of the precepts. The scholarly nuns distinguished themselves by giving lectures on scriptures and monastic rules or by writing commentaries on scriptures, most often the *Lotus Sutra,* the *Vimalakīrti Sutra,* the *Nirvana Sutra,* the *Flower Garland Sutra,* and the *Perfection of Wisdom Sutra in 8,000 lines.*

Continuation of the Lives of Nuns contains the biographies of two hundred nuns. While the general categories used in discussing the earlier collection of lives are applicable here, the most striking difference is the large number of nuns who practiced Chan Buddhism, reflecting its rising popularity since the Tang. They studied with some of the most prominent Chan masters, for instance, Huineng (638–713), Dahui (1089–1163), Mingben (1263–1323), and Zhuhong (1535–1615).

The ability to chant sutras was still a highly valued trait. The *Lotus Sutra* remained the favorite, and the *Diamond Sutra, Flower Garland Sutra,* and *Smaller Amitābha Sutra* follow closely. The *Perfection of Wisdom Sutra* and the *Vimalakīrtī Sutra* are only occasionally mentioned. In terms of religious practice, Chan and Pure Land dominated. The ability to compose commentaries, give lectures on the sutras, or observe the Vinaya rules finds scant mention. From some of the lives, it appears that the nuns were quite free in combining elements from different Buddhist schools in their practices.

In recent years, scholars have made strides in the study of nuns and Buddhist women in the Song and Qing. Although there is a rhetoric of equality based on the Chan philosophy of nonduality, the institutional setting was not hospitable to women practitioners. In the Song, male teachers began using a peculiar expression, *da zhangfu* (great hero), to refer to female Chan masters worthy of praise. The implication of this rhetoric of heroism is of course that these female masters were exceptions and did not represent nuns in general. They had transcended the gender limitation, and this was exactly why they should be emulated. Clearly, since ordinary nuns did not receive this appellation, they were not treated as equals with monks. However, some nuns were abbesses and Dharma teachers. Some were poets and, through their literary work, participated in and contributed to Buddhism of the Song and the late imperial period. Through these activities and accomplishments, they raised the profile of the nuns and received recognition from literati and officials, who often became their followers and patrons.

The 265 nuns discussed in these two works constitute a small sample of the nuns who lived in the past sixteen centuries. The very fact that they were patronized by the emperors and the royal family, were admired by the wealthy and powerful, built temples, and led large numbers of monastics and laypeople means that they were not ordinary nuns. The social backgrounds of the nuns in the *Lives* were clearly elite. Even in *Continuation of the Lives,* where we find more diversity, they still represent the exception rather than the rule, for it was precisely because they stood out from the masses that their stories were collected and told. Generally, it is hard to detect much difference between nuns' and monks' reputations except that women, in addition to having to refuse marriage, sometimes had to fight off sexual advances. In terms of asceticism, ability to work miracles, willingness to sacrifice their lives for the Dharma, expertise in sutra exposition, and great feats in chanting scriptures, the nuns noted were in no way inferior to monks. Those who wrote commentaries clearly were not only highly literate but also proficient in their understanding of doctrines. It is a great pity that none of the texts have been preserved. In the end, this small group of nuns provides a window into the religious lives of women from the early medieval period to the twentieth century. Although their life stories are a mixture of hagiographies and biographies, we are richer for being able to visualize what nuns could achieve under the right conditions.

In addition to the historical record, scholars today can supplement their study with fieldwork. As a result, we have come to know the condition of today's monastic order much better. This is especially true of Buddhism in Taiwan. Much scholarship deals with Humanistic Buddhism, which emphasizes social engagement. In the Buddhist revival of the last several decades, nuns have played a leading role. Scholars have been impressed by the quality and the size of the nuns' order. Taiwanese nuns today are highly educated and greatly outnumber monks, both unprecedented in the history of Chinese Buddhism. Chapter 9 will examine one community of nuns as a case study.

Discussion Questions

1. Why was the Buddhist monastic order met with opposition from its critics?
2. What measures did the state use to regulate the monastic order?
3. Describe the procedure for becoming a monastic.
4. Name some of the functions the monastic order served in China.
5. What opportunities did the Buddhist order provide for Chinese women to pursue their religious goals?

Further Reading

Chen-hua. *In Search of the Dharma: Memoirs of a Modern Chinese Buddhist Pilgrim.* Edited with an introduction by Chün-fang Yü. Translated by Denis C. Mair. Albany: SUNY Press, 1992.

Gernet, Jacques. *Buddhism in Chinese Society: An Economic History from the Fifth to the Tenth Centuries.* Translated by Franciscus Verellen. New York: Columbia University Press, 1995.

Kieschnick, John. *The Eminent Monk: Buddhist Ideals in Medieval Chinese Hagiography.* Honolulu: University of Hawai'i Press, 1997.

Tsai, Kathryn Ann. *Lives of the Nuns: Biographies of Chinese Buddhist Nuns from the Fourth to Sixth Centuries.* Honolulu: University of Hawai'i Press, 1994.

Welch, Holmes. *The Practice of Chinese Buddhism 1900–1950.* Cambridge, MA: Harvard University Press, 1967.

Notes

1   Wei-cheng Lin, *Building a Sacred Mountain: The Buddhist Architecture of China's Mount Wutai* (Seattle: University of Washington Press, 2014), 150.

2   Erik Zürcher, *The Buddhist Conquest of China.* (1959; repr., Leiden: Brill, 1972), 258.

3   Zürcher, *The Buddhist Conquest of China,* 284.

4   Chün-fang Yü, "Chung-feng Ming-pen and Ch'an Buddhism in the Yüan," in *Chinese Thought and Religion under the Mongols,* edited by Hok-lam Chan and Wm. Theodore deBary (New York: Columbia University Press, 1982), 185–187.

5   Kenneth Ch'en, *Buddhism in China: A Historical Survey* (Princeton, NJ: Princeton University Press, 1964), 242.

6   Ch'en, *Buddhism in China,* 232.

7   Gernet, *Buddhism in Chinese Society,* 9.

8   Ch'en, *Buddhism in China,* 245–246.

9   Chen-hua, *In Search of the Dharma.*

10   Welch, *The Practice of Chinese Buddhism,* 287. See his chapter 9, "Entering the Sangha," for a full description of the ordination session at Baohua.

11   Welch, *The Practice of Chinese Buddhism,* 298. Welch also quotes at length from Prip-Moller's eyewitness account of the application of moxa at Baohua. See 298–300.

12   Chen-hua, *In Search of the Dharma,* 59.

13   Gernet, *Buddhism in Chinese Society,* 142–191; Ch'en, *Buddhism in China,* 261–271.

14   Ch'en, *Buddhism in China,* 266.

15   Richard H. Robinson and Willard L. Johnson, *The Buddhist Religion: A Historical Introduction,* 4th ed. (Belmont, CA: Wadsworth, 1997), 74–75.

16   Kieschnick, *The Eminent Monk,* 111.

17   Kieschnick, *The Eminent Monk,* 143.

CHAPTER 5

The Doctrinal Traditions

Tiantai and Huayan

There is a saying among Chinese Buddhists that if one is interested in Buddhist doctrinal teachings, one should study either the Tiantai (Heavenly Terrace) or Huayan (Flower Garland) tradition, but if one is interested in religious practice, then one should follow either Chan or Pure Land. These four are the most important Chinese Buddhist schools. A school, or *zong*, is a doctrinal tradition based on a set of authoritative scriptures that has produced a body of commentarial and exegetical literature and is followed by a group sharing the same understanding and religious aspirations. Each school claims to have a lineage and venerates the founder and important masters as patriarchs. Chinese Buddhist schools are not sects as known in the West. A sect is usually defined as a group of people with different religious beliefs from those of a larger group to which they belong. For example, both the Catholic Church and Protestant denominations are Christian, but they differ in their institutional structure, ritual repertoire, and liturgical calendar. All Chinese Buddhist schools, in contrast, agree on these important points. The difference lies in their unique teachings based on their exegetical interpretation of scriptures and their emphasis on certain religious practices. The Chinese Buddhist schools are not exclusive to one another, and many monastics study with teachers of different schools.

The Chinese Buddhist schools also differ from Indian Buddhism. Within each of the two Buddhist traditions, Hinayana and Mahayana, further divisions developed. This came about because the Buddha never created an overarching ecclesiastical structure. When he was about to enter nirvana, he did not name a successor as his disciples requested.

Instead, he told them that they should be "lamps to themselves." In other words, he told them to practice the religion as they had been taught, taking the Dharma (teaching) and Vinaya (monastic rules) as their guides. As Buddhism was first established in north India and gradually spread to the rest of India, groups of Buddhist monks gathered around teachers in various places. Over time, different understandings of the Vinaya developed. The first split of the monastic community happened at the time of Emperor Aśoka (c. 268 BCE) and concerned precisely how strictly the rules of the Vinaya should be observed. The Sthaviras or "elders" pushed for the tightening of discipline on some points of the Vinaya, while the Mahasamghikas or "those of the great assembly" believed things should remain the way they were.

Subsequently more divisions evolved based on different interpretations of doctrines. Some schools developed their own Vinayas. Traditionally there were said to be eighteen schools by the time Mahayana appeared. The Sarvastivadins, who held the doctrine that all things of the past, present, and future existed, and the Sri Lankan Theravadins, who advocated the teachings of the elders, were the two most important schools traced to the Sthaviras. With the rise of the Mahayana around the beginning of the Common Era, Buddhism underwent a critical change. For the Mahayanists, who claimed to be following the Great Vehicle, all members of Buddhist schools that did not share their views (found in the new Mahayana sutras) were followers of Hinayana or the Lesser Vehicle. However, because there was no separate Mahayana Vinaya, the schism was primarily doctrinal. In the early stages of the Mahayana movement, for instance, monks who held Mahayana beliefs lived together with Hinayana monks in the same monasteries and observed the same Vinaya rules.

After the important Mahayana scriptures known as the *Perfection of Wisdom* appeared, treatises written by Nāgārjuna, who lived in 150 CE, led to the creation of the Madhyamaka or the Middle Way school, named after his most famous treatise, the "Verses on the Middle Way." Since everything is *śunya* (empty) because it lacks an intrinsic nature, neither positive nor negative statements are appropriate. The Buddha taught an ethical Middle Way: neither physical indulgence nor physical austerity was the right way to live. That same ideal was now understood in a philosophical and epistemological sense. In contrast, the brothers Asanga and Vasubhandu, who lived in the fourth century, favored other sutras and wrote treatises that formed the philosophical foundation of the Yogācāra school.

It claims that everything is a creation of the mind. We will first discuss these two Mahayana philosophical traditions because they had a general impact on Chinese Buddhism. They also inspired Chinese Buddhist thinkers to create their own exegetical traditions. The Three-Treatise school, founded by Jizang (549–623), represented a further refinement of the dialectics of Madhyamaka, while the Consciousness-Only School, founded by the great pilgrim and translator Xuanzang (596–664), was the Chinese version of Yogācāra.

Madhyamaka and Yogācāra

Nāgārjuna (c. 150–c. 250) was the founder of the Madhyamaka (Middle Way) school, which was a philosophical development based on the *Perfection of Wisdom* scriptures. For Nāgārjuna, the cause of suffering is our failure to know that emptiness is the true nature of everything. Because of this ignorance, we become attached to all kinds of wrong views that are all partial and lead to emotional turbulence. The insight of emptiness can only be arrived at through abolishing views. This is done through the negation of conventional thought patterns formed by language. The Madhyamaka method, as used by Nāgārjuna, is to take the view of one's opponent and through a dialectic process known as the Middle Path of Eightfold Negations deny the validity of all antithetical assertions about all things. This is summed up by the famous declaration "there is no production, no extinction, no annihilation, no permanence, no unity, no diversity, no coming, no going." The eightfold negations are arrived at by the Four Points of Argument: namely, by refuting something as existent, as nonexistent, as both existent and nonexistent, and as neither existent nor nonexistent. This is different from Aristotelian logic: the main points are not just A and not A; it is necessary to go further by adding two more alternatives: both A and non-A, neither A nor non-A. To assert any of the four as true is an extreme and falls short of the Middle Way. It is necessary to deny each one through the dialectic method until finally emptiness, which is the absolute middle, is reached.

Nāgārjuna begins the famous "Verses on the Middle Way" with a critique of causation. Causation, as represented by the Law of Dependent Origination, is the fundamental teaching of Buddhism. It is through the discovery of the law of causation that the Buddha became enlightened. The first verse says, "There absolutely are no things, nowhere and none, that arise [anew]; Neither out of themselves nor out of non-self, nor out of both, nor at random."[1] This statement means that the relationship between cause and effect cannot be logically established. If a thing is self-caused, then there is no difference between cause and effect. There will be infinite self-production. In contrast, if a thing is caused by another thing, then everything could come from everything else. It is therefore impossible for an entity that is inherently real and has independent existence to produce another entity with the same characteristics. If entity A produces B, and they are both distinct and independent of each other, then there is no actual explanation of causation. If we call C the effect of B, C would be the effect of A as well, since in both cases the supposed cause and effect are inherently distinct. Therefore, real causation does not exist. If a thing is not caused by itself or by another thing, how about the other two alternatives, by both or by neither? Nāgārjuna demolishes them with equal force. "Neither could there be origination from both self and other, since this argument would be prone to the faults of both positions. Nor from no cause at all, for then everything would be produced continually and everywhere, and also it would become quite pointless."[2] The purpose of this analysis is to show that there cannot be a cause-and-effect relationship between entities whose true nature is empty. We cannot explain logically how causation works. No view about causation can be established.

However, this is not to say that Nāgārjuna does not recognize that there is constant change in the world of our everyday life. In fact, it is precisely because everything is empty and has no inherent and independent existence that change is possible. The two truths of Buddhism provide us with a double vision. On the level of ultimate truth, since everything is empty, it is beyond conception and verbalization. Because it is inconceivable, all views fail to express this truth. However, on the level of conventional truth, we use concepts, language, and theories to explain events and communicate with our fellow human beings.

Jizeng was the founder of the Three Treatises School. It was the first Chinese philosophical school and was much influenced by the Madhyamaka philosophy. He was a scholar-monk with broad learning and was honored as one of the ten great virtuous Buddhist masters of the empire. The three treatises that inspired Jisang were translated by Kumārajīva. Two were written by Nāgārjuna, including the "Verses on the Middle Way," and the third by his disciple Deva. Jisang's father was Parthian and his mother Chinese. To avoid a vendetta, his ancestors first migrated to the area between Hanoi and Canton and later to Nanking, where he was born. His father became a monk, and he himself became a novice at the age of seven. He was reputed to be highly intelligent and understood right away what he heard. He wrote commentaries on the three treatises and a short treatise called "Meaning of the Two Truths." Building on Nāgārjuna's dialectical method, Jisang proposed that the two truths be understood on three levels as outlined below:

Conventional Truth	Ultimate Truth
1. Affirmation of being	1. Affirmation of nonbeing
2. Affirmation of either being or nonbeing	2. Denial of both being and nonbeing
3. Either affirmation or denial of both being and nonbeing	3. Neither affirmation nor denial of both being and nonbeing[3]

Jisang proposes three increasingly advanced levels of negation. The first two levels represent the Four Points of Argument of Madhyamaka. Jisang's contribution is the third level. For him, since the highest level of truth cannot be stated logically; it is revealed only when nothing is affirmed or denied.

Jisang achieved great fame during his lifetime. In 606, Emperor Yang of the Sui dynasty, a patron of Buddhism, invited him to the capital, where over ten thousand monks and laymen heard him preach. In addition to the three treatises of the Madhyamaka school, he also specialized in the *Perfection of Wisdom* scriptures, *Lotus Sutra, Vimalakīrtī Sutra,* and *Nirvana Sutra.* The Three Treastises school deepened Chinese Buddhists' understanding of the philosophy of emptiness and the Middle Way, but it did not continue to exist as a distinct school after the Tang dynasty.

The philosophy of emptiness and the subtle dialectic of Madhyamaka are counterbalanced by the Yogācāra school, founded by the brothers Asanga (c. 310–390) and Vasubandhu (c. 320–400). Yogācāra means practice of yoga. It puts primacy on meditation and offers a rich road map of the mind. The experience of meditation leads to the realization that the only reality is mind or consciousness, the world we experience is constructed by mind or consciousness, and mind or consciousness is composed of eight levels. Early Buddhism recognizes six kinds of consciousness, those corresponding to the five senses and the mind, which is the sense center that coordinates the other five. The contribution of Yogācāra to Buddhist psychology is its discovery of two more levels of consciousness: the seventh or *manas* consciousness, which is responsible for the mistaken belief in a self, and the eighth or *ālaya* consciousness, which serves as the base of all the other seven. *Ālaya* consciousness is called the storehouse consciousness because all the karmic seeds are stored in it.

Yogācāra is interested in how the world of samsara comes about, because when we know the answer, we can end our suffering. One explanation is the twelve links of the Law of Dependent Origination. The first link of ignorance starts the whole process. But how does ignorance come about? The *Perfection of Wisdom* scriptures and Madhyamaka do not ask this question. The insight of emptiness describes the true nature of our world without explaining the origin of either the world or us suffering humans living in it. The realization of emptiness frees us, but the steps we have to go through in order to reach this realization are not spelled out. Yogācāra provides both the explanation of samsara and the way of our release from it.

Both the world and the sense of ego evolve from consciousness. For this reason, nothing exists external to consciousness. This school is therefore called Mind Only or Consciousness Only. The *ālaya* consciousness is a storehouse of the seeds or residues of karma from time without beginning. Every thought or deed performed leaves a lingering spiritual energy that is stored in it. *Ālaya* is inactive. It is like a mirror or smooth ocean. The *manas,* the self-conscious mind or thought center, mistakes *ālaya* as ego and develops defiling vexations such as ignorance, self-love, pride, and so on. *Manas* is responsible for the belief in an ego as well as the belief in an external world. It creates the dualism of subject and object out of the unity of *ālaya.* Just as the *manas* turns to *ālaya* to create the subjective perceiver, it works with the mind and five senses to create the perceived world. The six senses start to function mechanically, and what they experience is reported back to *manas,* which gathers the information received, perceives and discriminates, and then gives orders back to the six senses. Since it is also connected with *ālaya,* it adds the seeds of actions and thoughts committed by the subject to the seeds already there. *Ālaya* is therefore constantly supplied with new seeds. There is a circularity: the seeds in *ālaya* consciousness constantly influence external manifestations, and these manifestations in turn add new seeds to *ālaya.* This process is summarized by a verse of the school:

A seed produces a manifestation;
A manifestation perfumes a seed;
The three elements (seed, manifestation, and perfuming) turn
      on and on;
The cause and effect occur at one and the same time.[4]

Since *manas* plays a central role in the evolution (or devolution) of ego and the world, enlightenment must start there. This is accomplished through a meditative process called turning consciousness into wisdom. It can only be achieved by a revolution in the base of consciousness through the discipline of meditation.

How we know the world is an important concern for Buddhism. Both Madhyamaka and Yogācāra propose that we fail to see things as they really are. Because we hold wrong views about the world due to this, we suffer. Salvation from suffering is possible only when we achieve enlightenment by gaining correct knowledge. Whereas the Four Noble Truths claim that suffering is caused by desire, Mahayana regards ignorance, or the inability to see the true nature of things, as the real cause of suffering. Soteriology is epistemology. What then are the different ways to see and know the things in the world? Is there a hierarchy of knowledge? The Madhyamaka school proposes that there are two ways of knowing the world, and they are the two levels of truth, the conventional and ultimate. Yogācāra has three levels of knowledge, called the three natures, which represent three ways of experiencing the world. The first is *parikalpita,* the mentally constructed or imagined. The second is *paratantra,* the other-dependent. The third is *pariniṣpana,* the absolutely accomplished or perfect knowledge.

The *parikalpita* nature is both the commonsensical view of the world projected by the deluded mind and the deluded mind itself. The subject experiences the world as objects with imaginary concepts and words. The *paratantra* nature is the realization that everything results from causes and conditions, known as dependent origination. In contrast, the *pariniṣpana* nature is perfect because one knows the world is projected by the mind. The experiencer and the experienced are not separate. One knows the world as Suchness, which is devoid of the duality of subject and object. It is called Suchness because reality is beyond concepts and verbal description. There are several analogies for the three kinds of knowledge. *Parikalpita* is like the illusory hairs seen by a person with cataracts, or when one sees water in a mirage or mistakes a rope for a snake. *Paratantra* is like the realization that the illusory hairs are produced by the cataract, or when one knows that the water is actually a mirage, or the snake is really a rope. *Pariniṣpana* is like the unconfused objects seen by one with sound eyes, or the complete lack of water in the mirage, or the realization that the snake is a projection of the mind.

Because one has a cataract, one sees nonexistent hairs, water, and a snake. But when there is no cataract, one sees hairs, mirage, and a rope as they are. However, from the perspective of the third level of knowledge, even the mirage and rope are not really real but are produced by the mind. The first and second levels of knowledge are comparable to the conventional truth, and the third level is comparable to the ultimate truth of Madhyamaka. Whereas Madhyamaka claims that ordinary people fail to realize that things do not have intrinsic nature and are empty, Yogācāra claims that they fail to realize that everything is projected by the mind.

Yogācāra thought was introduced to China by the Indian monk Paramartha (499–569), whose Chinese name was Zhenti, meaning "ultimate truth." Emperor Wu of the Liang dynasty, a pious Buddhist believer, admired his fame as a great scholar and sent envoys for him. He arrived in Canton in 546 and two years later was welcomed by the emperor in present-day Nanking, the capital. Emperor Wu planned to have Paramartha head a translation bureau and direct a large-scale project. However, this failed to materialize because the emperor died under house arrest after a rebellion by his general broke out. Paramartha was forced to spend the rest of his life going from place to place in southern China, and he was often homesick and depressed. Yet with the help of his disciples, he was able to translate as many as three hundred volumes of Yogācāra texts into Chinese before he died at the age of seventy. One of his most important translations was Asanga's *Compendium of the Mahayana,* which he translated in 563, six years before he died. It served as the basis for the Shelun school, which was replaced by the Consciousness Only school founded by Xuanzang and his disciple Kueiji (632–682), the Chinese version of Yogācāra. Although Paramartha was a great translator, because of the chaotic conditions in which he lived, he was not as fortunate as Kumārajīva, active more than a hundred years before him. But just as the latter provided the textual basis for the rise of the Three Treatises school, Paramartha paved the way for the Consciousness Only school.

Xuanzang is commonly known as Master Tripitaka, a title conferred by the emperor for his broad knowledge of Buddhist scriptures. He was born in a place near Luoyang and entered the monastic order when he was thirteen. He was confused by his teachers' different interpretations of the *ālaya* consciousness found in the *Compendium of the Mahayana* and decided to go to India to find the correct answer. He traveled alone through the deserts and mountains of Central Asia and encountered many life-threatening dangers. He arrived in India in 633, at the age of thirty-seven, and spent the next ten years studying at different centers of Buddhist learning, including the famous Nalanda University. He returned to the capital, Chang'an, in 645, once more by way of Central Asia, bringing back 657 Buddhist texts. He received a royal welcome and devoted the rest of his life to translating as many as seventy-five works from Sanskrit. Although his Chinese translations were regarded as peerlessly accurate, they were not as popular as those by Kumārajīva. Furthermore, the Consiousness Only school did not enjoy the same level of importance as Tiantai, Huayan, and Chan. There are two reasons for this. The first is that its literature is very technical and scholastic. The second and more important reason is philosophical. There are both pure and impure seeds in the *ālaya* consciousness in everyone, and they are mixed together. When the pure seeds mature through religious cultivation, they purify the impure seeds. The seeds will stop manifesting in the phenomenal world and discrimination between subject and object will cease. This is englightenment and buddhahood. Reflecting the Hindu caste system, according to the Yogācāra school, there are hierarchically different spiritual lineages in which the so-called *icchantika*s or evil people occupy the lowest rank. Because the Consciousness Only school claims that the *icchantika*s have only impure seeds, they can never achieve enlightenment. Being more Indian in spirit, both features went against the general grain of Chinese Buddhism. Interestingly, the school received renewed interest among Buddhists and intellectuals in the early twentieth century. They found its sophisticated analysis of consciousness comparable, if not superior, to Western psychology.

Although the school connected with him did not flourish, Xuanzang is the most famous Buddhist monk and greatest pilgrim in Chinese history. He wrote an account of his travels in India and the Central Asian countries between India and China. It is one of the most valuable records we have of those countries in the seventh century.[5] It also inspired an author in the sixteenth century to write *Journey to the West*,[6] one of the great novels in Chinese literature, making the adventures of Master Tripitaka and his three disciples widely known to Chinese people from all walks of life. It has been shared through storytelling and drama in the past and movies and TV shows in modern times.

The Chinese Buddhist schools are different from the schools of early Buddhism (which disagreed with each other mainly on some points in the Vinaya). Although the Vinayas of the four Indian Buddhist schools were all translated into Chinese, the *Vinaya in Four Divisions* (*Sifenlü*) of the Dharmaguptaka school has been observed in China since the sixth century. However, the Chinese Buddhist schools bear some resemblance to the schools of Mahayana Buddhism discussed above, although they differ in their selective emphasis on certain sutras and their respective philosophical points of view. There are two major differences that account for the unique features of Chinese Buddhist schools. The first is an overarching scheme created to accommodate the entire Buddhist canon. This is the scholastic system called "doctrinal classification" (*panjiao*), which was used to construct a hierarchical order of the translated sutras. The second is the nonsectarian nature of Chinese Buddhist schools. The four schools interacted with one another and were combined in the religious lives of the people. A person might be attracted to Tiantai teaching but be a Pure Land practitioner. Another person might be interested in Huayan philosophy but be a Chan practitioner. In fact, this pattern has characterized Chinese Buddhism since the Song dynasty (960–1279). This is how the common saying mentioned at the beginning of the chapter came about. This is also a major difference between Chinese Buddhism and Japanese Buddhism, which upholds the strict separation of different schools.

Chinese Buddhist schools came about due to historical circumstances. As discussed in the introduction, Buddhism was not introduced into China in a systematic fashion. Instead, Buddhist sutras were brought by missionary monks from various parts of India and Central Asia. Scriptures of both early and Mahayana Buddhism produced at different time periods were translated into Chinese randomly. A scripture composed later in time might be translated into Chinese before another scripture produced earlier in time. As we have seen, some sutras, such as the *Perfection of Wisdom* scriptures, the *Lotus Sutra,* the *Vimalakīrti Sutra,* and the *Nirvana Sutra* immediately became popular. During the first four hundred years, monks and intellectuals studied these scriptures without asking how they were related to one another and, more broadly, how these Mahayana sutras were related to the scriptures of early Buddhism. When China became unified under the Sui dynasty (581–618), there was a movement to consolidate

Buddhist teachings. Monk-scholars had long felt the need to account for the corpus of translated scriptures. They believed that all were the "word of the Buddha." But why did the scriptures differ from and even contradict each other? Was there any relationship among them? If so, how were they related? For faithful Buddhist believers, these were not just intellectual questions but spiritual ones. It is understandable that they felt the need to create a cohesive system and order for the translated corpus of scriptures. The scholastic system of doctrinal classification was the answer.

The attempt to explain conflicting statements in the Buddha's teaching began in India. The earliest method was to distinguish between the teachings whose meaning was explicit and those whose meaning required interpretation. With the rise of Mahayana Buddhism, the two levels of truth, conventional and ultimate, as well as the concept of *upāya* (expedient means) were two favorite methods used to achieve the same purpose. Although Tiantai and Huayan created different systems of doctrinal classification, they shared the same methodology. First, they created a hierarchical order of all Buddhist teachings, early and Mahayana, and ranked them as progressing from elementary to intermediate to the most profound. The highest position was assigned to the sutra most revered in one's own tradition: the *Lotus Sutra* for Tiantai and the *Flower Garland Sutra* for Huayan. Second, they assigned different types of teachings to different stages of the Buddha's life or to his different teaching methods. In this way, as the Buddha advanced in age, his teachings became progressively more advanced, ending with one specific Mahayana sutra as representing the supreme truth. Doctrinal classification served two purposes: it provided an overview of all the Buddha's teachings, and it served a partisan interest by giving the favored scripture of one's tradition the supreme position over all the other scriptures. In addition to constructing doctrinal taxonomies, Chinese Buddhist schools produced new and creative philosophical theories about the nature of reality. We will now discuss the two major philosophical schools: Tiantai and Huayan.

Tiantai

Tiantai was named after Mount Tiantai (Heavenly Terrace), located in Zhejiang province. Zhiyi (538–597), the founder of Tiantai, lived for many years on the mountain in the sixth century and made it the base of his teaching career. Responding to the Chan claim that it represented the original teaching of the Buddha, the Tiantai tradition also claimed to trace its teachings to the Buddha through a lineage of patriarchs. It regarded Nāgārjuna as the first patriarch, who was succeeded by two Chinese patriarchs before Zhiyi, the fourth patriarch, brought the school to its full development. The myth of patriarchal transmission originated in the Chinese Buddhists' great veneration of Indian Buddhism. Although historically there was no teacher-disciple relationship between Nāgārjuna and the Chinese patriarchs, the authority of famous Indian masters had to be invoked to give the newly established Chinese Buddhist school legitimacy. Chan was the school that took the patriarchal transmission most seriously. Although Chan did not exist in India, it nevertheless had to construct a link to Indian masters. The Chan tradition claims Mahākāśyapa as its first Indian patriarch and Bodhidharma, the twenty-eighth Indian patriarch, who brought Chan to China, as the first Chinese patriarch. Other schools, including Tiantai, followed the example set by Chan and created their own lineages based on patriarchal transmission.

Zhiyi was one of the greatest scholars in East Asian Buddhism. He was the first to create a comprehensive doctrinal classification of the Buddhist canon. He was also an original thinker. He was born in present Hunan province during the rule of the Buddhist Emperor Wu of the Liang (r. 502–549). His biography contains many miraculous events, indicating his extraordinary life. He was conceived when his mother dreamed of swallowing a white mouse. The white mouse was taken to be a transformation of the white elephant who entered the Buddha's mother, Queen Māyā. On his birthday, two monks appeared at his home and predicted that the boy would become a monk when he grew up. At a young age, whenever he saw an image of the Buddha, he would worship it. When he was seven, he impressed the monks at a temple by reciting the words of a sutra after listening to it only once. He came from an illustrious clan, prominent since the Jin (265–420). His father was an official and received honors from the royal houses of the states in southern China. Zhiyi enjoyed a comfortable life during his childhood. However, when he was seventeen years old, after the Western Wei in the north defeated the Liang, his family became refugees. His parents also died the next year. Deeply shaken by the sense of impermanence, he took the tonsure and became a monk.

In 575, after studying under Huisi (515–577), the third patriarch, Zhiyi came to Mount Tiantai when he was thirty-eight. Huisi was a meditation master. Due to his influence, Zhiyi stressed the necessity of both scriptural study and systematic meditation throughout his teaching career.

His fame attracted the patronage of both the emperor of the Chen (557–589) and, later, the emperor of the Sui. He was an early advocate of not killing living creatures. He persuaded fishermen to give up fishing along the seashore under Mount Tiantai. He further bought up the fishing rights and asked the court to issue a decree prohibiting fishing in the area.

Zhiyi made contributions in three areas that became the essential teachings of the Tiantai school. The first is his doctrinal taxonomy, the Tiantai scheme of doctrinal classification. The second is the doctrine of three truths. The third is the concept of nature inclusion, which says that all beings possess both good and evil in their nature. Although other schools created their own systems of doctrinal taxonomy, the latter two teachings are unique to Tiantai.

Zhiyi divided the Buddha's teaching career into five periods and assigned representative sutras to each period, beginning after the Buddha's enlightenment. The first period lasted only three weeks. The sutra taught was the *Huayan* or *Flower Garland Sutra*. But because it was too profound, no one understood it. The second period lasted twelve years, during which the Buddha taught the Hinayana Āgama scriptures of the Four Noble Truths, the Noble Eightfold Path, and the Law of Dependent Origination. These are teachings suitable for people of lesser ability. The third period lasted eight years, during which the Buddha taught elementary Mahayana sutras called Vāipulya (*fangdeng*, "broad and equal"). These scriptures exalt the superiority of Mahayana over Hinayana and the bodhisattva ideal over that of arhat. The fourth period lasted twenty-two years, during which the Buddha taught the *Perfection of Wisdom* scriptures, which represent the mature Mahayana teaching of *śunyatā*. The fifth period covers the last eight years of the Buddha's life. He taught the *Lotus Sutra* and the *Nirvana Sutra*, which proclaim buddhahood for all. They represent the Buddha's final and most profound teaching.

According to tradition, the Buddha was originally reluctant to teach after his enlightenment because he thought people would not understand the profound truth he had discovered. It was only after the god Brahma asked him that the Buddha agreed to teach. As we shall see, the *Flower Garland Sutra* is indeed a very complex and deeply philosophical scripture. It was a very strategic move for Zhiyi to place it in the first period. He used the traditional story to justify his evaluation of *Huayan*: while it is profound, it cannot be considered a perfect and highest teaching like the *Lotus Sutra*. For Zhiyi, the *Lotus Sutra* was the pinnacle of the Buddha's teaching. His lectures on the *Lotus Sutra* were recorded by his disciple Guanding (561–632) and have remained the classics of the Tiantai school. The Tiantai doctrinal classification, like that of the Huayan school, was an attempt to include all Buddhist scriptures within the teaching career of the Buddha in an ascending order. While this did not accord with historical reality, it demonstrated a spirit of inclusiveness and comprehensiveness.

Both the doctrine of three truths and that of nature inclusion are unique to Tiantai. The three truths are the truth of emptiness, the truth of temporariness, and the truth of the mean. While they are based on the two truths Nāgārjuna taught in his "Verses of the Middle Way," they represent a creative synthesis. The two truths refer to the ultimate truth and the conventional truth. Because all things are dependent on causes and have no independent nature, they are said to be empty. This is the ultimate truth. Although they are empty, things are not nonexistent because they do exist contingently. This is the conventional truth. The third truth of the mean or the middle way is the insight that all things are empty and temporary at the same time in reality. The three truths should not be viewed as separate or sequential, but as three integrated and simultaneous ways of understanding the ultimate reality. This threefold vision infuses the world right here and now with ultimate meaning. There is no reality outside and beyond the phenomenal world. If we see everything around us this way, then nirvana is not separate from samsara. This philosophical doctrine affirms this world of ours. It is no wonder that Tiantai became a leading Chinese Buddhist school. It accords with the traditional Chinese worldview, which does not segregate the sacred from the secular.

There are ten Dharma realms in Tiantai cosmology. They include the traditional six realms of *deva*s, asuras, humans, animals, hungry ghosts, and hellish beings. Tiantai adds four more realms: buddhas, bodhisattvas, *pratyekabuddha*s (self-enlightened buddhas), and voice hearers or disciples. Just as the three truths are integrated with each other, these ten Dharma realms are similarly integrated. The Tiantai saying "the three thousand worlds in one instant of thought" is used to describe this vision. The "three thousand worlds" refers to the totality of phenomena, and the "one instant of thought" refers to the mind. This means that mind and phenomena are nondual. Mind as an instant of thought is not ontologically prior to phenomena, nor the other way around. Unlike Consciousness Only thought, held by Yogācāra, the three thousand worlds in one instant of thought does not mean that all phenomena are produced by the mind, nor that the mind.

contains all phenomena. For Zhiyi, "it is not only that every instant of thought includes all phenomena, but also that any one phenomenon in any moment includes all other phenomena. This assertion implies that each phenomenon and each individual being intrinsically includes all other phenomena and beings, an idea that came to be referred to as nature inclusion."[7] When this is applied to the ten Dharma realms, each realm includes the nine other realms. Consequently, not only buddhas but also hungry ghosts, animals, and hell beings possess buddhahood. Following the same logic, buddhas also possess the same evil nature as hungry ghosts, animals, and hell beings.

Everyone therefore has two natures: one good, the other evil. The buddha and the *icchantika* are not different in their nature because they are both good and evil. They have the potential to do both good and evil. The Buddha is aware that he has the potential to do evil, but he chooses to cultivate good instead. The *icchantika* is not aware that he has the potential to do good; therefore, he continues to cultivate evil. Enlightened beings such as the Buddha have fully developed their good nature, while unenlightened beings such as ordinary people are dominated by their evil nature. However, the two natures are not separated but are mutually included. Just as good nature and enlightenment exist in us potentially, the fully enlightened Buddha retains the evil nature in a state of dormancy. Precisely because the Buddha shares the evil nature with us (although unlike in us, it is unmanifested), he is not cut off from us. If the Buddha had nothing in common with us, he would not be able to understand our suffering. In that case, the image of the Buddha as the compassionate father found in the *Lotus Sutra* could not be established. As discussed, the *Nirvana Sutra* declares that because everyone has Buddha nature, everyone can achieve buddhahood, including the incorrigible *icchatika*s. They can do so when their good Buddha nature emerges as a result of religious cultivation. The usual understanding in Buddhism is that enlightenment happens when the impure vexations such as ignorance and desire are eliminated. The Tiantai doctrine of nature inclusion drastically changes this traditional view. Good and evil exist in all beings. Just as we can activate our good nature and become buddhas, we are still linked to the Buddha on account of our shared evil nature. This revolutionary view led to the striking conclusion reached by Zhanran (711–782), the ninth patriarch, who declared that even grasses and trees can achieve buddhahood because Buddha nature is found not only in sentient beings but also in insentient ones.

Following his teacher, Huisi, Zhiyi put equal emphasis on scriptural study and meditation. Traditionally Buddhism divides meditation into *śamatha* and *vipaśyanā*. The former leads to cessation and the various states of concentrative absorption known as *jhāna*, while the latter leads to insight and nirvana. Tiantai uses the same terminology, translated as *zhi* (concentration) and *guan* (insight) in Chinese. Zhiyi's masterpiece, the *Great Calming and Contemplation* (*Mohe zhiguan*), is a classic for all Tiantai Buddhists in East Asia.

One practices *zhi* in order to stop the flow of false ideas and realize the nonexistence of phenomena and the truth of emptiness. One practices *guan* in order to realize that although phenomena are like dreams and illusions, they nevertheless have a temporary existence, and thereby achieves insight into the truth of temporariness. The meditative practices are carried out for the sake of a religious life lived in the middle way, which enables one to not become attached to either samsara or nirvana.

Tiantai declined after the Huichang Persecution of 845. Teaching centers were destroyed and many writings were lost. But it began a vigorous new life after the king of Wuyue sent envoys to Japan and Korea to obtain important Tiantai texts in the tenth century. Both Zhili and Zunshi, the two masters we met in chapter 3, played important roles in the revival during the Song. It was also during this time that Tiantai faced a crisis of identity when it split into two factions, known as Off Mountain and Home Mountain. They differed on two critical issues: the nature of the mind and the method of meditation. The Off Mountain group was much influenced by Zanran, who lived at a time when Huayan came into prominence. For him, reality was One Mind or True Suchness, as stated by the *Awakening of Faith*. In this view, as discussed in chapter 1, everything issues from the mind, which is intrinsically pure. Ignorance is an illusion that obscures the pure mind. For Off Mountain adherents, the object of meditation is therefore the pure mind, not the defiled mind. When one is awakened to this pure mind, one realizes one's true nature and achieves enlightenment. This view is very similar to that of Chan.

Zhili was the spokesman for the Home Mountain group, which claimed to represent the Tiantai orthodoxy. He denounced the Off Mountain group as heretical. Following Zhiyi, he believed in the mutual inclusion of all phenomena or the "three thousand worlds." The Buddha realm includes the other nine Dharma realms, just as each Dharma realm includes all of the other nine Dharma realms, including the Buddha realm. True Mind is no different from poison and purity is no different from pollution, for they are all contained in each person. Zhili regarded evil and impurity as very real and felt that they must be dealt with. For although evil, like good, cannot be dissipated in the ultimate sense, one can change its configuration through practice. Repentance ritual practice was therefore very important for him. The climactic moment after making confession is to observe or discern one's defiled mind. As in the Great Compassion Repentance, although one cannot remove evil, by repenting and identifying with Guanyin through discernment, one can deactivate evil and activate good, which is contained in oneself from the beginning. Thus, by ritually "playing" Guanyin, one can eventually hope really to act as the bodhisattva.

Although there was controversy between the two groups during his lifetime, Zhili's Home Mountain and his ideas on nature inclusion became the Tiantai orthodoxy. He had many disciples who carried on his legacy, whereas the adherents of the Off Mountain group did not have successors to continue their cause. When the Tiantai chronicles were compiled in the thirteenth century in response to the Chan genealogical histories called lamp records, they recognized Zhili's Home Mountain group as the true representative of the Tiantai tradition. The concept of nature inclusion as interpreted by Zhili is the most significant difference setting Tiantai apart from Huayan and Chan. With the support of local officials and imperial patronage, many monasteries were designated as Tiantai monasteries. Institutionally speaking, there were only two types of monasteries: teaching (*jiao*), represented by Tiantai, and meditation, represented by Chan. Huayan and Pure Land did not have their own monasteries.

Huayan

The Huayan school is named after the scripture of the same name. It appeared after Tiantai in the Tang, when the Chan school was on the way to becoming the dominant movement. Whereas the Tiantai school holds the *Lotus Sutra* as the summit of the Buddha's teaching, the Huayan school regards the *Flower Garland Sutra* as the Buddha's ultimate teaching. Like Tiantai, it created a system of doctrinal classification of the Buddha's teachings and a comprehensive scheme covering the entire corpus of Buddhist scriptures. They are listed in the following (ascending) order:

1. The teaching of the disciples as found in the Agama scriptures of the Hinayana. While it teaches that the self does not exist in an individual, dharmas or elements do exist.

2. The elementary Mahayana teaching of *śūnyatā*. It teaches that not only the individual but all dharmas lack an intrinsic nature. This is represented by the Yogācāra or Consciousness Only school founded by Xuanzang (596–664). It is considered elementary because it does not hold that all beings have Buddha nature.
3. The final Mahayana teaching represented by the Tiantai school, which teaches the temporary existence of all things although they are ultimately empty.
4. The abrupt Mahayana teaching represented by the Chan school. It teaches sudden enlightenment when both existence and nonexistence are negated because language fails to express the truth of nonduality.
5. The perfect Mahayana teaching represented by the Huayan school. It teaches that not only are all things in the world identical with and interpenetrating the mind, but all things are also identical with and interpenetrating each other. In contrast to the Tiantai slogan "all in one and one in all," the Huayan slogan is "all in all."

The *Flower Garland Sutra* was translated from Sanskrit three times, the first in 420. The three versions are of different lengths, consisting of sixty, eighty, and forty volumes, respectively. The forty-volume version constitutes the last forty chapters of the other versions and is titled "Entering the Dharmadhātu (Realm of dharmas)." The ultimate reality for the *Flower Garland Sutra* is Dharmadhātu. It is the world of all the dharmas, whose true nature is empty. According to Buddhist metaphysics, everything in the world consists of dharmas, the irreducible unit of phenomena. Modern scholars equate the dharmas to atoms. "Entering the Dharmadhātu" describes the pilgrimage of a youth named Sudhana who travels all over the world in search of supreme enlightenment. He seeks instructions from fifty-three teachers, who are called "good friends" and come from all walks of life. They are bodhisattvas, gods, goddesses, kings, bankers, householders, hermits, laymen, laywomen, boys, maidens, a ship's captain, and a courtesan. Each of them instructs Sudhana in one aspect of the Ultimate Truth and sends him on his way to the next teacher. The pilgrimage of Sudhana has served as the subject of Buddhist art in China, Japan, and Indonesia (where the monumental art complex of Borobudur provides a grand vision of his paradigmatic journey). At the end of his pilgrimage, led by Maitreya, Sudhana enters the Vairocana

Tower, which represents the Dharmadhātu, the world as seen by enlightened bodhisattvas. The buddha who teaches in the *Flower Garland Sutra* is Vairocana or Illuminator Buddha, who is not the historical Śākyamuni Buddha in his physical form or Rūpakāya. Instead, this is his Dharmakāya, his Truth Body. Dharmadhātu is the Dharmakāya and is represented by the Vairocana Tower.

Why is the Buddha in the *Flower Garland Sutra* called Vairocana? To answer this question, we have to know the Mahayana Buddhology or theory about the Buddha. The Buddha has three bodies, each representing one aspect of him. The Rūpakāya (Transformation Body) is the physical body of the historical Śākyamuni Buddha. He was born as a man, achieved enlightenment, and passed into nirvana upon death. The Sambhogakāya (Enjoyment Body) is the glorified body of the Buddha who preaches to bodhisattvas in his Pure Lands. This is the form of the Buddha worshiped by the faithful. It is also the form attained by a practitioner upon achieving buddhahood. Amitābha, the buddha worshiped by the Pure Land school, is the most famous Enjoyment Body. The Dharmakāya (Truth Body) is the highest of the three bodies and serves as the basis for the other two. The entire body of Buddha's teachings was originally called the Dharma. With the development of Mahayana philosophy, the Dharma refers to the truth of emptiness (*śūnyata*), which describes all things as they truly are. Since all things are empty, there is no intrinsic difference between one thing and another. All beings are potentially buddhas. The flip side of emptiness is Buddha nature. The Chinese Buddhist tradition prefers the positive way of referring to the real nature of everything. Dharmakāya is a religious way to express this insight. The Truth Body is the cosmos as it truly is. For Huayan Buddhism the Dharmadhātu is the cosmos seen by the Buddha in his Truth Body appearing as Vairocana Buddha.

Just as Tiantai claimed superiority by presenting Śākyamuni as the eternal Buddha who preaches the *Lotus Sutra*, Huayan tradition claimed that it was Vairocana Buddha, the Truth Body, who preached the *Flower Garland Sutra*. According to Fazang (648–712), the third patriarch and founder of the Huayan school, the *Flower Garland Sutra* was preached during the second week after the Buddha's enlightenment, when he was still seated under the Bodhi tree and immersed in the "samadhi of oceanic reflection." For Fazang, it "symbolized the Buddha's enlightened vision in which the harmonious interrelationship of all phenomena in the entire universe simultaneously appeared as if reflected on the surface of a vast, tranquil ocean."[8] The universe seen by Vairocana Buddha in this mystic vision is called Dharmadhātu, which is also the Truth Body. What is it like? We can get some ideas from the *Flower Garland Sutra,* which in many passages provides tantalizing descriptions:

> The realm of the Buddhas is inconceivable;
> No sentient being can fathom it. . . .
> The Buddha constantly emits great beams of light;
> In each light beam are innumerable Buddhas. . . .
> The Buddha-body is pure and always tranquil;
> The radiance of its light extends throughout the world; . . .
> The Buddha's freedom cannot be measured—
> It fills the cosmos and all space. . . .
> With various techniques it teaches the living,
> Sound like thunder, showering the rain of truth. . . .
> All virtuous activities in the world
> Come from the Buddha's light. . . .[9]

> In all atoms of all lands
> Buddha enters, each and every one,
> Producing miracle displays for sentient beings:
> Such is the way of Vairocana. . . .
> In each atom are many oceans of worlds,
> Their locations each different all beautifully pure;
> Thus does infinity enter into one,
> Yet each unit's distinct, with no overlap. . . .
> In each atom are innumerable lights
> Pervading the lands of the ten directions,
> All showing the Buddhas' enlightenment practices,
> The same in all oceans of worlds.
> In each atom the Buddhas of all times
> Appear, according to inclinations;
> While their essential nature neither comes nor goes,
> By their own power they pervade the worlds.[10]

Since Vairocana means illumination, the Dharmadhātu seen by the Buddha is full of light. Just as light penetrates everywhere without obstruction, things in that world interpenetrate with each other yet retain their individual uniqueness. The pilgrim Sudhana witnesses the wonder of this world when he enters the Vairocana Tower.

> To Sudhana's wondering gaze, the interior of the Tower reveals itself as being as wide as the sky. . . . Moreover, within the tower there are hundreds of thousands of towers, each one as exquisitely adorned . . . and each one, while preserving its individual existence at the same time offering no obstruction to all the rest. . . . He sees Maitreya and other bodhisattvas entering into *samādhi* and emitting from the pores of their skin multitudes of transformation bodies of various kinds. He also hears all the teachings of the Buddha melodiously issuing from every single pore of the skin of all the bodhisattvas. He beholds all the Buddhas, together with their respective assemblies, and is the spectator of their different activities. In one particularly high, spacious, and exquisitely decorated tower, of incomparable beauty, he sees at one glance the entire trichiliocosm . . . and in each one of these worlds he sees Maitreya's descent to earth, his nativity, and all the subsequent events of his final existence.[11]

Fazang used "Indra's net" as a metaphor for the Dharmadhātu, which is represented by the Vairocana Tower. It is characterized by nonobstruction, identity, interpenetration, and interdependence. All the towers are identical, but the many towers which are within the Tower are dependent on it, just as the Tower is dependent on those many towers. Not only do the Tower and the towers interpenetrate one another, the many towers themselves also interpenetrate one another. Francis Cook describes Indra's net this way:

> Far away in the heavenly abode of the great god Indra, there is a wonderful net which has been hung by some cunning artificer in such a manner that it stretches out infinitely in all directions. In accordance with the extravagant tastes of deities, the artificer has hung a single glittering jewel in each "eye" of the net, and since the net itself is infinite in dimension, the jewels are infinite in number. There hang the jewels, glittering like stars in the first magnitude, a wonderful sight to behold. If we now arbitrarily select one of these jewels for inspection and look closely at it, we will discover that in its polished surface there are reflected all the other jewels in the net, infinite in number. Not only

that, but each of the jewels reflected in this one jewel is also reflecting all the other jewels, so that there is an infinite reflecting process occurring. The Hua-yen school has been fond of this image, mentioned many times in its literature, because it symbolizes a cosmos in which there is an infinitely repeated interrelationship among all the members of the cosmos. This relationship is said to be one of simultaneous mutual identity and mutual intercausality.[12]

Both Tiantai and Huayan were firmly grounded in the Mahayana teachings of dependent origination and emptiness. However, like Tiantai, Huayan created unique concepts and vocabularies in constructing its philosophy. The ultimate reality is called *li* (universality), and things in the phenomenal world, *shi* (particularity). Both terms are familiar to Chinese speakers but not found in Buddhist scriptures. *Li* originally refers to the vein in jade, while *shi* refers to an object or event. By extension, *li* is the underlying essence and *shi* is the outward manifestation of *li*. In Huayan teaching, *li* represents emptiness or Buddha nature as seen by enlightened bodhisattvas, while *shi* represents everyday things and events as experienced by ordinary people. *Li* and *shi* represent two sides of *sūnyatā*. While *li* refers to its static aspect, *shi* refers to its dynamic aspect. They are fundamentally inseparable, although they can be contemplated and discussed separately. Huayan patriarchs speak of four Dharmadhātus. This does not mean that there are four different kinds of Dharmadhātu; rather, the Dharmadhātu should be viewed from four different perspectives: the Dharmadhātu of principle or *li,* the Dharmadhātu of phenomena or *shi,* the Dharmadhātu of the nonobstructed interrelationship between *li* and *shi,* and the Dharmadhātu of the nonobstructed interrelationship among *shi.*

The best example of using the fourfold way to see how the Dharmadhātu works was offered by Fazang, the third patriarch of the Huayan school. He regarded the Dharmadhātu of nonobstructed interrelationship among *shi* as the highest realization. Fazang's ancestors originally were from Sogdia in Central Asia, but he was born in the Tang capital, Chang'an. Like a number of Buddhist masters, he had a life full of supernatural signs and omens. According to his biography, Fazang was conceived after his mother dreamed that she swallowed the sun and moon. He was attracted to Buddhism at an early age. When he was sixteen, he burned one finger as an offering to Buddha's relic in a stupa. He traveled

everywhere in search of a teacher when he was seventeen and was not satisfied with any. He then lived as an ascetic hermit on a mountain for several
years and returned home only because his parents were ill. One night he
dreamed that his house was entirely illuminated by heavenly light. He
took this as a sign that a great teacher must be teaching nearby. It turned
out that Zhiyan (602–668), the second patriarch, was indeed lecturing on
the *Flower Garland Sutra* in the capital. He went to see Zhiyan the very
next morning and became his disciple as a layperson. He was ordained as
a monk finally at the age of twenty-eight, which was rather late among his
contemporaries. Empress Wu (624–705) appointed him as the abbot of a
new temple in the capital. Fazang was a prolific writer and great lecturer.
He gained national fame and served as preceptor for four rulers, and
Empress Wu was his most famous student. She was the only woman who
ruled in her own right in Chinese history. She promoted Buddhism as the
state religion and was particularly fond of the Huayan teachings. The fortune of various Buddhist traditions rose and fell in close connection with
royal patronage. Tiantai prospered during the Sui because Zhiyi enjoyed
imperial patronage, and Yogācāra was popular because Xuanzang was
admired by the Tang emperors. In order to differentiate herself from rulers
in the Sui and Tang, Empress Wu favored Huayan. Tiantai and Yogācāra
receded into the background.

In addition to his broad learning, Fazang was apparently a good
teacher. One time, when the empress was listening to Fazang's exposition
of the fourfold Dharmadhātu, she had difficulty understanding its com-
plexity. Using a skillful device, he pointed to the golden lion guarding the
palace for illustration. The "Essay on the Golden Lion" was written down
afterward and became the most famous work in Huayan literature. The
golden lion represents the Dharmadhātu, which can be examined from
four different perspectives. When the empress concentrates on the gold
only and not the lion, she sees the realm of *li*. Gold as *li* is *śūnyatā*, the
ultimate reality. When she concentrates on the lion and not the gold, she
sees the realm of *shi*, the phenomenal particulars. But when she realizes
that the gold cannot be separated from the lion, she sees the nonobstructed
interrelationship between *li* and *shi*. Without the gold, the lion cannot be
cast. By the same token, without the form of the lion, gold is not manifested. This is the same truth of "form is emptiness, emptiness is form;
form is no other than emptiness, emptiness is no other than form," proclaimed by the *Heart Sutra*. Finally, when she realizes that each part of the

lion is identical with and interpenetrates every other part of the lion, she sees the nonobstructed interrelationship among *shi*. This is so because all the parts of the lion are made of gold; they are identical. Furthermore, since all the parts of the lion are of one nature, that of gold or emptiness, they penetrate into each other and also the lion as a whole. The relationship between the gold as *li* and the lion as *shi* is similar to that between water and waves, which is a favorite metaphor found in the *Awakening of Faith*. Fazang describes their relationship in the section titled "Ten Mysterious Gates" in his essay:

> The various organs of the lion, down to each and every hair, all include the whole lion, in so far as they are all the gold. Thus each and every one of them permeates the eyes of the lion. The eyes are the ears, the ears are the nose, the nose is the tongue, and the tongue is the body. They each are freely established and do not impede one another. This is called the theory of mutual freedom among things. In the lion's eyes, ears, limbs, and every separate hair, the gold lion is present. The lion of all the hairs, taken together, is at the same time all found within a single hair. Thus these many hairs have an infinitude of lions, and these infinitude of lions of these many hairs is further contained within each single hair. In this way there is an endless doubling and redoubling, like the jewels in Indra's net.[13]

Fazang adopted different techniques in his teaching. Just as he used the golden lion as a pedagogical tool to teach Empress Wu, he constructed a hall of mirrors to show his disciples how Indra's net looks. He prepared ten mirrors, with eight placed at the eight points of the compass, one above, and one below, all facing one another. In the center he put a statue of the Buddha, lighted by a bright torch. The Buddha image was now reflected in the ten mirrors, and the image in each mirror was also reflected in all the other mirrors. Moreover, the many images reflected in each mirror were also reflected in every other mirror. There was thus the doubling and redoubling of the images, just as the many jewels being reflected in each jewel of the net were also reflected in every other jewel.

It is no wonder that Indra's net was a favorite metaphor for the Huayan masters. If we imagine the net as the world and the jewels as human beings in the world, we immediately see the existential significance. The net cannot exist without the many jewels, just as the many jewels cannot exist without the net. Furthermore, each single jewel has the same interdependent relationship with both the net and the other jewels. When even one single jewel is missing, the net will not be able to remain the same. Similarly, just as our existence depends on the world, the world is also dependent on each one of us. Such a realization endows us simultaneously with a sense of gratitude and a sense of responsibility. Indra's net is a cosmic ecology that views existence as one organic unity in which all things are identical in their emptiness, and in which each part is dependent on the whole and simultaneously contributes to the whole because of the law of dependent origination.

Zongmi (780–841) was the fifth patriarch and made important contributions to Huayan thought. He studied the Confucian classics and, like his learned contemporaries, planned to enter officialdom by taking the civil examination. However, when he was twenty-seven, he was deeply impressed by a Chan master he met and decided to become a monk instead. He at first followed the Chan practice, but after he read the commentaries on the *Flower Garland Sutra* written by Chengguan, the fourth patriarch, who also studied under Chan teachers, he became the latter's disciple. Aside from their familiarity with Chan, the teacher and student shared another thing in common. Both Chengguan and Zongmi created their doctrinal classifications and drew ideas from the *Awakening of Faith*. As pointed out by Peter Gregory, Zongmi identifies Dharmadhātu with *tathāgatagarbha* and gave the teaching of *tathāgatagarbha* the highest position in his doctrinal classification instead of the *Flower Garland Sutra*. He called it "the teaching that reveals the nature." Nature, otherwise known as One Mind, Suchness, or *tathāgatagarbha,* gives rise to everything. All phenomena therefore originate in nature. This is known as nature origination.

> The teaching of the one vehicle that reveals the nature holds that all sentient beings without exception have the intrinsically enlightened true mind. From [time] without beginning it is permanently abiding and immaculate. It is shining, unobscured, clear and bright ever-present awareness. It is also called Buddha-nature, and it is also called tathāgatagarbha. From time without beginning deluded thoughts cover it, and [sentient beings] by themselves are not aware of it. Because they only recognize their inferior qualities, they become indulgently attached, enmeshed in karma, and experience the

suffering of birth-and-death. The Great Enlightened One took pity upon them and taught that everything without exception is empty. He further revealed that the purity of the numinous enlightened true mind is wholly identical with that of all Buddhas.[14]

As discussed in chapter 1, according to the *Awakening of Faith,* there is only one reality, which is the One Mind. The One Mind has two aspects: Suchness and ignorance. It is possessed by both buddhas and sentient beings. It gives rise to all things because it is the totality of everything. Within this One Mind, the absolute and the phenomena, enlightenment and unenlightenment, nirvana and samsara, coexist. They are mutually inclusive. Under the influence of Suchness, one becomes enlightened, but under the influence of ignorance, one becomes entangled in the world and suffers as a result. The One Mind is always pure and luminous even when we are not aware of it. Enlightenment is none other than becoming aware of our original enlightened nature. In this regard, Zongmi differs from his teacher, Chengguan, for he holds that *tathāgatagarbha,* not the unobstructed interrelationship of all phenomena, is the main teaching of Huayan.[15] Like Chan, Zongmi also emphasizes that our essential task is to become aware of our originally enlightened nature. For this reason, Zhongmi was revered in both Huayan and Chan. He was also responsible for advocating the combination of doctrinal schools with Chan, a feature unique in Chinese Buddhism and not found in Japanese Buddhism.

This chapter began with a discussion about how a Chinese Buddhist school differs from a sect. It then discussed the two Mahayana Buddhist schools in India. While Madhyamaka and Yogācāra exerted much influence on Chinese Buddhist thinkers, Tiantai and Huayan are two philosophical schools unique to Chinese Buddhism. While the Tiantai teaching is described as round and gradual, that of Huayan is described as perfect and sudden. The doctrine of nature inclusion of Tiantai can be contrasted with the doctrine of nature origination of Huayan. Even though each elevates one particular sutra as the final teaching of the Buddha, both traditions are indebted to the *Awakening of Faith.* The difference is that while Huayan emphasizes the pure and enlightened mind of Suchness, Tiantai stresses the deluded and defiled mind in the world of phenomena. Historically, Huayan had a close connection with Chan and Tiantai with Pure

Land. Many Chan masters favored the *Flower Garland Sutra,* and many Pure Land lay societies, as we will discuss in chapter 7, were founded by Tiantai masters during the Song. Both Huayan and Chan emphasize that our mind is originally pure and that sudden enlightenment is triggered by this realization. Tiantai, because of its belief in nature inclusion, is keenly aware of the precarious nature of the human condition and the need for confession and repentance. Devotion is as essential for Tiantai as it is for Pure Land.

The Buddhist schools of Tiantai and Huayan, like Chan and Pure Land, discussed in the next two chapters, were Chinese Buddhist creations not found in India. They were introduced into Japan and Korea and became distinctive features of East Asian Buddhism. Their philosophical foundations are *śūnyatā,* nonduality, and universal buddhahood, emphasized in many Mahayana scriptures. However, echoing the positive language of One Mind, True Suchness, and *tathāgatagarbha* of the *Awakening of Faith,* Tiantai calls the ultimate reality One Mind, while Huayan calls it *li.* Their doctrines have direct consequences for how we view our world and our life. They affirm the religious value of the earth and endow everyday life with spiritual significance. They agree with the indigenous Chinese tradition, which does not demarcate the secular from the sacred. Rather, we are microcosms corresponding to the macrocosm, and with spiritual and moral cultivation, humans can form a trinity with heaven and earth.

Discussion Questions

1. What is a Chinese Buddhist school?
2. Why did Chinese Buddhists create doctrinal classifications?
3. How do you understand nature inclusion as taught by Tiantai?
4. What does the Huayan metaphor of Indra's net signify?
5. How do some of the ideas studied in this chapter apply to our contemporary ecological and environmental concerns?

Further Reading

Chan, Chi-wah. "Chih-li (960–1028) and the Crisis of T'ien-t'ai Buddhism in the Early Sung." In *Buddhism in the Sung,* edited by Peter N. Gregory and Daniel Getz Jr., 409–441. Honolulu: University of Hawai'i Press, 1999.

Cook, Francis. *Hua-yen Buddhism: The Jewel Net of Indra.* University Park: Pennsylvania State University Press, 1977.

Gregory, Peter N. *Tsung-mi and the Sinification of Buddhism*. Princeton, NJ: Princeton University Press, 1991.

Williams, Paul. *Mahāyāna Buddhism: The Doctrinal Foundations*. London: Routledge, 1989.

Wriggins, Sally Hovey. *Xuanzang: A Buddhist Pilgrim on the Silk Road*. Boulder, CO: Westview Press, 1996.

Notes

1   *The Teachings of the Compassionate Buddha: Early Discourses, the Dharmapada and Later Basic Writings*, edited, with commentary, by E. A. Burtt (New York: New American Library, 2000), 147.

2   Williams, *Mahāyāna Buddhism*, 66.

3   Fung Yu-lan, *History of Chinese Philosophy* (Princeton, NJ: Princeton University Press, 1953), 2:295.

4   Wing-tsit Chan, *A Sourcebook in Chinese Philosophy* (Princeton, NJ: Princeton University Press, 1963), 371.

5   *On Yuan Chwang's Travels in India, 629–645 A.D.*, translated by Thomas Watters, 2 vols. London: Royal Asiatic Society, 1904–1905.

6   *Journey to the West*, translated by Anthony C. Yu, 4 vols. (Chicago: University of Chicago Press, 1977–1983).

7   Chi-wah Chan, "Chih-li (960–1028) and the Crisis of T'ien-t'ai Buddhism," 411.

8   Gregory, *Tsung-mi and the Sinification of Buddhism*, 130.

9   Thomas Cleary, trans., *The Flower Ornament Scripture* (Boulder, CO: Shambhala, 1984), 1:66–69.

10 Cleary, *The Flower Ornament Scripture*, 190–201.

11 Sangharakshita, *The Eternal Legacy* (London: Tharpa Publications, 1985), 229–231.

12 Cook, *Hua-yen Buddhism*, 214.

13 Fung Yu-lan, *A History of Chinese Philosophy*, translated by Derk Bodde (Princeton, NJ: Princeton University Press, 1953), II:350.

14 Gregory, *Tsung-mi and the Sinification of Buddhism*, 165.

15 Gregory, *Tsung-mi and the Sinification of Buddhism*, 167.

CHAPTER 6

The Meditation Tradition
Chan Buddhism

Chan is the Chinese transliteration of the Sanskrit word *dhyāna,* which means meditation. It is number seven on the Noble Eightfold Path and an essential training in all Buddhist traditions. However, Chan Buddhism was a unique Chinese creation that did not exist in India and was later transmitted to Japan, Korea, and Vietnam. Westerners came to know it as Zen, which is the Japanese pronunciation of *Chan,* because the teachers who first introduced it to the West after the Second World War were Japanese.

Meditation was never exclusive to Chan. As we saw in previous chapters, different teachers taught different forms of meditation. Anshigao taught the observation of breath and impurity. Huiyuan taught the mindfulness of Buddha. Zhiyi's four forms of samadhi were based on the Tiantai method of concentration and insight. Until the tenth century, authors compiling biographies of eminent monks routinely included monks renowned for their meditation abilities in a section called "Meditators." Chan simply meant a person who practiced meditation. Although meditation was a common practice of all Buddhists, Chan called itself the Meditation school because it claimed to be the only tradition representing the original teaching of Śākyamuni, the historical Buddha. Unlike Tiantai and Huayan, which find legitimizing authority in scriptures, Chan advocates mind-to-mind transmission. One achieves enlightenment by meditating like the Buddha did, without relying on scriptural study or religious rituals. Truth was transmitted from the Buddha's mind to his disciple Mahākāśyapa, who, in turn, carried out the transmission to his disciples, the Chan patriarchs. Chan, which developed later than Tiantai and Huayan, tried to establish its superiority by tracing its lineage back to the Buddha through patriarchal transmission. Bodhidharma (424–535) was the twenty-eighth Indian patriarch, brought the Chan lineage to China, and became known as the First Patriarch.

The Chan identity is well characterized by a four-line stanza attributed to Bodhidharma:

> A separate transmission outside the teachings,
> Not setting up scriptures.
> Pointing directly at a person's mind.
> Seeing into the nature and attaining buddhahood.

The last two lines reflect the thought of Buddha nature prevalent during the sixth century. When a person realizes the original nature of his mind, he achieves buddhahood. This idea, as we have seen in chapter 5, is shared by Huayan. The first two lines, however, are unique to Chan. They refer to a seminal Chan origin myth. It tells the story of how, one time at an assembly, instead of preaching a sermon as usual, the Buddha held a flower while remaining silent. Everyone was confounded except for Mahākāśyapa, who was known as the wisest among the disciples. Without saying a word, he suddenly smiled. The Buddha declared that his true teaching, the Buddha mind or the Dharma eye, was now transmitted to Mahākāśyapa in this wordless fashion. It was a direct mind-to-mind transmission, a teaching separate from scriptures. This mythical account has been widely accepted as the origin of Chan in East Asia.

Recent scholarship, however, makes clear that this claim of Chan being a separate transmission was a Song construction. It did not appear suddenly but went through a long and complicated process of development, culminating with the *Transmission of the Lamp of the Jingde Era*, dated 1004, the earliest of the Chan genealogical histories known as lamp records. It was further bolstered by successive Chan genealogical histories in the next several centuries until it became the orthodoxy. According to T. Griffith Foulk, Chan monasteries, like all public monasteries in the Song, had facilities for meditation practice, sutra study, and group recitation of sutras in ritual settings. All Buddhist monks, including those affiliated with Chan, were required by the state to be versed in both sutras and Vinaya (monastic rules) in order to qualify for the novice and full ordinations.[1] He further suggests that the Chan made its unique claim for two reasons. The first was to defend itself against attack by the Tiantai school, which already claimed that their revered *Lotus Sutra* was the true teaching of the Buddha. It was therefore the sutra that transmitted the Buddha's Dharma. As discussed in the last chapter, Tiantai underwent a revival under Zhili and Zunshi. They succeeded in lobbying the court to have a number of public monasteries designed as teaching monasteries and to have Tiantai writings introduced into the canon. Much later, during the twelfth and thirteenth centuries, Tiantai genealogical histories were composed in imitation of Chan histories. Instead of the robe traditionally handed down from one Chan patriarch to the next, a fly whisk and incense burner served as the insignia of a Tiantai patriarch. The second reason Chan claimed to represent a separate transmission was to establish its institutional dominance. As T. Griffith Foulk puts it,

> The controversies that simmered in the Sung over the status of the Ch'an heritage as a "separate transmission," in short, were more about securing prestige, patronage, and special privileges within the Buddhist order than about practical matters of monkish training or spiritual cultivation. The "separate transmission" slogan was used successfully by proponents of Ch'an to argue that members of their lineage, having inherited the enlightenment of the Buddha in a direct line of "mind-to-mind transmission," were the monks most qualified for positions of leadership within the exiting Buddhist monastic institution.[2]

We will now look at how the Chan tradition presents its history.

Bodhidharma

There are several stories about Bodhidharma. While they may contain some historical facts, it is better to regard them as myths, for each story expresses something of fundamental significance about Chan to its followers. The first is about the interview between Bodhidharma and Emperor Wu (r. 502–549) of the Liang dynasty. Modeling himself upon Emperor Aśoka of India, the emperor was a great devotee and patron of Buddhism. He promoted vegetarianism, gave up meat and wine himself, and ordered his subjects to use fruits and vegetables instead of living creatures in sacrifice. The emperor not only gave lectures on some Buddhist scriptures himself but also wrote commentaries on the *Vimalakīrti, Nirvana,* and *Perfection of Wisdom* scriptures. He honored monastics and held Dharma assemblies. He constructed many temples. More strikingly, on three occasions he offered himself to a Buddhist temple to serve as a menial laborer. The courtiers then had to redeem him. The emperor did this as a clever strategy to raise money for the temple.

Bodhidharma. China. Seventeenth century. Ming (1368–1644).
Metropolitan Museum of Art

In the story of the meeting between Emperor Wu and Bodhidharma, the emperor is used as a foil to highlight the master's superior insight. When the emperor received Bodhidharma, he greeted him and asked if by performing so many good deeds on behalf of Buddhism, he had accumulated much merit. Fully expecting to receive a positive answer and be praised, he received instead a curt reply: "No merit whatsoever!" The meeting naturally ended abruptly, and Bodhidharma sailed across the Yangtze River on a leaf and went to Shaolin Temple to meditate, facing a wall for nine years. There are three points the story tries to make. The first is to show that despite the emperor's devotion and patronage of Buddhism, he had not really understood the truth of emptiness taught by the *Perfection of Wisdom* scriptures. Although on the level of conventional truth, Buddhism affirms the distinctions between good and bad, or merit and demerit, on the level of ultimate truth, such distinctions are dissolved by the insight of emptiness and nonduality. On the level of ultimate truth, the perfection of giving is achieved only when one gives without being self-consciously aware of the giver, the receiver, and the gift. Since Emperor Wu was fully conscious of the good things he had done on behalf of Buddhism, he spoke from the point of view of conventional truth. Bodhidharma, on the other hand, spoke from the level of ultimate truth. It was no wonder that the two did not have a meeting of the minds.

The story of Bodhidharma's sailing across the river on a leaf is a favorite theme in Chan paintings. Similarly, painters also like to depict Bodhidharma sitting cross-legged facing a wall, practicing "wall gazing," which he was supposed to have done for nine years without lying down. According to both Hinduism and Buddhism, meditation leads to a number of supernormal abilities called *siddhi*s. They include hearing things far away, seeing things far away, knowing the minds of others, knowing the past and present and future, becoming invisible, traveling in the sky, walking on water, and so on. Great meditators were great magicians. The fantastic manner of his travel indicated that Bodhidharma was an accomplished meditator and possessed supernormal powers. Although the Chinese word *biguan* literally means "wall-gazing," scholars agree that it actually refers not to the manner of his meditation but to the degree of difficulty. Since Bodhidharma was reportedly practicing a formless meditation (not using any image or traditional method), it was as difficult as scaling a cliff.

He did not actively recruit followers, but as his fame spread, people came to him for instruction. The meeting and interview between Bodhidharma and his first Chinese disciple, Huike, who was later regarded as the Second Patriarch, was celebrated in the Chan hagiography. Bodhidharma kept Huike waiting outside his cave chamber in the snow for three days and nights to test the latter's sincerity. He relented only after Huike cut off his left arm to demonstrate his determination. Bodhidharma asked Huike, "Why did you come here?" and Huike said, "My mind is not at peace." Bodhidharma then said, "Hand me over your mind and I shall pacify it." This unexpected answer was said to have led to Huike's enlightenment.

The final story about Bodhidharma concerns his choice of successor. The Chan tradition describes the scene this way:

> Nine years have passed and Bodhidharma now wishes to return to India. He called his disciples and said, "The time has now come. Why does not each of you say what you have attained?"
>
> Tao-fa replied, "As I see it, [the Truth] neither adheres to words or letters, nor is it separate from them. Yet, it functions as the Way."
>
> The Master said, "You have attained my skin."
>
> Then a nun, Tsung-chih, spoke, "As I understand it, the truth is like the auspicious glimpse of the Buddha Land of Akshobya, it is seen once, but not a second time."
>
> The Master said, "You have attained my flesh."
>
> Tao-yü said, "The four great elements are originally empty, the five skandhas have no existence. According to my belief, there is no dharma to be grasped."
>
> To him the Master replied, "You have attained my bones."
>
> Finally, there was Hui-k'o [Huike]. He bowed respectfully and stood silent.
>
> The Master said, "You have attained my marrow."[3]

By remaining silent, Huike demonstrated that the truth is ineffable and beyond verbal expression. He was the true heir of Vimalakīrti, the lay bodhisattva and hero in the sutra named after him. Bodhidharma recognized Huike as the Second Patriarch and handed him the robe, a sign of the Dharma. However, despite the colorful myths, Bodhidharma was quite traditional in his teaching. This is clearly shown in his surviving essay, "Treatise on the Two Entrances and Four Practices":

> Now, in entering the path there are many roads. To summarize them, they reduce to two types. The first is entrance by principle and the second entrance by practice. Entering by principle means that one awakens to the thesis by means of the teachings, and one deeply believes that all living beings, common and sagely, are identical to the True Nature; that it is merely because of the unreal covering of adventitious dust that the True Nature is not revealed. If one rejects the false and reverts to the real and in a coagulated state abides in wall examining, then self and other, common man and sage, are

identical; firmly abiding without shifting, in no way following after the written teachings—this is mysteriously tallying with principle. It is nondiscriminative, quiescent, and inactive; we call it entrance by principle.

Entering by practice means the four practices, for all other practices are included within these. What are the four? The first is the practice of requiting injury; the second is the practice of following conditions; the third is the practice of having nothing to be sought; and the fourth is the practice of according with Dharma. What is the practice of requiting injury? If the practitioner who is cultivating the path encounters suffering, he thinks to himself: I, from the past, across innumerable eons, have become estranged from the root and followed after the branches, have flowed along in various existences, producing a great deal of ill will and hatred, antagonizing and harming others endlessly. Though there is no transgression on my part in the present, this suffering is the ripening of bad karma fruits of the faults of my past lives. It is something that neither the gods nor men have put upon me. With satisfaction I will bear and accept it, with absolutely no ill will or complaining. . . . When this thought arises, one is yoked with principle. Taking ill will as an opportunity, one advances on the path, and therefore it is called the practice of requiting injury. As to the second, the practice of following conditions, sentient beings lack a self and are all whirled around by conditions and karma; suffering and joy are to be equally accepted, for both arise from conditions. If I encounter excellent karmic recompense, such as honor and so forth, it is in response to causes in my past lives. Even if I should encounter such recompense in the present, the necessary conditions for it will exhaust themselves, and it will again cease to exist. What is there to be joyful about in its existence? Gain and loss follow conditions. Mind has neither increase nor decrease. Unmoved by the winds of joy, one is mysteriously in accordance with the path. Therefore, it is called the practice of following conditions. As to the third, the practice of having nothing to be sought, worldly people are in a perpetual state of delusion; everywhere they are covetous and attached, and this is called seeking. The person of insight awakens to reality: Principle is the obverse of the conventional; quiet mind and practice no action; forms follow the turnings of fate; the ten thousand existences are thus void; wish for nothing. Merit and Darkness always follow each other. A long time dwelling in the three realms is like liv-ing in a burning house. Having a body is all suffering; who can attain peace? If one comprehends this locus, then in his various existences he will stop thoughts and have no seeking. . . . We clearly know that seeking nothing truly is practice of the path. As to the fourth, the practice of according with Dharma, the principle of intrinsic purity is viewed as Dharma. According to this principle, all characteristics are void, without defilement and without attachment, without this and that. . . . The one of insight who is able to believe in and understand this principle should practice according to Dharma. The Dharma substance has no stinginess; in terms of your life and property, prac-tice giving, your mind free of parsimony. You will comprehend the three voidnesses, solicit nothing, and transform sentient beings and yet not grasp characteristics. This is self benefit, but, in addition, it can benefit others; it also can ornament the path of enlightenment. When you give in this spirit, the other five perfections follow suit. In order to eliminate false thought, one practices the six perfections, and yet there is nothing that is practiced. This is the practice of according with Dharma.[4]

In this essay, we come across familiar terms such as "nondiscrimina-tion," "no-action," "voidness (emptiness)," and the "six perfections." "Wall-gazing" ("wall-examining") is defined here not as a physical act but a state of mind that accords with reality. It is a steady state of nonduality in which "self and other, common man and sage, are identical," a state achieved by not "following after the written teachings."

In the two hundred years after the death of Bodhidharma, there were meditation teachers active in different areas in China, each teach-ing distinctive methods of meditation. Zongmi, the Huayan scholar and Chan practitioner we met in chapter 5, was familiar with the different Chan traditions in his lifetime. He described their characteristics in his writings, and rejection of scriptural study was not one of them. On the contrary, Chan monks studied scriptures like everyone else. This is evi-dence that Chan was not a separate transmission in the ninth century. Zongmi himself studied Chan with a teacher who traced his lineage from Shenxiu (c. 605–706), a prominent master patronized by the court and a leading monk under the Fifth Patriarch. But as the result of ener-getic promotion by Shenhui (670–762), who claimed to be the disciple of

Huineng (638–713), a rather obscure figure during his lifetime, only one of the teachers became recognized as the true representative of Chan. Shenhui campaigned for Huineng and declared the latter the Sixth Patriarch, the Dharma heir in the lineage tracing back to Bodhidharma, and not Shenxiu. Shenhui attacked Shenxiu for teaching gradual enlightenment in contrast to the sudden enlightenment taught by Huineng. The controversy centered on whether enlightenment happened suddenly or as a result of gradual practice. "Sudden enlightenment followed by gradual cultivation," a slogan proclaimed by Zongmi, might be seen as a skillful compromise. Because Shenxiu was active in the north and Huineng in the south, they became known as the founders of Northern and Southern Chan, respectively. It was Huineng's Southern Chan that succeeded in becoming the orthodox Chan tradition not only in China but also throughout East Asia. This was due mainly to the influence of his ideas as contained in the *Platform Sutra,* a text compiled by his disciples. It is significant that this work bears this title. "Sutra" is traditionally reserved for teachings of the Buddha. Of all the writings by Chinese Buddhists, this is the only one with that title. It implies that Huineng is on the same level as the Buddha and that his teaching has the same authority as the "word of the Buddha."

Huineng, the Sixth Patriarch

The *Platform Sutra* begins with a brief biography of Huineng that portrays him as a saintly figure. He was the son of an official originally from Fanyang, near modern Beijing. The father was dismissed from his job and exiled to Xinzhou, in a remote part of Canton, and died when Huineng was still a child. He and his widowed mother moved to Nanhai (modern-day Guangzhou), the provincial capital, and lived in poverty. Huineng took care of his mother by selling firewood in the marketplace. One day when he delivered some firewood to a customer staying in a lodging house for officials, he heard someone chanting the *Diamond Sutra.* Huineng was deeply impressed by the sentence "Without dwelling in anything whatsoever, allow this mind to arise" and achieved a sudden awakening. He asked the person where he had obtained the scripture and was told that he got it from Hongren (601–674), the Fifth Patriarch, who was teaching at the East Mountain in Yellow Plum County in modern Hubei province. The man further said that there were a thousand disciples studying under Hongren, who told them that if they recited this one-volume *Diamond*

Sutra, they could see into their own natures and with direct apprehension become buddhas. Huineng decided to travel north to study with the Fifth Patriarch.

The encounter between Hongren and Huineng and their dialogue recall the earlier interactions between Bodhidharma and Huike. Hongren asked Huineng where he was from and why he had come. Huineng answered that he was from Xinzhou and sought the Buddha Dharma. At that time the south was commonly regarded as uncivilized by people living in the north. So Hongren challenged him, saying that since Huineng was a southern barbarian, how could he hope to become a buddha? But Huineng retorted, "Although people from the south and people from the north differ, there is no north and south in Buddha nature. Although my barbarian's body and your body are not the same, what difference is there in our Buddha nature?" Satisfied with the answer, Hongren allowed Huineng to stay and work in the kitchen, pounding rice for eight months. Huineng was presented as a simple illiterate commoner, but in this anecdote he emerged as someone who had an innate understanding of the doctrine of Buddha nature, the core teaching of the *Nirvana Sutra.* Similarly, his immediate comprehension of the teaching of emptiness in the *Diamond Sutra* underscores his wisdom, independent of book learning. Both stories highlight the Chan democratic belief that enlightenment and buddhahood are available to everyone regardless of social class.

Echoing the manner in which Bodhidharma chose his successor and transmitted the Dharma to the Second Patriarch, Hongren chose the Sixth Patriarch by holding a verse contest. One day he gathered his disciples and asked them to write a verse to demonstrate their understanding about the original nature, an alternate term for Buddha nature. He would give his robe and the Dharma to the person who won. Since Shenxiu was the monk most advanced in learning, all the monks expected that he would be the one to succeed Hongren and therefore decided not to write anything. Instead of handing in a verse to the master, Shenxiu wrote a verse at midnight on the wall in the south corridor reserved for a painting illustrating scenes from the *Lankāvatāra Sutra,* a scripture favored by Bodhidharma as well as Hongren.

> The body is the Bodhi tree,
> The mind is like a clear mirror.
> At all times we must strive to polish it,
> And must not let the dust collect.

When Hongren saw it in the morning, he dismissed the painter hired to paint on the wall and told the monks to recite the verse so that they could practice in accordance with the poem and gain benefit. Knowing that it was Shenxiu who had written it, Hongren called him to his room and said, "This verse you wrote shows that you still have not reached true understanding. You have merely reached the front of the gate but have yet to be able to enter it. If common people practice according to your verse they will not fall. But in seeking the ultimate enlightenment (bodhi) one will not succeed with such an understanding. You must enter the gate and see your own original nature. Go and think about it for a day or two and then make another verse and present it to me. If you have been able to enter the gate and see your own original nature, then I will give you the robe and the Dharma."[5]

Shenxiu failed to come up with another verse. Because Huineng was a menial laborer working in the threshing room, he was not aware of what was happening in the temple. But one day he overheard a novice reciting this verse while passing by. He immediately realized that the verse did not demonstrate true insight. Since he could not read or write, Huineng asked someone to write his own verse on the wall in the west corridor.

> The Bodhi tree is originally not a tree,
> The mirror also has no stand.
> Buddha nature is always clean and pure;
> Where is there room for dust?

This verse met with Hongren's approval, but he did not give Huineng public recognition. Instead, he called Huineng to the hall at midnight to teach him the *Diamond Sutra*. Huineng understood it immediately after hearing it only once. Hongren then transmitted to him the Dharma of Sudden Enlightenment and the robe, saying: "I make you the Sixth Patriarch. The robe is the proof and is to be handed down from generation to generation. My Dharma must be transmitted from mind to mind. You must make people awaken to themselves."[6] He told Huineng to leave the temple right away, for otherwise he would come to harm from those who were jealous of him. Huineng returned to Canton and lived in seclusion for many years before he started teaching in Caoxi after he became a tonsured monk.

In many ways this is a very fantastic story. Hongren did not choose an erudite monk to be his successor, but a poor laborer who was not only illiterate but also a layman. Huineng's verse was the sole proof of his superior understanding. His verse is a direct rebuttal of Shenxiu's verse. What are the differences between the verses? Mirror and dust represent the mind and passions in Buddhism. According to the Buddhist tradition, although our mind is naturally pure and luminous, it can be covered over by human passions such as ignorance, greed, and anger. It is for this reason that we must be vigilant in our religious practice. The Noble Eightfold Path of morality, meditation, and wisdom is designed to achieve this goal. By affirming the need to constantly polish the mind/mirror to prevent the gathering of passions/dust, Shenxiu stands for the traditional Buddhist methods of cultivation. Since the practice is continuous and cumulative, enlightenment

Liang Kai (1175–1248), "The Sixth Patriarch Cutting Bamboo." Tokyo National Museum

happens only at the end of a gradual process. In contrast to this view, Huineng negates the very existence of dust because Buddha nature is always "clean and pure." Since there is no place for dust to settle, why is there a need to do any polishing? While Shenxiu recognizes the duality between body and Bodhi tree, mind and mirror, purity and dust, Huineng negates all dualities: no tree, no mirror, and no dust. Indeed, this is the nonduality of the *Perfection of Wisdom* found in the *Diamond Sutra* and *Vimalakīrti Sutra*. Since such realization is not the end result of a gradual cultivation but immediate insight into the empty nature of all pairs of opposites, enlightenment comes suddenly.

Huineng's teachings as found in his sermons are all based on the doctrine of Buddha nature and the nonduality taught by the *Perfection of Wisdom* scriptures. We will focus on three key points: identity of wisdom and meditation, samadhi of oneness, and no thought, nonform, nonabiding.

The Noble Eightfold Path of Buddhism is divided into morality, meditation, and wisdom. Each is necessary for the others, but each is also distinct from them. The traditional understanding is that we must practice meditation in order to achieve wisdom. Meditation is the means and wisdom the end. Huineng, however, emphasizes the nonduality of the two. For him, they cannot be separated. He reiterates the identity of wisdom and meditation several times: "Good friends, my teaching of the Dharma takes meditation and wisdom as its basis. Never under any circumstances say that meditation and wisdom are different; they are one unity, not two things. Meditation itself is the substance of wisdom; wisdom itself is the function of meditation. . . . Students, be careful not to say that meditation first gives rise to wisdom, or that wisdom first gives rise to meditation, or that meditation and wisdom are different from each other. To hold this view implies that things have duality."[7]

To highlight their identity, he compares the relationship between meditation and wisdom to that between a lamp and its light. The two appear together and are mutually containing: "Good friends, how are concentration and wisdom concurrent? It is like a lamp and its light. [Only] when there is a lamp, is there light; without a lamp there is no light. The lamp is the essence of the light, and the light is the functioning of the lamp. Although they have two names, in essence they are not two."[8] When we separate the two, we make the mistake of thinking wisdom or enlightenment is something to be sought outside ourselves and to be obtained in the future. However, since we are endowed with wisdom and Buddha nature, enlightenment is already present here and now. To teach the nonduality of concentration and wisdom as Huineng does is the sudden teaching, and to affirm this is the sudden practice. It is not to be realized through a step-by-step gradual process. His other two central doctrines, samadhi of oneness and no thought, nonform, nonabiding, follow naturally. In putting forward these ideas, Huineng refers to the *Vimalakīrti Sutra* several times. It is clear that he was by no means the illiterate rustic presented in the *Platform Sutra*.

The *samādhi* of oneness is direct mind at all times, walking, staying, sitting, and lying. The *Vimalakīrti Sutra* says: "Direct mind is the place of practice; direct mind is the Pure Land." . . . Just practicing direct mind only, and in all things having no attachments whatsoever, is called the *samādhi* of oneness. The deluded person clings to the characteristics of things, adheres to the *samādhi* of oneness, [thinks] that direct mind is sitting without moving and casting aside delusions without letting things arise in the mind. This he considers to be the *samādhi* of oneness. This kind of practice is the same as insentiency and is the cause of an obstruction to the Tao [Dao]. Tao must be something that circulates freely; why should he impede it? If the mind does not abide in things, the Tao circulates freely; if the mind abides in things, it becomes entangled. If sitting in meditation without moving is good, why did Vimalakīrti scold Shariputra for sitting in meditation in the forest?[9]

Huineng not only gave a totally new explanation about meditation and wisdom, he also showed meditation in a new light. For him, meditation does not mean to sit motionless in a special place and cast away all thoughts. To do so is to become attached to an outward form of meditation by making a distinction between sitting and moving, thinking and not thinking. The correct meditation is simply to have a direct mind in daily activities, be it "walking, staying, sitting, or lying." What is the direct mind? It is the mind of nonduality. It is not to discriminate between sitting and not sitting, thinking and not thinking, but to remain centered and aware in all circumstances. Only in this way is the mind free-flowing like the Dao. A nonjudgmental mind is like a mirror. It reflects whoever and whatever is appearing in front of it. The mirror does not judge, not does it cling to and fixate on the reflection. The reflection also does not remain fixed in the mirror. This is what the *Diamond Sutra* calls a nonabiding mind. As soon as we discriminate, we become judgmental and our mind becomes fixated on that one thing. This is the way ignorant people function, and that is why they suffer.

The practice of direct mind or the samadhi of oneness leads naturally to the last triad of no thought, nonform, and nonabiding.

Good friends, in this teaching of mine, from ancient times up to the present, all have established no-thought as the main doctrine, non-form as the essence and non-abiding as the basis. Non-form is to be separated from form even when associated with form. No thought is not to think even when involved in thought. Non-abiding is the original nature of man. Successive thoughts do not stop; prior thoughts, present thoughts, and future thoughts follow one after the other without cessation. . . . If one instant of thought attaches, then successive thoughts attach; this is known as being fettered. If in all things successive thoughts do not attach, then you are unfettered. Therefore, non-abiding is made the basis. Good friends, being outwardly separated from all forms, this is non-form. When you are separated from form, the substance of your nature is pure. Therefore, non-form is made the substance. . . . Men of the world, separate yourselves from views; do not activate thoughts. If there were no thinking, then no-thought would have no place to exist. "No" is the "no" of what? "Thought" means "thinking of what?" "No" is the separation from the dualism which produces the passions. "Thought" means thinking of the original nature of True Reality. True Reality is the substance of thoughts; thoughts are the function of True Reality. If you give rise to thoughts from your self-nature then, although you see, hear, perceive, and know, you are not stained by the manifold environments, and are always free. The *Vimalakīrti Sūtra* says, "Externally, while distinguishing well all the forms of the various dharmas; internally, he stands firm within the First Principle."[10]

Of the triad, no thought is perhaps most difficult to understand. Huineng defines it thus: "No thought is not to think even when involved in thought." It is a paradox: how can we not think while we are thinking? Peter Gregory offers a good explanation.

To make sense of this definition and the explanation that ensues, it is helpful to note that the word translated as "thought" (*nian*) is being used in two different senses. In its primary sense, "thought" (T1) refers to the entire spectrum of mental activity, which includes everything that we see, hear, perceive and are aware of. This is the thought that continues without interruption from moment to moment without abiding. In its secondary sense, "thought" (T2) refers to the mental act of interrupting the natural flow of thoughts and taking one of those moments of thought as an object, as when we "think on" or "dwell on" something. Hence the definition of no-thought could be glossed: "No-thought means not to think (T2) in the midst of thoughts (T1)."[11]

We can now summarize Huineng's main teachings. Since our Buddha nature is pure, enlightenment is seeing it directly without resorting to a long, gradual, and laborious process. To see it, we have to: (1) not have views and not discriminate among external objects and cling to them. This is no-form; (2) to not dwell on any thought but allow our mind to be aware of every thought. This is no thought; (3) to be able to live life conforming to the above, not abiding in anything or any thought. This is nonabiding; (4) to live life this way is meditation, which in turn is no other than wisdom.

Although the image of Huineng constructed by the *Platform Sutra* is one of an illiterate simple rustic, his teaching, as we have seen, is firmly grounded in the *Perfection of Wisdom,* the doctrines of emptiness and Buddha nature. How can we apply his teaching to our daily lives? Let us see how this works in relation to people and events. We meet different people every day: men and women, old and young, rich and poor, beautiful and ugly, and so on. According to Huineng, when we meet them, we should be fully attentive to them. However, we should not make conscious evaluations and pass judgment about them, thinking, "This is an attractive person," or "How come he is so short?" If we can do this, we remain in a state of bare awareness and will not become entangled with the opposing emotions of like and dislike. Once the meeting is over, we move on and do not dwell upon what has happened. Similarly, when some event happens in our life, such as losing a cherished object or getting a job promotion, while we are fully conscious of the feelings of sadness or happiness, we do not stay in that state by dwelling on the experience. This is what Huineng meant by nonabiding and no thought. This makes sense because ultimately people and things lack intrinsic nature and are empty. Although we live in the world of phenomena with various characteristics, they do not have form, and thus they have "no form." Seeing the world this way is wisdom. Maintaining this insight is meditation. Meditation and wisdom are therefore two sides of the same coin. The mind of no thought and nonabiding functioning in the world of no form is a free-flowing mind. It is by no means a static mind empty of thoughts. On the contrary, precisely because it does not discriminate or evaluate, it does not become stagnant and is not fixated on anything but is ever ready to experience and deal readily and effectively with new events in life.

Chan Buddhism after the Sixth Patriarch

By the middle of the ninth century, the Southern school of Chan had won the day. It regarded Huineng as the Sixth Patriarch. It was from the Southern school that all later Chan subschools were to trace their line of descent. Historians speak of "Five Houses," of which Linji and Caodong have continued to the present day. They are known as Rinzai and Sōtō in Japan. The difference between the two lay mainly in the methods taught to aspiring students. Like Bodhidharma's wall gazing, Huineng's samadhi of oneness appealed to people of intuitive insight, or what Buddhism called sharp roots. Chan at first did not provide any concrete guidelines or techniques to a practitioner.

But if Chan claims that everyone is endowed with Buddha nature, how can a person realize this truth? This democratic promise must be accomplished by a practical method of practice. The founders of the Five Houses established their traditions and taught distinctive methods according to the differences in the students' abilities. The methods provided by Linji and Caodong are respectively the use of "public cases" (*gong'an;* Japanese: *koan*), and the quiet sitting known as "silent illumination." Linji Chan was named after Master Linji (d. 867) and was traced to Mazu (709–788); Caodong Chan was named after two masters, Caoshan (807–869) and Dongshan (840–901), and traced to Shitou (700–790). Mazu and Shitou were two famous masters in the Sixth Patriarch's lineage.

The *Record of Linji* provides some striking examples of his teaching style. It contains talks to his disciples at the lecture hall. When a master gave a formal talk, he "ascended the hall," which means he sat on a chair in front of the gathered assembly.

> The Master ascended the hall and said, "There in the lump of red flesh there is a True Man with no rank. Constantly he goes in and out of the gates of your face. If there are any of you who don't know this for a fact, then look! look!"
>
> At that time there was a monk who came forward and asked, "What is he like—the True Man with no rank?"
>
> The Master got down from his chair, seized hold of the monk and said, "Speak! Speak!"
>
> The monk was about to say something, whereupon the Master let go of him, shoved him away, and said, "True Man with no rank—what a shitty ass-wiper!"
>
> The Master then returned to his quarters.[12]

The "True Man of no rank" refers to the Buddha, although the term occurred in the writings of the Daoist philosopher Zhuangzi, who used it to describe an enlightened person. Linji was saying that Buddha was in each of us. When a disciple asked him what the True Man without rank was like, instead of giving him an answer, Linji resorted to an unexpected action. He got up from his chair, seized the disciple, and ordered him to answer. Linji's behavior was most unconventional in Chinese society. There were strict protocols governing the interactions between a teacher and student, just as there were between people of different social classes and genders. A teacher would never bodily seize a student. Linji increased the shock by ordering the disciple to give a spontaneous reply. However, just as he was about to give an answer, Linji dealt the disciple a final shock by telling him that the True Man of no rank or the Buddha was equivalent to a stick used when there was no toilet paper at hand!

To liken the Buddha to a shit stick shows the highest degree of irreverence. However, to abolish all views based on duality, what can be more effective than this? The Daoist thinker Zhuangzi employed the same pedagogy. He also identified the Dao or Way with what is commonly held to be the most impure.

> Master Easturb inquired of Master Chuang, saying, "Where is the so-called Way present?"
>
> "It's in ants," said Master Chuang.
>
> "How can it be so low?"
>
> "It's in panic grass."
>
> "How can it be still lower?"
>
> "It's in tiles and shards."
>
> "How can it be still lower?"
>
> "It's in shit and piss."
>
> Master Easturb did not respond.[13]

Master Easturb, like the monk, must have been thrown into a state of total bewilderment and confusion.

On another occasion, Linji delivered a sermon encouraging disciples to have faith in themselves because they were endowed with Buddha nature. But the message was delivered with shocking blasphemy.

> Followers of the Way, if you want to get the kind of understanding that accords with the Dharma, never be misled by others. Whether you're facing inward or facing outward, whatever you meet up with, just kill

it! If you meet a buddha, kill the buddha. If you meet a patriarch, kill the patriarch. If you meet an arhat, kill the arhat. If you meet your parents, kill your parents. If you meet your kinfolk, kill your kinfolk. Then for the first time you will gain emancipation, will not be entangled with things, will pass freely anywhere you wish to go.[14]

Linji, like all great Chan masters, was a skillful teacher. Shocking language and nonverbal actions were devices to bring home a point. But as this talk shows, he also taught his disciples to be spontaneous and natural: "Followers of the Way, the Dharma of the buddhas calls for no special undertakings. Just act ordinary, without trying to do anything particular. Move your bowels, piss, get dressed, eat your rice, and if you get tired, then lie down. Fools may laugh at me, but wise men will know what I mean."[15]

This advice is quite similar to that of Zhuangzi. Linji even used the Way (Dao) for Dharma. Both thinkers believed that we are already enlightened, because we either are endowed with Buddha nature or came from the Dao. However, because of wrong thoughts and mistaken views due to discrimination, we became alienated from our original nature. If we can get rid of discrimination, then we will become enlightened. Enlightenment does not come from outside of ourselves. We do not have to acquire anything in order to become enlightened. It appears when we give up deluded thought and remain natural and spontaneous.

The use of *gong'an* or koans as a meditation device started rather late in Chan history. It became popular only during the Song dynasty (960–1279). The first two hundred years, from the time of Bodhidharma to Huineng, the Sixth Patriarch, there were no koan exercises to induce enlightenment. During the eighth and ninth centuries, koans were likewise not used consciously or systematically by Chan masters such as Linji. They would use everyday events, homely examples, or nonverbal "body language" such as a slap, a blow, a kick, a shout, or a roar of laughter to answer disciples' questions about "the meaning of Chan" or "the purpose of Bodhidharma's coming to the east"—typically coded phrases about the Ultimate Reality. Sometimes they might quote an anecdote or a saying of an earlier master to help them bring home a point. However, there was no compilation of recorded koans in existence, nor did they use koans in such collections regularly. The early masters created many koans unselfconsciously but did not assign any specific koan to their disciples as a meditation topic. By the eleventh century, koans of earlier masters were eagerly collected. This gave rise to new literary genres called lamp records and recorded sayings. Some famous examples are *The Transmission of the Lamp,* compiled by Daoyuan in 1004, which consists of more than a thousand koans. *The Record of Blue Cliff* of 1125 contains one hundred koans and was collected by Xuedou (980–1052), with annotations and commentary by Yuanwu (1063–1135). *The Gateless Gate* of 1228 contains forty-eight koans and was compiled with commentary and verses by Wumen (1183–1260).

There was a reason for this new emphasis on koan collections. After the persecution of Buddhism in 845, within fifty years a most illustrious generation of Chan masters died one by one. Chan Buddhism—unlike Tiantai and Huayan, which prized scriptural knowledge, or Pure Land, which emphasized piety—had always placed the most stress on personal religious experience: namely, the experience of enlightenment. Enlightenment could not be taught by words or concepts. On the contrary, words and concepts would involve a person in discrimination and intellectualization, which would lead him further away from realizing the truth. The ideal condition for enlightenment was to work under a master who was already enlightened. Through his skillful hints and merciless prodding, one could be forced to break through the customary mode of thinking and acting to a new mode of being. By the tenth century, with the death of great masters, a keen need was felt to find a new way of training disciples. If true masters could not always be found to serve as "midwives" in the miracle of self-transformation called enlightenment, was there perhaps a substitute, an alternative? The alternative found is the koan. It was hoped that through the collection of earlier koans and through the concentrated investigation of the critical phrases contained in the koans, the original experience of enlightenment could be re-enacted.

Chan of Koan Investigation (Kanhua Chan)

What is a koan? As used by Chan Buddhists, "koan" always refers to a dialogue or an event between a Chan master and his student. In a sense, all the stories about Chan masters, both short and long, are koans. The dialogues usually consist of a student's question and the master's answer. The unique characteristic of the answer is its paradoxical nature. During the Song, when Chan came into full development, Chan monks rarely used the term "koan"; instead, they liked to use *huatou*. While "koan" refers to the whole situation or event, *huatou* means specifically the critical words or points of the situation. The distinction between a koan and a *huatou* may be illustrated by the following famous exchange between the Tang master Zhaozhou and a monk: "A monk asked Master Zhaozhou, 'Does a dog have the Buddha nature?' Zhaozhou answered, '*Wu!*' (meaning 'No')." The entire dialogue is called a koan, but a Chan practitioner who meditates on this should not think of the question and the answer. Instead, he should concentrate wholeheartedly on the critical word *wu*— this is his *huatou*.

During the Southern Song, both the Linji and the Caodong schools were active. The Linji master Dahui (1089–1163), unlike many other Chan masters who used koans together with sitting meditation in the training of Chan monks, insisted upon the exclusive use of koan in Chan meditation and opposed the practice of quiet sitting. He believed that this practice was conducive to lifeless emptiness and passive escapism. He called the Caodong masters who taught quiet sitting heretics and referred to their Chan practice as the "heretical Chan of silent illumination." His own tradition came to be known as the "Chan of koan investigation." Scholars regard Dahui as a seminal figure in the development of Chan Buddhism, a view also shared by Chinese Buddhists since Dahui's time. He is important mainly for his successful creation of an "orthodox" teaching on the use of koan in Chan, and to some extent in Japan as well, through the activities of the Tokugawa Rinzai Zen master Hakuin (1686–1769), who also belonged to this tradition.

Dahui stressed the importance of concentrating on the *huatou,* or the critical phrase within a koan, to the exclusion of all other interests, pursuits, and preoccupations. This investigation is not the same as "thinking about." In fact, it is the exact opposite of our ordinary discursive thinking processes. Take the koan of Zhaozhou's "*Wu,*" which is case 1 in *The Gateless Gate.* How is one seriously to think about this "*Wu*"? Surely it makes no "sense." Since we know that all sentient beings are endowed with Buddha nature, and a dog is surely a sentient being, why is the answer "No"? The entire exchange between the disciple and Zhaozhou is unintelligible and cannot be thought about or understood rationally no matter how hard one tries. Actually, the very opaqueness to reason and making them difficult to "figure out" are intrinsic features of koans and constitute their effectiveness as meditative devices.

One useful way to understand a koan or *huatou* is to regard it as an opening wedge for the sudden and intuitive apprehension of a new reality. Its effectiveness lies in its ability to create in the meditator a sense of doubt and the accompanying feelings of bewilderment, frustration, anxiety, and anger. If the meditator takes his koan seriously, he will be impelled to "solve" it by the strong sense of urgency this painfully disquieting doubt produces. In actual practice, there were probably few monks who could sustain their effort without constant prodding from their teachers. That was why before his enlightenment, Dahui was chastised by his master that he did not "doubt words [his *huatou*] enough." Chan masters have always recognized the crucial role this sense of doubt plays in the mechanics of enlightenment. Some six hundred years after Dahui, Hakuin regarded the "Great Doubt" as the indispensable driving force behind every enlightenment experience. He claimed that the greater the doubt, the greater would be the enlightenment. But if there was no doubt, there would be no enlightenment.

And how does a *huatou* generate doubt? It works as a shock, a surprise, which breaches the meditator's taken-for-granted expectations. In traditional vernacular novels and plays, *huatou* means "opening statement." The speaker delivers a short opening speech, sets up the proper dramatic situation, and provides the occasion for the unfolding of the succeeding events. In the case of a koan, however, what follows is not a rational sequence of statements or events but a totally unrelated and sometimes illogical statement, a non sequitur. The meditator is thus caught by surprise. He is estranged from the familiar world of reasonableness and becomes vulnerable, open to transformation. A *huatou* produces the "shock" that catapults the meditator into enlightenment.

Chan of Silent Illumination (Mozhao Chan)

Was Dahui justified in attacking Caodong for teaching "the heretical Chan of silent illumination"? Like those in other Chan schools, Caodong masters used koan and *huatou,* but unlike Dahui, they did not use them exclusively. They also did not emphasize the central importance of doubt leading to enlightenment, as did Dahui. For them, there was no need to consciously seek enlightenment because we are already endowed with Buddha nature. Concentration or meditation is to sit quietly and not dwell on any thought. This is what is meant by "silence." Insight or wisdom is to let our original nature shine forth like a bright mirror. This is what is meant by "illumination." According to this understanding, our Buddha nature is manifested in all the mental and physical activities of daily life. Silent illumination is the functioning of our Buddha nature in sitting meditation.

Seen in this light, far from heretical, the Chan of Silent Illumination might be more in accord with both the teachings of the Sixth Patriarch and the *Awakening of Faith*. Dahui's Chan of Investigating *Huatou* stresses the importance of concentrating wholeheartedly on a *huatou* in order to reach the moment when enlightenment suddenly erupts. Investigation of the *huatou* is thus the means to an end. Meditation is clearly differentiated from wisdom. This contradicts Huineng's core teaching of the nonduality of meditation and wisdom and the samadhi of oneness. It also separates the inherent enlightenment from the incipient enlightenment found in the *Awakening of Faith*. It is dualistic. The Chan of Silent Illumination teaches the opposite. It does not separate meditation (silence) from wisdom (illumination). By letting the mind flow freely without becoming fixated on a *houtou,* we are already in the state of enlightenment. The inherent enlightenment spoken of in the *Awakening of Faith* is thus not separated from the incipient enlightenment. In contrast to Dahui, this is nondualistic. That is why Morten Schlütter concludes: "It was Dahui himself who was unorthodox in his unabashed de-emphasis of inherent enlightenment and his new meditation technique strongly focused on working toward a moment of breakthrough enlightenment. By insisting on enlightenment as a goal that must always be kept in mind, Dahui might have been seen as open to criticism for being both dualistic and gradualistic."[16]

The height of the dispute was during the Southern Song. Just as Chan's early claim of being a "separate transmission" was motivated by its drive for patronage, according to Schlütter, the same factor played an important role in this dispute as well.[17] Religion was never separated from worldly concerns about power. In later periods, Chan masters used both koans and silent sitting in training their students. For instance, Master Shengyan in recent years taught both methods. He would teach koan meditation first and the silent illumination meditation only after the student had made enough progress. Because no koan is used and a student has nothing to rely on while engaged in Mozhao Chan, it is considered to be more demanding.

How Did Chan Become the Dominant Tradition in Chinese Buddhism?

Most Chinese Buddhist monasteries nowadays identify themselves as Chan, even if the abbots are learned in Tiantai or Huayan philosophies. The late Master Shengyan was an example. Although he was a renowned Chan master, he wrote extensively on Tiantai and Huayan. The temple he established in Taipei in the 1980s is called Farming Chan (Nongchan). In the 1990s Shengyan founded Dharma Drum Mountain, one of four large Buddhist communities in Taiwan. Its mission is to teach Chan. Intensive meditation retreats known as Chan Seven are a popular way to introduce Chan to interested laypeople. During the seven-day period, participants live on the premises and engage in meditation under the guidance of a teacher. They must keep silent and not communicate with either their fellow participants or people on the outside. They should not read or write. Another popular Buddhist ritual is to attend Buddha Seven to carry out an intensive Buddha invocation. It is modeled upon the Chan-Seven. Although this is a Pure Land practice, it often takes place in a Chan monastery.

Chan reached maturity during the Song and succeeded in becoming the dominant Buddhist school in China. Institutional, social, and cultural factors all played important roles. As mentioned in chapter 4, there were public and private monasteries. During the Song, the state, with the support of local officials, converted many private monasteries into public monasteries. By the early thirteenth century, half of the public monasteries were designated Chan, meaning the abbot must be a monk who was a Dharma heir in a Chan lineage. It was also during the Song that two important developments happened in Chan history: the construction of lineages based on Dharma transmission, and the compilation of lamp records to record the lineage transmissions. Chan lineages were similar to family trees in secular genealogy. Although all Chan monks regarded Huineng, the Sixth Patriarch, as their "ancestor," there were different lines of descent from him. These are the lineages linking Dharma masters to their Dharma heirs who have received the transmission. Literati and prominent officials sponsored the compilation of the lamp records, which were then introduced into the canon with imperial approval.

Unlike the biographies of eminent monks, the lamp records include the enigmatic sayings and unconventional actions of the Chan masters. Like the recorded sayings and the koan collections, the lamp records were literary productions that delighted the literati. Furthermore, many Chan masters were accomplished poets, writers, and painters. They were befriended by the literati and officials, who sometimes became their lay disciples. Chinese elite culture was deeply influenced by Chan Buddhism, and the latter, by turn, was enthusiastically embraced and supported by the literati.

Since the government designated most public monasteries as Chan during the Song, Chan has remained the dominant Chinese Buddhist tradition, irrespective of the lineages. This is very different from the situation in Japan. Unlike Linji and Caodong, their Japanese counterparts, Rinzai and Sōtō, have retained their sectarian distinction based on their institutional separation.

Discussion Questions

1. What does "Chan" in Chan Buddhism mean? How is it different from other Buddhist traditions?
2. What do the stories about Bodhidharma tell us about the identity of Chan?
3. Why did the verse by Huineng receive the master's approval?
4. How do you understand the teaching of "no thought" of the *Platform Sutra?*
5. What is a koan? Why is it so important for Chan practitioners?

Further Reading

Broughton, Jeffrey L. *The Bodhidharma Anthology: The Earliest Records of Zen.* Berkeley: University of California Press, 1999.

Foulk, T. Griffith. "Myth, Ritual, and Monastic Practice in Sung Ch'an Buddhism." In *Religion and Society in T'ang and Sung China,* edited by Patricia Buckley Ebrey and Peter N. Gregory, 147–208. Honolulu: University of Hawai'i Press, 1993.

———. "Sung Controversies concerning the 'Separate Transmission' of Ch'an." In *Buddhism in the Sung,* edited by Peter N. Gregory and Daniel A. Getz Jr., 220–294. Honolulu: University of Hawai'i Press, 1999.

McRae, John R. *Seeing through Zen: Encounter, Transformation, and Genealogy in Chinese Chan Buddhism.* Berkeley: University of California Press, 2003.

Poceski, Mario. *Ordinary Mind as the Way: The Hongzhou School and the Growth of Chan Buddhism.* Oxford: Oxford University Press, 2007.

Schlütter, Morten. "Silent Illumination, Kung-an Introspection, and the Competition for Lay Patronage in Sung Dynasty Ch'an." In *Buddhism in the Sung,* edited by Peter N. Gregory and Daniel A. Getz Jr., 109–147. Honolulu: University of Hawai'i Press, 1999.

———. *How Zen Became Zen: The Dispute of Enlightenment and the Formation of Chan Buddhism in the Song Dynasty.* Honolulu: University of Hawai'i Press, 2008.

Schlütter, Morten, and Stephen F. Teiser, eds. *Readings of the Platform Sūtra.* New York: Columbia University Press, 2012.

Weller, Albert. *Monks, Rulers, and Literati: The Political Ascendancy of Chan Buddhism.* Oxford: Oxford University Press, 2006.

Yampolsky, Philip B. *The Platform Sutra of the Sixth Patriarch.* New York: Columbia University Press, 2012.

Notes

1 Foulk, "Myth, Ritual, and Monastic Practice."

2 Foulk, "Sung Controversies," 221.

3 Henri Dumoulin, *A History of Zen Buddhism* (Boston: Beacon, 1969), 73.

4 Jeffrey L. Broughton, *The Bodhidharma Anthology: The Earliest Records of Zen* (Berkeley: University of California Press, 1999), 9–12.

5 Wm. Theodore deBary, ed., *The Buddhist Tradition* (New York: Modern Library, 1969), 215.

6 DeBary, ed., *The Buddhist Tradition,* 217.

7 Yampolsky, *The Platform Sutra of the Sixth Patriarch,* 135. Peter N. Gregory, "The Platform Sūtra as the Sudden Teaching," in *Readings of the Platform Sūtra,* ed. Morten Schlütter and Stephen F. Teiser (New York: Columbia University Press, 2012), 96.

8 Gregory, "The Platform Sūtra as the Sudden Teaching," 96.

9 Yampolsky, *The Platform Sutra of the Sixth Patriarch,* 136.

10 Yampolsky, *The Platform Sutra of the Sixth Patriarch,* 139.

11 Gregory, "The Platform Sūtra as the Sudden Teaching," 100–101.

12 Burton Watson, trans., *The Zen Teachings of Maser Lin-chi: A Translation of the Lin-chi lu* (New York: Columbia University Press, 1999), 13.

13 Mair, Victor H., ed., *Wandering on the Way: Early Taoist Tales and Parables of Chuang Tzu* (Honolulu: University of Hawai'i Press, 1994), 217.

14 Mair, ed., *Wandering on the Way,* 52.

15 Mair, ed., *Wandering on the Way,* 31.

16 Schlütter, *How Zen Became Zen,* 173.

17 Schlütter, "Silent Illumination, Kung-an Introspection, and the Competition for Lay Patronage in Sung Dynasty Ch'an," 109–147.

CHAPTER 7

The Devotional Tradition
Pure Land Buddhism

Since at least the 1950s, Americans have known Chan and its Japanese form, Zen. But few have heard of Pure Land, the type of Buddhism practiced by the majority of Chinese Buddhists. As the common saying goes, "Everybody knows how to chant *Omituofo* [Amitābha], and every household worships Guanyin." While Guanyin is the most popular bodhisattva, Amitābha is the most famous buddha. Pure Land practice has always been a part of Chinese Buddhism. It is mentioned in the *Awakening of Faith,* and the Tiantai master Zhiyi incorporated meditation on Amitābha as one method for achieving samadhi (concentration). Even the *Platform Sutra* mentions Buddha mindfulness. Faith in Amitābha and his Pure Land was never restricted to any specific school. According to a study by Daniel Getz, "Pure Land was not a distinct institutional entity with a self-conscious lineage or doctrinal system. Rather, until the Southern Song (1127–1279) Pure Land existed as one facet of religious life alongside others, and with the appearance of various doctrinal and cultivational systems in the Sui (581–618) and T'ang (618–907) it became an integrated element functioning within the precincts of institutional settings not exclusively identified with Pure Land."[1]

However, standard textbooks count Pure Land as one of the major Chinese Buddhist schools. But Pure Land is very different from Tiantai, Huayan, and Chan, discussed in the previous two chapters. Unlike Chan, Pure Land does not have a lineage based on patriarchal transmission. It was provided with a patriarchal transmission similar to that of Chan and Tiantai by two Southern Song Tiantai masters, Zongxiao and Zhipan, when they composed genealogical histories to establish the Home Mountain branch led by Zhili as orthodox Tiantai. Although both masters regarded Huiyuan as the first patriarch, they differed in naming the subsequent ones. Unlike Tiantai and Huayan, which recognize one scripture as teaching the highest truth, Pure Land practitioners do not agree on the absolute authority of either one or a group of scriptures. There are actually two distinct traditions within Pure Land. While both emphasize the practice of *nianfo* (being mindful of the Buddha/invoking the Buddha's name), their interpretations of it differ. Huiyuan represents one tradition, in which the *Scripture of Prolonged Samadhi* (Banzhou sanmei jing) is regarded as the authoritative scripture. In this tradition, *nianfo* means mental concentration on Amitābha Buddha. The goal is to have a vision of Amitābha in samadhi through visualization. Shandao (613–681), the second patriarch recognized by both Zongxiao and Zhipan, represented a different tradition that can be traced back to Tanluan (476–542) and Daocho (562–645). The authoritative scriptures in this tradition are the so-called Three Scriptures of the Pure Land—The *Shorter Sukhāvatīvyūha Sutra,* the *Longer Sukhāvatīvyūha Sutra,* and the *Visualization of Amitāyus Sutra. Nianfo* for this tradition means the oral invocation of the name of Amitābha. Rebirth in the Western Paradise (Sukhāvatī) is regarded as the final goal by both groups, but the former stresses the importance of "seeing Buddha" during samadhi in this life—a concern not shared by the latter. The divergence of the two traditions lies with their interpretation of the term *nianfo,* which is the Chinese translation for the Sanskrit term *Buddhānusmrti.* It means originally the recollection or the bearing in mind of the attributes of a buddha. But the character *nian* can also mean calling the name of the Buddha. Although *nianfo* means either Buddha contemplation or Buddha invocation, it is the latter that has become the accepted Pure Land practice.

The Scriptures, the Buddha, and His Pure Land

Amitābha means "Measureless Light." He is also known by another name, Amitāyus (Measureless Life). He has two names because his lifespan is infinite and because of his limitless radiant light. The *Shorter Sukhāvatīvyūha Sutra* provides an explanation. "Why is this Buddha called 'Amita'— 'measureless'? . . . This Buddha's beaming light is measureless. It shines without obstruction into buddha-fields in the ten directions. Therefore, he is called 'Amita'. . . . Furthermore, this Buddha's life-span, and the life-spans of the human beings in his buddha-field as well, has a duration of measureless, boundless, countless, cosmic ages. For this reason too he is

Amitābha Attended by Guanyin and Dashizhi. Cave 57. (618–712). Duanhuang Research Institute

called 'measureless.'"[2] He resides in Sukhāvatī, the Land of Bliss, located to the west of our world system. It is therefore called the Western Paradise. Mahayana Buddhist cosmology conceived of the universe as made up of many world systems that undergo infinite cycles of creation and destruction. It also teaches that there are many buddhas residing in their buddha fields, which are their spheres of spiritual influence. These buddha fields are also called pure lands.

Of all the buddhas' pure lands, we have a special affinity with Amitābha's Pure Land, because he created it for us by making a series of

Amitābha Attended by Guanyin and Dizang. Eighth century. Tokyo National Museum

great vows long before he became Amitābha. The origin story forms the central theme of the *Longer Sukhāvatīvyūha Sutra*. According to the scripture, there was once a monk by the name of Dharmakara who lived many aeons ago. He gave rise to the thought of enlightenment and made forty-eight bodhisattva vows. The Pure Land tradition puts special emphasis on the eighteenth, nineteenth, and twentieth vows. These vows declare that he will not achieve complete enlightenment and become a buddha unless he creates a pure land for beings who are virtuous, sincerely want to be reborn there, and single-mindedly think of him. The fact that Dharmakara is now Amitābha in the Western Paradise proves that his vows have been fulfilled and that we are guaranteed rebirth there. Not only will the faithful be reborn in the Pure Land, but even before they die, Amitābha will come to welcome them together with other bodhisattvas, chief among them being Guanyin:

> May I not gain possession of perfect awakening if, once I have attained Buddhahood, any among the throng of living beings in the ten regions of the universe should single-mindedly desire to be reborn in my land with joy, with confidence, and gladness, and if they should bring to mind this aspiration for even ten moments of thought and yet not gain rebirth there.
>
> May I not gain possession of perfect awakening if, once I have attained Buddhahood, any among the throng of living beings in the ten regions of the universe resolves to seek awakening, cultivates all the virtues, and single-mindedly aspires to be reborn in my land, and if when they approached the moment of their death, I did not appear before them, surrounded by a great assembly.
>
> May I not gain possession of perfect awakening if, once I have attained Buddhahood, any among the throng of living beings in the ten regions of the universe hear my name, fix their thoughts on rebirth in my land, cultivate all the roots of virtue, and single-mindedly dedicate this virtue desiring to be born in my land, and yet do not attain this goal.[3]

As the vows indicate, although Amitābha's Pure Land is created by his compassionate vows, in order for us to be reborn there, our virtue, aspiration, and concentrated "ten moments of thought" (*nian*) are necessary. Clearly, it means mental contemplation, not calling his name. Similarly, the *Shorter Sukhāvatīvyūha Sutra* emphasizes the importance of focusing the mind on the name of Amitābha, which is the only requirement for being reborn in the Pure Land:

Shariputra, if good men or good women hear this explanation of the qualities of the Buddha Amita, and embrace his name, and keep it in mind single-mindedly and without distraction, be it for one day, or for two, for three, for four, for five, for six, or for seven days, then, when their lives come to an end, the Buddha Amita, together with his holy entourage, will appear before them. At the time of their death, their minds free of any distorted views, they will be able to be reborn forthwith in Amita Buddha's Land of Supreme Bliss.[4]

While the *Longer Sutra* puts equal stress on Amitābha's compassion and our own effort, the *Shorter Sutra* states that our rebirth in the Pure Land is entirely due to Amitābha's grace. The difference between the two is conventionally expressed as self-power versus other-power. The third Pure Land scripture, the *Visualization of Amitāyus Sutra*, differs from the other two and offers other methods to achieve rebirth. Scholars suggest that it was composed in the area of Kashmir and incorporated a number of Chinese interpolations. It was one of a group of scriptures that emphasize visualization of buddhas and bodhisatvas. It claims to be the teaching given by Śākyamuni Buddha to Queen Vaidehi, who was imprisoned by her evil son, Ajātaśatru. The queen wishes to be reborn in a place free of suffering and asks the Buddha if there is such a place. The Buddha tells her that the land of Amitābha is not far away. She can be reborn there if she engages in visualizations. The Buddha instructs Queen Vaidehi how to perform visualization in a step-by-step sequential fashion. Because the Pure Land is situated to the west of our world system, she should begin by visualizing the setting sun and continue with the various features of the Pure Land, next Amitābha and the two attending bodhisattvas, and finally the holy triad, Amitābha, Guanyin, and Dashizhi, which guarantees the queen's rebirth. This demanding regime, though much more detailed and precise, is typical of the first kind of *nianfo* as Buddha meditation, found in the two Pure Land sutras. Similarly, it is also found in the *Scripture of Prolonged Samadhi* followed by Huiyuan. Concentrated contemplation leads to a direct vision of Amitābha before one's death, and having this vision is a sure sign that he will go to the Pure Land.

There are two crucial points unique to the *Visualization Sutra*. They led scholars to suggest that these are Chinese interpolations. The first is the nine grades of rebirth based on a person's virtuous or immoral behaviors in life. The grades of superior, middle, and inferior rebirth are each further differentiated into three subgrades of superior, middle, and inferior. The nine grades are: superior-superior, superior-middle, superior-inferior, middle-superior, middle-middle, middle-inferior, inferior-superior, inferior-middle, and inferior-inferior. No matter which grade they are in, everyone will be reborn in the Pure Land enclosed in a lotus flower. But the grade determines the length of time before the flower opens and one sees the Buddha. While the lotus enclosing a person of the superior-superior grade opens right away, enabling him to see the Buddha immediately, a person of the inferior-inferior grade has to wait twelve greater kalpas before it opens. The nine grades of rebirth shows a bureaucratic mentality and might reflect the Chinese ranks of officials. In fact, an exact model of dividing officials into the nine grades was first suggested by Chen Qun (b. 237), an official living in the period of Three Kingdoms (220–280). The second noteworthy feature of the scripture has much greater impact and most likely played an important part in making the second kind of *nianfo,* invocation of Amitābha, the prevalent practice in the Pure Land tradition. The scripture promises salvation to the evil person of the inferior-inferior grade. Even if he cannot engage in visualizing the Buddha, as long as he follows someone's advice and utters the name of Amitāyus ten times without interruption before dying, he will be reborn immediately in the Pure Land, although he will have to wait a very long time to see Amitābha and the two bodhisattvas. It is not hard to see how attractive this message was to the vast number of people incapable of practicing meditation. Although a person is without any virtue and has not practiced Buddhism all his life, he can still be reborn in the Pure Land by calling the Buddha's name for as few as ten times. The oral calling of the name by chanting "*Namo Omituofo* (Adoration of Amitābha)" has become such a favorite Buddhist practice that it was not limited to Pure Land followers only.

What is the Pure Land, and why is it so attractive? The Pure Land is the opposite of our world, and life there is completely different from our life here on this earth. To be reborn there is never to be reborn in the six realms of rebirth. In contrast to this world, living beings there are free from all kinds of suffering but enjoy all forms of happiness. The Pure Land sutras contain lavish descriptions of paradisiacal beauty and splendor. The ground is made of gold. Trees and pavilions are made of the seven precious gems: gold, silver, lapis lazuli, crystal, coral, red pearls, and agate. There are pools made of the seven gems as well, filled with limpid and sweet-tasting water. Lotus flowers of many colors as large as cart wheels grow in the pools. A gentle breeze carries celestial music.

Moreover, one is taught the Dharma not only by Amitābha and his companion bodhisattvas; even birds created magically by the Buddha proclaim the tenets of his teaching with their melodious voices. The birds are magical creations, because the three evil rebirths of animals, hungry ghosts, and hell beings are not found in the Pure Land. The Pure Land is therefore more than a paradise for sensual enjoyment. It is a place where one can achieve enlightenment more quickly with the constant reminder of and easy access to the Dharma.

As with the *Lotus Sutra,* the interest shown in the Pure Land scriptures was soon reflected in art. One of the earliest Amitāyus triads dates to 402 CE. Sculpted in stucco, it can be found in Cave 169 of Binglin Temple, which is located in eastern Kansu. The names of the bodhisattvas are clearly identified on the inscribed cartouches. Guanshiyin (Guanyin) is on the left side of Amitāyus and holds a lotus bud in one hand. Most likely inspired by Huiyuan's energetic promotion of the Pure Land faith, art began to reflect the belief in Amitābha/Amitāyus as well as the Pure Land itself. The depiction of the Pure Land and the triad would become major themes in Chinese Buddhist art in later periods. There are images of the triad, which is known as the Three Holy Ones of the Western Paradise, in almost all Chinese Buddhist temples today.

Depiction of the Pure Land in the Visualization Sutra. Cave 172. (712–781). Dunhuang Research Institute

Pure Land Masters

Two Tiantai masters in the thirteenth century retroactively created a patriarchal transmission lineage for Pure Land. Some of the patriarchs not only did
not have a teacher and disciple relationship but also were actually separated by
several hundred years. It is therefore very different from Chan. Tanluan (476–
542) was not included in the Pure Land lineage, yet his importance to the tradition is probably second only to Huiyuan's. He was born near Mount Wutai,
the holy mountain believed to be the abode of the bodhisattva Mañjuśrī. He
was originally interested in Daoism before he was converted by the famous
translator Bodhiruci around 530. The latter told Tanluan that Buddhism was
superior to Daoism because it offered a way to everlasting life. Subsequently,
Tanluan spent the rest of his life promoting Pure Land teaching. Like Huiyuan, he also advocated meditating on Amitābha. He wrote about meditating
on Amitābha's name, characteristics, merits, wisdom, and extraordinary facul-
ties, but he put special emphasis on the oral invocation of the name. He organized Buddha-invocation societies. When he was near death, his disciples, all
three hundred, chanted "*Omituofo*" collectively by his side. Buddha-invocation
societies became very popular in the Song and after. Similarly, the collective
chanting of Amitābha's name by the side of the dying to help the person focus
their thoughts on the Buddha has remained a popular practice. Today in Taiwan "lotus friends" belonging to groups known as "assisting invocation groups"
often visit the dying in hospitals, hospices, and private homes.

Daozhuo (d. 645), like Tanluan, was also not included in the patriarchal lineage, yet his importance to the Pure Land was equally great. He
wrote the *Collection of Essays on the Western Paradise* to demonstrate how
ignorant people could go to the Pure Land in the Age of Decline of the
Dharma. As discussed, according to Buddhist eschatology, the Buddhadharma would go through three periods after Śākyamuni's nirvana: the Age
of True Dharma, lasting five hundred years; the Age of Counterfeit Dharma,
lasting a thousand years; and the Age of Decline of the Dharma, lasting ten
thousand years. During the Age of True Dharma, Buddhism flourished and
people could achieve enlightenment without difficulty. During the Age of
Counterfeit Dharma, Buddhism retained its external form but lost its inner
spirit. Not only was it difficult to achieve enlightenment, but also people
had less faith in Buddhism. Finally, during the Age of Decline of the
Dharma, it is impossible to achieve enlightenment. Even monasteries,
monastics, scriptures, and stupas will eventually disappear from the face of

the Earth. Daozhuo, like all Buddhists after the sixth century, believed that he was living in this last period. According to him, Pure Land was the teaching most appropriate for this period. His advice to his followers was to practice exclusively the oral chanting of Amitābha's name. He instructed them to use beans to keep track of the number of times they called the name. There were cases of *nianfo* marathons. One monk chanted the name a million times in seven days. It was reported that the beans marking the times one nun chanted (*nian*) the Buddha's name came to eighty piculs (one picul is the weight measure equivalent to what one can carry on one's shoulder). Daozhou later strung seeds of the mulan tree together and kept track of the recitation by moving the seeds. This was the origin of the rosary.

Shandao (613–681) was recognized as the second patriarch. He met Daozhuo when the latter lectured on the *Visualization Sutra* and became convinced that the Pure Land path was the best Buddhist practice. He taught two kinds of activities that would lead to rebirth in the Pure Land. The oral invocation of the name was the primary activity, while chanting the sutras, meditating on the Buddha, worshiping the image of the Buddha, and singing praises of the Buddha were the four auxiliary activities. He kept a statue of Amitābha in his room, and whenever he was there, he would kneel down and invoke the name with all his might, stopping only when he was exhausted. Even on extremely cold days, he would perspire as a result of his effort. For thirty years he preached Pure Land teachings without a moment's relaxation. With the income he received from donations, he made one hundred thousand copies of the *Shorter Sukhāvatīvyūha Sutra* and had frescoes painted depicting the scene of the Pure Land on three hundred temple walls. Because of his evangelical work, an incalculable number of monks and laypeople in the capital were converted to the Pure Land faith. Some of his followers recited the *Shorter Sukhāvatīvyūha Sutra* one hundred to five thousand times. Others invoked the Buddha's name as many as one hundred thousand times daily; still others attained samadhi through Buddha contemplation. Once someone asked Shandao if one could achieve rebirth in the Pure Land by calling the Buddha's name. He answered, "As soon as you call the name, your wish will be fulfilled." He wrote the following verse to encourage people to practice Buddha invocation:

> Gradually your skin becomes puckered and your hair turns white;
> Slowly your steps become infirm.
> Even if you have a roomful of gold and jade,

How can you escape from disease and old age?
Despite much enjoyment and happiness,
Death will eventually come upon you.
There is only one shortcut in cultivation.
That is to recite *Omituofo*.

Fazhao (d. 822), another Pure Land patriarch, followed the teachings of
Shandao and Daozhuo. He had several visions of the Pure Land during his
lifetime. In 769 he created the method of invoking the name of Amitābha in
five tunes called "five assembly of Buddha invocation." He claimed that he
received the inspiration from Amitābha. It refers to a method of sequentially
invoking the Buddha's name in five consecutively altered tunes. The tempo of
invocation changes from slow to fast and the level of voice from low to high as
one proceeds from the first to the fifth. Throughout the sequence one concentrates on the Three Treasures (Buddha, Dharma, and Sangha) and keeps one's
mind free of all extraneous thoughts. During the first assembly, one calls out
"na-mo O-mi-tuo-fo" slowly and in an even tune. During the second assembly, one still calls out the name slowly, but now in a slightly higher tune. During the third assembly, one calls out the name in a way that is neither slow nor
fast. The same is done at a much faster tempo during the fourth assembly.
Finally, during the fifth assembly, one simply calls out the four syllables
"O-mi-tuo-fo" at an extremely fast tempo. It starts with a low voice and builds
to a crescendo. It uses the sound of the invocation as a device to achieve mental concentration. One time while he was leading collective Buddha invocation, the monastery became enveloped in five-colored clouds, and he saw
Amitābha with his two attendant bodhisattvas. When he made a pilgrimage
to Mount Wutai, he received a direct revelation from Mañjuśrī Bodhisattva.
When he entered the lecture hall of the Bamboo Forest Monastery, he saw
Mañjuśrī standing in the east and Puxian (Samantabhadra) in the west, each
preaching the Dharma. He paid the two bodhisattvas his respects and asked
for the best path to pursue in the Age of the Decline of the Dharma. Mañjuśrī
told him that Buddha invocation was the superior path and that he himself
had achieved supreme knowledge precisely because he had practiced it in the
past. After this vision, Fazhao continued to advocate chanting the name in
five tunes in north China. It is said that Emperor Dezong (r. 779–804) often
heard voices reciting the Buddha's name coming from a northeasterly direction. The emperor therefore sent messengers to seek out Fazhao and invite
him to teach members of the imperial family to practice it.

As discussed in chapter 3, Tiantai masters Zunshi and Zhili were Pure Land believers. Zunshi composed two manuals for performing Pure Land repentance rituals that circulated widely among monastics and laypeople. Daniel Stevenson describes the first one, the *Rite for Repentance and Vows for Rebirth in the Pure Land,* as "a regimen of ritual penance and meditation that is to be applied in isolated retreat lasting from one week to seven weeks or longer. At each of the six intervals of the day and night, the retreatants perform ritual repentance and profession of vow for rebirth before Amitābha Buddha, followed by recitation of Pure Land sutras and circumambulation of the central altar. For the remainder of the period they withdraw to a separate location for seated meditation, where they mentally visualize the form of Amitābha and the Pure Land, or, if lacking in contemplation skills, they verbally intone the Buddha's name."[5] Zunshi designed the rite in the convention of the Tiantai four samadhis. The goal was to remove karmic obstacles, achieve a vision of Amitābha by concentrated meditation, and "lay the foundation for rebirth in the Pure Land." The second manual, titled *Ten Moments of Mindfulness,* stipulates a rite for morning worship. Zunshi based the rationale on what the *Longer Sukhāvatīvyūha Sutra* says about the "ten moments" at the time of death. For him, the phrase "ten moments" means not thinking of the Buddha but calling his name. The rite calls for the recitation of the Buddha's name and concludes with a vow. He created this simple rite "both as a minimum daily quota of Pure Land practice and a dress rehearsal for the deathbed."[6]

Eager to convert people from "heretical cults" of blood sacrifice to Buddhism, Zunshi promised them worldly benefits in addition to spiritual ones: "Pure Land devotees will be protected by the Buddhist guardian gods and great bodhisattvas, never to suffer affliction by ghosts, demons, and other forms of calamity. Amitābha will enfold them in his radiance, eliminating their past sins and affording them nightly dreams of his person and realm. They will be blessed with a joyous heart, radiant disposition, and brimming vitality; their actions will produce auspicious outcomes; and they will receive respect from whomever they encounter."[7]

Both Zunshi and Zhili promoted the organization of Buddha-invocation societies for laypeople. This was part of their proselytizing to revive Tiantai, together with converting local deities, feeding hungry ghosts, releasing living creatures, burning fingers, and making vows of self-immolation. We have accounts of followers of Zhili engaging in marathon *nianfo* feats. During the thirteenth century, people used rosaries to mark the number of their Buddha invocations. A new device called recitation charts were used to record the number. Pure Land devotees included both literati and common people. A scholar-official named Qiu formed a Pure Land society in present-day Ningbo, encouraged people to chant the Buddha's name, and had recitation charts printed to gain merit. An ironsmith, Mr. Qi, lost sight of both eyes when he was seventy. After he received one of the charts distributed by Qiu, he recited the Buddha's name 360,000 times. When his invocations filled four charts, he regained his vision.[8]

Under the promotion of Tiantai masters, Pure Land became a mass movement after the Song. Beginning in the twelfth century some charismatic leaders formed societies to chant the Buddha's name, practice vegetarianism, and engage in philanthropic work. These were exactly the type of pious activities encouraged by Zunshi and Zhili. However, unlike the earlier societies under monastic leadership, these new-style societies did not have direct connections with monks or monasteries. They were regarded with suspicion and censured by both the government and the Buddhist establishment. Getz may be right in suggesting that the Pure Land patriarchate was created in reaction to this situation. A Pure Land lineage of patriarchs was constructed in order to differentiate the orthodox Pure Land tradition led by monks from these new sectarian religions led by laypeople.[9]

The Joint Practice of Pure Land and Chan

During the Tang dynasty, when both Chan and Pure Land began to forge an identity and competed for followers, monks who proclaimed allegiance to one school seldom approved of those who followed the other. In fact, they had engaged in mutual criticism since the early Tang. Fazhao, for instance, harshly criticized Chan monks as arrogant and undisciplined, although he did not question the value of Chan practice itself. Chan monks tended to regard Pure Land devotion as simple-minded and suitable only for the ignorant. To counter Chan criticism, the Pure Land adherents had long argued that *nianfo* was really a form of koan. This is because the samadhi reached by Buddha contemplation is similar to the state of awakening reached by dwelling on a Chan koan. One uses the contemplation of Amitābha as a means to reach the nondualistic state of having no mind and no thought. The movement of joint practice of Chan and Pure Land is generally traced to Yanshou (904–975), who provided a persuasive argument for the basic compatibility between *nianfo* and Chan meditation.

Yanshou served as a tax official under the king of Wuyue. He used government funds to buy fish and shrimp to set them free. When this was discovered, the king, who was a patron of Buddhism, instead of having him executed (which was the designated punishment), ordered his subordinates to test Yanshou. He told them that if Yanshou became frightened and changed his expression, he should be executed and if not, he should be pardoned. Yanshou showed no fear and was forgiven. After that, he became a monk and practiced the meditation of the Tiantai school. His conversion to Pure Land took place during a midnight vision. One night, while he was performing the penitential rituals formulated by Zhiyi and doing circumambulation, he saw the statue of Puxian holding a lotus flower in his hand. Not sure of its significance, he made out two divination lots. One lot said: "Practice meditation and concentration all your life"; the other lot said: "Recite sutras, perform good acts, and glorify the Pure Land." After much praying, he cast the lots, and the second one came up seven consecutive times. From that time on, he devoted himself to Pure Land practice. In 961, he went to Yongming Monastery in Zhejiang and taught the dual cultivation of Chan and Pure Land. It is said that he recited the Buddha's name a hundred thousand times daily, and every night the sound of Buddha invocation reverberated from the mountaintop. He told people that in Buddhism, mind was the underlying principle, and attainment of awakening was the goal. Using mind as a basis, he also tried to harmonize the doctrines of the Tiantai, Huayan, and Yogācāra schools. In contrast to the traditional Chan denigration of Pure Land, Yanshou accorded it a position equal, if not superior, to Chan. His attitude is perhaps best illustrated by this famous "fourfold summary" of Chan and Pure Land.

> With Chan but no Pure Land, nine out of ten people will go astray. When death comes suddenly, they must accept it in an instant.
>
> With Pure Land but no Chan, ten thousand out of ten thousand people will achieve rebirth. If one can see Amitābha face to face, why worry about not attaining enlightenment?
>
> With both Chan and Pure Land, it is like a tiger who has grown horns. One will be a teacher for mankind in this life, and a Buddhist patriarch in the next.
>
> With neither Chan nor Pure Land, it is like an iron bed with bronze posters. For endless kalpas one will find nothing to rely on.[10]

The joint practice of Chan and Pure Land rested on the assertion that the two paths were essentially the same because they led to the same goal: the stopping of wrong thoughts and the end of the cycle of samsara. A number of Chan monks after the time of Yanshou promoted the practice. For them, joint practice did not mean the simultaneous practice of Chan meditation and *nianfo*. Instead they regarded *nianfo* as another form of Chan meditation. Since the end result was to terminate discursive thought, it had the same effect as koan meditation. The invocation of *O-mi-tuo-fo* was therefore called *nianfo* koan. One asks, "Who is the one calling the name of the Buddha?" Using *nianfo* in this fashion became a means to arouse the "feeling of doubt," the critical mental tension that drove one to reach awakening.

Zhuhong (1535–1615), the eighth Pure Land patriarch, systemized this joint practice by providing a theoretical foundation. Following Zongmi (780–841), the Huayan master who was also revered by the Chan tradition, Zhuhong distinguished four categories of *nianfo,* enumerated in the following order: (1) calling the name of Amitābha in the manner prescribed in the *Shorter Sukhāvatīvyūha Sutra;* (2) concentrating one's attention on a statue of Amitābha made of earth, wood, bronze, or gold; (3) contemplating the miraculous features of Amitābha with the mind's eye in the manner described in the *Visualization Sutra;* (4) contemplating Amitābha as no different from oneself, since both Amitābha and one's own nature transcend birth and extinction, existence and emptiness, subject and object. Indeed, since contemplation is free from the characteristics of speech, name, and mental cognition of external phenomena, it is therefore contemplation of the Buddha in accordance with reality. The fourth kind of *nianfo* arrives at the famous saying favored by Zhuhong: "The Pure Land is no other than the Mind, Self-nature is the same as Amitābha." According to this fourfold classification, Buddha invocation would correspond to the first kind of *nianfo,* while Buddha contemplation could refer to any of the other three kinds. Thus, Huiyuan and Fazhao practiced primarily Buddha contemplation, while Shandao practiced mainly Buddha invocation. Yanshou, consistent with his general effort to harmonize Buddhist schools, advocated both invocation and contemplation. Zhuhong modeled himself after Yanshou. Through a creative interpretation of the Tiantai concept of One Mind and the Huayan concepts of *li* and *shi*, Zhuhong sought to establish the ultimate identity underlying the various forms of *nianfo.*

Zhuhong's teaching is based on the *Shorter Sukhāvatīvyūha Sutra,* which tells people to "embrace the name and keep it in mind single-mindedly and without distraction." In his commentary on this sutra, Zhuhong provides a detailed explanation of One Mind (single-mindedness) and "taking hold of the name." These two ideas constitute the core of his theory of *nianfo,* which serves to justify the joint practice of Chan and Pure Land. Why is it necessary to invoke the name with One Mind? According to Zhuhong, even though the mind is originally pure and devoid of thought, sentient beings, because of their ignorance, have been accustomed to delusive thoughts since time immemorial. It is very difficult to make people stop their random thoughts. But when they recite the name of the Buddha, this one thought can crowd out the multitude of others. It is like "using one poison to counteract another poison or using war to stop all wars." When delusive thoughts are thus stopped by the thought of *nianfo,* it is nothing other than enlightenment.

Zhuhong was a skillful teacher who was sensitive to the different types of practitioners. He lists three ways of performing *nianfo:* the invocation of the name in a clear voice; the silent contemplation of the name; and the recitation of the name with slight movement of the lips and tongue without uttering a sound. When reciting the name, one may or may not count the number of invocations. Unlike some Pure Land masters who promoted *nianfo* marathons, he was critical of the quantitative approach to Buddha invocation. Moreover, using the Huayan doctrinal formulation, he distinguishes two kinds of "taking hold," which are on two levels corresponding to the two levels of One Mind. The lower one is that of particularity (*shi*), and the higher one is that of universality (*li*). The latter is achieved through the former. To take hold of the name with uninterrupted recollection and mindfulness results in the One Mind of particularity.

> When you hear the Buddha's name, you must always remember it and dwell upon it. Tracing each syllable [*o-mi-tuo-fo*] distinctly, you must think of the name in continuous and uninterrupted succession; whether walking, standing, sitting, or lying, just have this one thought and let no second thought arise. You will then be undisturbed by greed, the *kleśa*s, or any other thought. This is to remain single-minded in leisure and quietude, to remain single-minded in various states of defilement. Whether you are praised or blamed, whether you win or lose, whether you are faced with good or evil, you always remain single-minded.

The One Mind of particularity can suppress delusion, but it cannot shatter delusion. This is so because it is achieved by the power of faith. It pertains only to concentration, not to wisdom.

The higher One Mind of universality is achieved with uninterrupted experience and embodiment. "When you hear the Buddha's name, you should not only remember and dwell upon it but also turn inward to contemplate, investigate, and observe it, and try to find out its origin. When investigation and observation are carried to the utmost limit, it will suddenly achieve an accord with your original mind."[11] Compared with the One Mind of particularity, the One Mind of universality is on a higher level. Zhuhong says that it can destroy delusion, for it leads not only to concentration but also to wisdom. Using this two-level interpretation of Buddha invocation, Zhuhong harmonizes the four traditional categories of *nianfo*. For the One Mind realized in Buddha invocation is not different from samadhi. Indeed, it is identical with the last and highest form of *nianfo*, that of contemplating Amitābha as no different from one's own self, for this One Mind is absolute reality.

According to Zhuhong, it is wrong for people to think *nianfo* is appropriate only for those of dull intelligence and that only Chan can lead them to enlightenment. Zhuhong points out that the deeper form of *nianfo* is in essence the same as Chan. The *nianfo* of "total experience and embodiment" has the same effect as working on koan to generate great doubt, as taught by Chan masters of earlier times.

Similarly, Zhuhong feels that those Chan practitioners who denigrate Pure Land also fail to understand the true meaning of *nianfo*. "Chan and Pure Land reach the same destination by different routes. Since the latter does not separate itself from the One Mind, it is identical with the Buddha, identical with *dhyāna*. Therefore, he who clings to Chan and denigrates the Pure Land is denigrating his own original mind; he is denigrating the Buddha. He is denigrating his own Chan doctrine. How thoughtless!"[12] In claiming that Pure Land and *nianfo* were not different from Chan meditation and that *O-mi-tuo-fo* was the same as a Chan koan, Zhuhong not only continued the tradition of joint practice of Chan and Pure Land but also brought it to culmination. Joint practice did not mean the simultaneous pursuit of both, but rather (1) that *nianfo* was not inferior to Chan; (2) that *nianfo* could achieve the same goal as Chan, the realization of one's true nature or original mind; and (3) that *nianfo* was more effective than Chan not only because of the efficacy of the name but also because of its suitability to the Age of Decline of the Dharma.

As a result of Zhuhong's promotion, the joint practice of Chan and Pure Land has been widely accepted in Buddhist circles. Nowadays Buddhist monasteries hold intensive seven-day sessions of Chan meditation (Chan Seven) as well as seven-day sessions of Buddha invocation (Buddha Seven). One works on a Chan koan during Chan Seven and either calls the name of Amitābha or uses the name as a koan by silently contemplating, "Who is the one doing *nianfo?*" and thus turns the name into a koan during Buddha Seven.

Humanistic Buddhism and Pure Land on Earth

The joint practice of Chan and Pure Land represents a belief in self-power. By realizing that one's true nature is no different from Amitābha, a person achieves enlightenment here and now. Pure Land is no different from our One Mind of Suchness. However, this understanding does not replace the more traditional view. The majority of Pure Land believers hope to be reborn in the Pure Land. Throughout the ages, many stories have been compiled about the faithful who succeeded in achieving this. Most often as a result of sincere faith and invocation of the Buddha's name, they obtained a vision of the Pure Land or saw the Buddha before their death. These miraculous events were confirmed by bystanders who witnessed signs such as bright light or fragrance.

The Pure Land tradition underwent another transformation in the twentieth century. It was a result of a crisis that the nation and the Buddhist sangha alike faced at the end of the Qing and into the early decades of the newly established Republic of China. As will be discussed in chapter 9, Chinese leaders were eager to modernize the country to deal with the threat from the Western imperialists. Traditional culture and religions, including Buddhism, were seen as backward. Critics charged that all the monks did was perform funeral services for the dead and that they made no contribution to society. Buddhists masters and lay believers came to the defense of Buddhism.

Taixu (1890–1947) emphasized that the purpose of Buddhism is the improvement of society and betterment of the world. Buddhism is concerned with human beings, not gods and ghosts. In his essay "The Purpose of Buddhism for Human Life," Taixu lists improving human life as the first of four goals, the other three being a better rebirth, release from samsara, and complete insight into reality. To improve human life Buddhists had to purify society through philanthropy, education, and culture. He coined the term "Buddhism for human life" to counter the prevailing perception that Buddhism was only concerned with death.

The term "Humanistic Buddhism" has been used by three Buddhist leaders in Taiwan: Xingyun (1927–), Shengyan (1931–2009), and Zengyan (1937–). It was first coined by Yinshun (1906–2005), who, due to his prodigious writings and wide circle of disciples, is universally regarded as the most influential thinker in modern Chinese Buddhism. Yinshun advocated Humanistic

Buddhism based on his belief that "the Buddha is in the human realm" but not in the other five realms. He explained how he came to this realization: "I read the *Ekottarāgama* and learned that 'All Buddhas become enlightened in the human realm, but not in heaven. . . . I thus became convinced that the Buddhadharma was the Buddha in the human realm' and it means that 'the human being is the principal manifestation' of Buddhadharma."[13]

Humanistic Buddhism differs from "Buddhism for human life" by only one Chinese character. Like Taixu, contemporary Buddhist leaders in Taiwan put their proselytizing energy toward the improvement of society. Like the engaged Buddhism promoted by American Buddhists, Humanistic Buddhism is characterized by activist social concern. Shengyan was a Chan master, but he used the Pure Land language in promoting Humanistic Buddhism. In his writings and lectures, he emphasized that the Pure Land was not located in a distant world system to the west of our world but could be established on Earth now. He liked to cite a saying in the *Vimalakīrti Sutra:* "If the bodhisattva wishes to acquire a pure land, he must purify his mind. When the mind is pure, the Buddha land will be pure."[14] Our mind is originally pure, but it is tainted by delusive thoughts. We can regain its original purity because we are endowed with Buddha nature. The recovery of the pure mind can be achieved through Chan meditation or Buddha contemplation. Once the mind is pure, we will naturally be compassionate to our fellow sentient beings and be caring of the Earth that is our home. According to Shengyan, it is through social ethics and environmental protection that we can establish the Pure Land on earth.

Discussion Questions

1. Who is Amitābha Buddha? Why is the Pure Land so attractive?
2. What are the two meanings of *nianfo?*
3. What is the main difference between Chan and Pure Land?
4. If Chan and Pure Land are different, how is the joint practice of Chan and Pure Land justified?
5. What is Pure Land according to Humanistic Buddhism?

Further Reading

Getz, Daniel A., Jr. "T'ien-t'ai Pure Land Societies and the Creation of the Pure Land Patriarchate." In *Buddhism in the Sung,* edited by Peter N. Gregory and Daniel A. Getz Jr., 477–523. Honolulu: University of Hawai'i Press, 1999.

Gomez, Luis O., trans. *The Land of Bliss: The Paradise of the Buddha of Measureless Light: Sanskrit and Chinese Versions of the Sukhīvyūha Sutras.* Honolulu: University of Hawaiʻi Press, 1996.

Yü, Chün-fang. *The Renewal of Buddhism in China: Chu-hung and the Late Ming Synthesis.* New York: Columbia University Press, 1981.

Notes

1 Getz, "T'ien-t'ai Pure Land Societies," 477.
2 Gomez, *The Land of Bliss,* 147–148.
3 Gomez, *The Land of Bliss,* 167–168.
4 Gomez, *The Land of Bliss,* 148.
5 Daniel B. Stevenson, "Protocols of Power: Tz'u-yun Tsun-shih (964–1032) and T'ian-t'ai Lay Buddhist Rituals in the Sung," in *Buddhism in the Sung,* edited by Peter N. Gregory and Daniel A. Getz Jr. (Honolulu: University of Hawaiʻi Press, 1999), 360.
6 Stevenson, "Protocols of Power," 362.
7 Stevenson, "Protocols of Power," 363.
8 Getz, "T'ien-t'ai Pure Land Societies," 500–501.
9 Getz, "T'ien-t'ai Pure Land Societies," 505–506.
10 Yü, *The Renewal of Buddhism in China,* 52.
11 Yü, *The Renewal of Bddhism in China,* 60.
12 Yü, *The Renewal of Buddhism in China,* 61.
13 Yishun, *A Rational and Timely Humanist Buddhism* (Taipei: Zhengwen, 1989), 3.
14 Burton Watson, trans., *The Vimalakirti Sutra* (New York: Columbia University Press, 1997), 28.

CHAPTER 8

Buddhism and Gender

For two thousand years, Chinese Buddhists have found encouragement and comfort in the good news that everyone can achieve buddhahood or, failing that, be reborn in the Pure Land. This optimism echoes the Confucian belief that everyone can become a sage. However, does it refer to both men and women? Just as we do not find female sages, we do not find female buddhas. The rhetoric of equality is not reflected in social reality. Moreover, even on the doctrinal level, there are conflicting views in Buddhism concerning the female gender. The attitude toward women is multivocal and complex. Chinese Buddhism is Buddhism with Chinese characteristics, but its views about gender have roots in Indian Buddhism. It is therefore necessary to review briefly how women were perceived in the greater Buddhist tradition.

Views of Women in India and Early Buddhism

As discussed in chapter 4, the Buddha was at first reluctant to establish the order of nuns. He relented only after repeated pleadings by Ānanda, who reminded him of the milk debt the Buddha owed to Mahāprajāpatī. By instituting the Eight Rules of Respect, the Buddha made the order of nuns subordinate to the order of monks. From our modern perspective, we often take this as anti-woman discrimination. But we should see it in the historical light of the time of the Buddha, the sixth century before the Common Era. According to the *Law of Manu*, which set forth the ethical norms for society, a woman has no independent agency and cannot remain unmarried. When she is young, she follows her father; when she is married, she follows her husband; when she is old, she follows her son. The subordination of nuns to monks is thus a monastic version of the social order. On the other hand, by establishing the order of nuns and providing women with the opportunity to carry out their religious pursuits, the Buddha recognized that women had the ability, just like men, to practice the Dharma and achieve enlightenment. Seen in their historical and social contexts, these conflicting attitudes reflected competing concerns of the Buddhist community.

Like Jesus, the Buddha did not write anything. His teachings were orally recited and handed down, until they were compiled into the Pali canon in the first century before the Common Era. Although the early Buddhist texts claim to be the "word of the Buddha" and indeed represent his views, they also contain ideas and beliefs significant to the community that emerged over some four hundred years after his death. Alan Sponberg finds that there are four distinctive attitudes toward women and the feminine in Buddhism: soteriological inclusiveness, institutional androcentrism, ascetic misogyny, and soteriological androgyny.[1]

Like monks, nuns in early Buddhism strove to become enlightened. *The Verses of Elder Nuns* (Therīgāthā) contains seventy-three short poems written by nuns over a period of three hundred years, beginning in the late sixth century BCE. The poems show their remarkable spiritual insight and intellectual ability. Many of the nuns became teachers and leaders of other nuns after achieving enlightenment.

For example, Patacara was a remarkable woman of independent spirit and strong character. She suffered unimaginable losses before she became a nun, but she achieved enlightenment and was a teacher of other nuns. When she was young, her parents arranged for her to marry a young man from a good family. But she was in love with one of the family servants and ran off with him to live in a place distant from home. When she was pregnant with her second child, she wanted to go back to her parents' home to give birth. Her husband was reluctant to let her go, but she went anyway with her first child. He followed and caught up with her. They encountered a great storm and had to build a shelter. When the husband went into the forest to gather wood and grass, he was bitten by a poisonous snake and died. Not knowing that he had died and thinking that she had been abandoned, she gave birth at night, covering the children with her body to shield them from the storm. When she discovered her husband's body the next day, she was overwhelmed with grief. However, she was determined to continue her journey. What happened next was tragic beyond belief: "She came to a river swollen with floodwaters. Too weak to carry both children across at once, she took the newborn first. On the far side, she placed the child on a pile of leaves, but was so reluctant to leave him that she looked behind her again and again. Halfway back across the river, she saw a hawk seize her newborn and carry him off. The hawk ignored Patacara's screams, but the older child, thinking his mother was calling him, came up to the riverbank, fell in, and drowned. In utter despair, all Patacara could do was resume her journey."[2]

But more tragedy was in store for her. When she finally reached the outskirts of her hometown and asked a man if he knew her family, she was told that her entire family had died when the house collapsed on them during a heavy rain. The news drove her out of her mind. She wandered aimlessly. Her clothing became rags and she was half naked. One day she came to where the Buddha was preaching. She asked the Buddha for help and was taught the Buddhist path. She asked to be ordained and was accepted into the order of nuns. Much later, Patacara wrote a poem describing her enlightenment:

> When they plow their fields
> and sow seeds in the earth,
> when they care for their wives and children,
> young brahmans find riches.
>
> But I've done everything right
> and followed the rule of my teachers.
> I'm not lazy or proud.
> Why haven't I found peace?
> Bathing my feet
> I watched the bathwater
> spill down the slope.
> I concentrated my mind
> the way you train a good horse.
>
> Then I took a lamp
> and went into my cell,
> checked the bed,
> and sat down on it.
> I took a needle
> and pushed the wick down.
>
> When the lamp went out
> my mind was freed.[3]

While the first two stanzas describe Patacara's struggle and frustration, the next three stanzas capture the moment of her enlightenment. The lamp going out is an apt metaphor for nirvana. But it is also the trigger for her final breakthrough after her intense concentration earlier.

Patacara became a renowned teacher. She is said to have had thirty disciples. Two nuns, Canda and Uttama, describe how they became enlightened under her guidance in their poems. The first one is by Canda:

> I was in a bad way,
> a widow,
> no children, no friends,
> no relations to give me food and clothes.
>
> I was a beggar with a bowl and stick
> and wandered
> house to house
> in the heat and cold
> for seven years.
>
> But I met a nun
> who had food and drink,
> and I went up to her and said,
> "Take me into the homeless life."
>
> She was Patacara.
> Out of pity she guided me
> in leaving home,
> encouraged me,
> and urged me to the highest goal.
>
> I took her advice.
> It wasn't wasted.
>
> I have the three knowledges.
> There are no obsessions in my mind.[4]

Uttama's poem describes her difficulties in carrying out religious practice and how she eventually achieved a breakthrough by following Patacara's teaching.

Four or five times
I left my cell.
I had no peace of mind,
no control over my mind.

I went to a nun
I thought I could trust.
She taught me the Dharma,
the elements of body and mind,
the nature of perception,
and earth, water, fire and wind.

I heard what she said
and sat cross-legged
seven days full
of joy.
When, on the eighth
I stretched my feet out,
the great dark was torn apart.[5]

It is clear that not only Patacara but also some of her disciples achieved enlightenment. Poems by other nuns describe similar extraordinary spiritual breakthroughs. Some are said to have realized the three knowledges, the same knowledges that the Buddha realized during the three watches of the night. These are the remembrance of past lives, the divine eye of seeing beings coming into and going out of existence according to their karma, and the destruction of mental defilements that bind one to samsara: sensual desire, desire for continued existence, and ignorance. Others are said to have become "cool" and "quenched," which are code terms for nirvana. These are the qualities that define the arhat, the highest status of a Buddhist. However, although the nuns are given the honorific title of eldress (*theri*), none of them is called an arhat, the title given to a monk who has achieved the same spiritual realization.[6]

The term "arhat" denotes someone worthy of receiving gifts. Ellison Findly suggests that the nuns were denied this title because the donors did not think them fully worthy of receiving gifts. They fell short on account of their female nature: "The content of the Therīgāthā indicates that many women fully achieved the soteriological requirements of *arahant* [arhat] status, yet these *theri*, or eldresses of their Sangha, might still have been perceived by potential donors as bound by impure bodies and thus were not granted *arahant* status by virtue of the prevailing social standard. Although *araha*nt status is accorded to specific women in later texts, early canonical texts remain shaped by Vedic views of menstruation and pollution that prevent the recognition of fully deserved spiritual achievement in women."[7]

The Indian attitude toward female renunciates was shared by the Buddhist community. Soteriological inclusiveness could coexist with institutional androcentrism, which Sponberg describes as "the view that women indeed may pursue a full-time religious career, but only within a carefully regulated institutional structure that preserves and reinforces the conventionally accepted social standard of male authority and female subordination."[8] The most often cited example is the Eight Rules of Respect that the Buddha stipulated for the community of nuns to follow, as we read in chapter 4.

If the lay donors regarded accomplished nuns as less worthy of gifts, the subordinate position of nuns in the monastic order could only reinforce this discrimination. The sangha received financial support from many female donors, but nuns enjoyed less prestige and financial support and fewer educational opportunities than monks. The nuns' second-class status led to their marginalized existence. Although Chinese pilgrims reported the existence of convents in the seventh century, it is not surprising that the order of nuns eventually disappeared in India.

The third attitude described by Sponberg, ascetic misogyny, is very different from the first two. Instead of focusing on a woman's spiritual potential or institutional role, the focus is her sexuality. For ascetic monks who try to observe celibacy, sexual desire is undoubtedly a troublesome obstacle. Since women are objects of sexual desire, demeaning and demonizing them would serve as an antidote. One of the ascetic practices favored by monks was the contemplation of dead bodies in a cremation ground. Such meditation leads to the realization of the Buddhist truths of impermanence, suffering, and no self. Liz Wilson finds many examples of monks' using mutilated and horrific female bodies in post-Aśokan Buddhist literature. Monks are described as having achieved insight by examining the "charming cadavers,"[9] bodies of especially beautiful women who died suddenly in their youth.

The story of Upagupta and the courtesan Vasavadattā is a famous example. Before he became a monk and later the leader of the sangha and advisor to King Aśoka, Upagupta was a young perfume merchant. Vasavadattā was a famous courtesan. She sent her servant to him twice to offer her services for free. But he refused to come. Some time later, she kills her lover in order to get a wealthier patron. When her crime is discovered, the king orders her hands and feet cut off as well as her nose and ears, which are the punishments for murderers and adulterers. She is then placed in the cremation ground together with her body parts. Only now does Upagupta come to see her. When she asks why, he replies, "Sister, I have not come to you impelled by desire, but have come to see the intrinsic nature of desires and impurities. When you were covered with clothes, ornaments, and other variegated externals conducive to passion, those who looked at you could not see you as you truly are, even when they made the effort. But now, free from outer trappings, your form may be seen in its intrinsic nature."[10] Viewing the disfigured courtesan enables Upagupta to achieve enlightenment and attain the status of a nonreturner, the stage prior to becoming an arhat.

In theory, Mahayana Buddhism stresses even more soteriological inclusiveness than early Buddhism. For early Buddhism offers enlightenment only to monks and nuns, while lay believers can only hope to become monastics in their future lives by making merit, mainly through donating to the sangha. Mahayana Buddhism, however, claims that enlightenment is available to both monastics and lay believers of both sexes. But this doctrinal egalitarianism does not translate into respect for real women. Misogyny is found in even more Mahayana scriptures than those of early Buddhism.

The chapter "The Tale of King Udayana of Vatsa" in the anthology *The Collection of Jewels* depicts women as polluting, evil, and destructive to men on a spiritual path.

> Like the overflow from a toilet
> Or the corpse of a dog
> Or that of a fox
> In the Śītavana cemetery
> Pollution flows everywhere.
> The evils of desire
> Are contemptible like these.
>
> Fools
> Lust for women

Like dogs in heat.
They do not know abstinence.

They are like flies
Who see vomited food.
Like a herd of hogs,
They greedily seek manure.
Women can ruin
The precepts of purity.
They can also ignore
Honor and virtue.

Like a multicolored bottle
Containing a potent poison,
The interior is feared
Though the external appearance is serene.

With a piece of bright silk
One conceals a sharp knife.
The ornaments on a woman
Have a similar end.

The dead snake and dog
Are detestable,
But women are even more
Detestable than they are.

Why should such fools
Be addicted to these,
To a skeletal post
Covered by skin and flesh?
Their stench is offensive
Like rotten food.

Women are like fishermen.
Their flattery is a net.
Men are like fish
Caught by the net.

The sharp knife of the killer
Is to be feared.

The woman's knife is to be feared
Even more so.

As a moth in a fire
Is singed,
Insects set afire
Have no refuge.

Confused by women
One is burned by passion.
Because of them
One falls into evil ways.
There is no refuge.[11]

In theory, the Mahayana teaching of emptiness, just like the teaching of no self in early Buddhism, should free Buddhists from holding such discriminatory views toward women. But because they were still members of Indian society, monks could not but share such views. Moreover, asceticism remained a strong value in Mahayana circles. It is interesting that although real women are denigrated, the feminine becomes exalted. In the *Perfection of Wisdom* scriptures, Prajñaparamitā is femininized as the "mother of all Buddhas" and worshiped as a goddess as early as the first century of the Common Era. She is praised in the *Perfection of Wisdom in 8,000 Lines,* the earliest of this group of scriptures:

The Buddhas in the world-systems in the ten directions
Bring to mind this perfection of wisdom as their mother.
The Saviours of the world who were in the past, and also
Those that are [just now] in the ten directions,
Have issued from her, and so will the future ones be.
She is the one who shows this world [for what it is], she is
The genitrix, the mother of the Jinas [= Buddhas].[12]

If the teaching of no self does not empower women to attain arhatship, the Mahayana teaching of emptiness and nonduality also does not result in female buddhas. The fourth attitude of soteriological androgyny described by Sponberg is found in Vajrayana, which appeared late in the seventh century and is represented by Tibetan Buddhism. Rather than achieving enlightenment as a man or a woman, the goal is integrating the feminine and masculine within the same practitioner. This is symbolized by the embrace of two divine figures, the feminine wisdom and the masculine method or expedient means. When the practitioner succeeds in integrating the masculine and feminine aspects within him- or herself, he or she transcends gender distinction. We can call this androgynous holy person both male and female, or neither male nor female. Whether a woman can become a buddha is therefore not a crucial issue.

But this is a very important question for Mahayana, and how the tradition deals with it is of concern for Chinese Buddhists. This is because Vajrayana does not have the same impact on Chinese Buddhism as Mahayana does. Despite the good news of universal buddhahood proclaimed by the *Lotus Sutra,* the Dragon Princess has to transform herself into a man before she can become a buddha. This is not an isolated case. Many other Mahayana scriptures tell similar stories. The "transformation of the female body" is a regular trope in the literature. The Goddess in the *Vimalakīrti Sutra* plays tricks on the monk Śāriputra by turning him into herself and herself into the monk. Using her magical power, she demonstrates her superior insight and teaches the nonduality of gender. The Goddess famously declares that according to the Buddha's teaching, "all phenomena are neither male nor female." But she is not a buddha. There is in both this story and that of the Dragon Princess the promise of enlightenment to women as well as the withholding of enlightenment.

The Pure Land attitude toward women is most problematic for contemporary Chinese Buddhists. According to the *Longer Sukhāvatīvyūha Sutra,* Amitābha's Pure Land is devoid of animals, hungry ghosts, and hells, the three evil paths. This is stated in Dharmakara's first vow. Moreover, the Pure Land is also without women. Women are thus grouped together with animals, hungry ghosts, and hells and viewed as equally defiling. Dharmakara's thirty-fifth vow declares: "May I not gain possession of perfect awakening if, once I have attained buddhahood, any woman in the measureless, inconceivable world systems of all the buddhas in the ten regions of the universe, hears my name in this life and single-mindedly, with joy, with confidence, and gladness resolves to attain awakening, and despises her female body, and still, when her present life comes to an end, she is again reborn as a woman."[13]

Women are not denied salvation. However, they are reborn in the Pure Land not as women but as men. This is similar to the idea that a woman can achieve enlightenment only by transforming her female body. We may understand this in two ways. The first explanation is connected with the theory of karma. It is generally believed that bad karma causes rebirth as a woman. Dharmakara clearly assumes that no woman wishes to be born as a woman in the next life. That is why he vows that by calling his name with faith and joy, a woman will not be reborn in the Pure Land with a female body. Seen from this perspective, instead of misogyny, a Pure Land where a woman is reborn as a man could be the fulfillment of her deepest yearning. Second, according to the Buddhist view of the human condition, desire is the cause of suffering. Of all the human desires, sexual desire is the most powerful and thus can cause the most suffering. Since there are no women in the Pure Land, sexual desire will no longer exist, and neither will its accompanying suffering.

Buddhists in Taiwan nowadays do not feel comfortable with this stark rejection of women from the Pure Land. Modern-day apologists would say that there are neither men nor women, for they are all asexual. More commonly, Buddhist women choose to concentrate on the attraction of the Pure Land while ignoring this particular vow.

Views of Women in Chinese Buddhism

As was the case in Indian Buddhism, how society viewed women influenced Chinese Buddhism. Like monks, nuns in traditional China were censured by Confucian literati-officials because they did not marry and bear children; they were regarded as selfish and unfilial by society at large. They were blamed for not contributing to economic production because they did not engage in farming and weaving. Nuns suffered additional censure because they defied the dictates of the Three Obediences (obeying their fathers, husbands, and sons), instead opting for independence.

Because there was no tradition of female renunciates in China, nuns were regarded in a more negative light there than in India. Such hostile attitudes were reflected in popular literature. Starting in the Southern Song (1127–1279), nuns were accused of a new crime: acting as go-betweens for illicit affairs. Due to the freedom they had to visit women in their homes, nuns were suspected of arranging trysts with admirers that would be consummated in secret chambers built for such purposes in the temples. Critics also said that when nuns encouraged laywomen to come to temples to worship or to go on pilgrimages to make merit, in fact they were conning gentry women into making donations. Buddhist nuns were customarily counted among the so-called three aunties and six grannies, a gaggle of meddling women, proverbially notorious troublemakers and women of dubious moral character. This view was so widespread that not only writers of novels and drama but also literati essayists used it as a standard trope. The early Ming writer Tao Zhunyi (fl. 1300–1360), for instance, has this to say about them: "The three aunties are Buddhist nun, Daoist nun, and female fortune-teller. The six grannies are match-maker, female human trafficker, female instructor, witch, female doctor and midwife. They are vicious as the penal punishments and six disasters. When a household is visited by one of the above, it is seldom that it does not fall into licentiousness and thievery. If one is cautious, stay away from them as one would snakes and scorpions. This might be said to be the method of purifying the household."[14]

One can find similar statements in novels such as the two collections of tales titled *Striking the Table in Amazement,* as well as *The Plum in the Golden Vase, Dream of the Red Chamber,* and handbooks instructing local officials how to rule and heads of households how to govern. The message is always that local officials should treat nuns as morally dubious characters in the same category as keepers of tea and wine shops, madams of brothels, and so forth. Similarly, good families must keep nuns at arm's length to protect their women from bad influences. The Ming novelist Ling Mengchu declares in the first volume of *Striking the Table,* "Buddhist nuns are most vicious. Using the pretext of the Buddha and the convents as refuge, they lure womenfolk of gentry families to burn incense and young men to come to visit. Behaving no different from monks, they interact with men with ease. But because they are women, they can also enter the inner chambers of womenfolk to recite sutras and chant the Buddha's name. As a result of their ease of interaction with men and women, nine out of ten incidents of illicit meetings between men and women in convents are engineered by nuns."[15]

Susan Mann cites the negative attitude of a Qing official, Huang Liuhong, toward nuns as typical of his contemporaries. He called nuns "female ruffians" and asked his fellow officials to prohibit them from visiting households of good families. "Female intermediaries, such as marriage brokers, procuresses, female quacks, midwives, sorceresses, or Buddhist or Taoist nuns, often act as go-betweens for people indulging in sexual debauchery. Many innocent women from good families are enticed by these female ruffians to engage in licentious acts. The magistrate should . . . post notices to the effect that Buddhist and Taoist nuns should remain in their monasteries performing their religious duties and are not permitted to visit any household."[16]

A more damaging public image was that of nuns as courtesans. Because some convents were notorious for entertaining male visitors, the entire population of nuns came under suspicion. According to a report, the Luminous Cause Convent in Hangzhou was one of the largest and most well-known convents in the Lower Yangzi area during the Southern Song period, and it continued to flourish throughout the late imperial period. In the Southern Song, it had a reputation for being a "nun station," "where monks, literati, and officials would regularly call upon the youngest and most beautiful of the resident nuns of entertainment."[17]

This same prejudice against nuns continued in the Qing (1644–1911). Zhu Yizun (1629–1709), a famous poet and scholar, lumped all nuns together and chastised them for being licentious, lazy, and up to no good. Part of a poem he wrote decries nuns thus:

> Spreading licentiousness in their monastic quarters,
> They fill their bellies with the best monastic cuisine.
> In this way, they sully people's customary ways;
> How will an end be put to all of their mischief?
> For women there is that which is women's work,
> The essence of which is sericulture and weaving.
> How is it then, in their monastic patchwork robes,
> That they sally forth from their Jetavana gardens?[18]

Reflecting societal views of its time, the novel *Dream of the Red Chamber* depicts most of the nuns who appear in it as worldly and promiscuous. They are usually said to come from the same background as actresses and are similarly "rented" to "perform" for special occasions.

In addition to the negative image of nuns as troublemakers of immoral character, their other prevailing image was as figures of tragedy. Speaking of nuns in the early twentieth century, the scholar Wing-tsit Chan declares in his *Religious Trends in Modern China* that the three main reasons a woman would become a nun were poverty, chronic illness, and disappointment in love. He assumes that no woman would voluntarily enter the "gate of emptiness."[19]

Such prejudice did not lessen much over the course of the twentieth century. In 1989, students in the Dance Department at the Taiwan National Academy of Arts planned to perform the popular Chinese opera *Longing for the Secular Life*. The opera was written by an anonymous author in the southern style of drama known as *kunqu*, which was popular in the Yuan dynasty (1260–1368). This particular work, which takes only about twenty minutes to perform, has enjoyed great popularity in China since 1700. It was usually performed as a prelude to more extensive pieces. An essential work in the training of young actors who played female roles, it is alluded to in the film *Farewell My Concubine*, where the protagonist who plays the nun has to demonstrate having mastered the role before he can be certified by his teacher. He is punished severely because instead of singing, "A young nun am I, sixteen years of age," he sings, "A young man am I, sixteen years of age."

Lin Yutang cited this very work as a "refined example of the literary handling of the sexual problems of the monks" in his *My Country and My People*. He translated its opening passages:

A young nun am I, sixteen years of age;
My head is shaven in my young maidenhood.
For my father, he loves the Buddhist sutras,
And my mother, she loves the Buddhist priests.
Morning and night, morning and night,
I burn incense and I pray. For I
Was born a sickly child, full of ills.
So they decided to send me here
Into this monastery.
Amitabha, Amitabha!
Unceasingly I pray.
Oh, tired am I of the humming of the drums and the tinkling of the
    bells;
Tired am I of the droning of the prayers and croonings of priors:
The chatter and the clatter of unintelligible charms,
The clamor and the clangor of interminable chants,
The mumbling and the murmuring of monotonous psalms,
Prajnaparamita, Mayura-sutra, Saddharmapundarika—
Oh, how I hate them all!
While I say mitabha, I sigh for my beau.

While I chant saparah, my heart palpitates so!
Ah, let me take a little stroll,
Let me take a little stroll.

In the following passages, the young nun expresses her hatred of the monastic life and her longing for a lover.

Whence comes this burning, suffocating ardor?
Whence comes this strange, infernal, unearthly ardor?
I'll tear these monkish robes!
I'll bury all the Buddhist sutras;
I'll drown the wooden fish,
And leave all the monastic sutras!
I'll leave the drums,
I'll leave the bells,
And the chants, and the yells,
And all the interminable, exasperating, religious chatter!
I'll go downhill, and find me a young and handsome lover—
Let him scold me, beat me!
Kick or ill-treat me!
I will not become a buddha!
I will not mumble *mita, prajna, para!*[20]

This opera not only depicts the young nun as a worldly creature tormented by sexual desire but also demonizes institutional Buddhism as inhumane in its suppression of that same desire, which the audience believes to be natural. From the Buddhist point of view, both are gross distortions, for returning to lay life when celibacy cannot be maintained has always been an option. But for centuries, Buddhists had to endure this defamation without being able to do anything about it.

A staple in the traditional repertoire, the opera was performed in Taiwan as late as 1979 without incident. Ten years later, however, things had changed. In 1989, under the leadership of a young activist nun named Zhaohui (1957–), who had formed an organization called the Association for Defending Buddhism, the Buddhist position saw a better outcome. Starting on January 14, when Zhaohui first learned about the upcoming performances on January 27–29, she wrote letters of protest to the Ministry of Education, which had authority over the content of performances, as well as to the administrators of the Academy of Arts and to newspapers and media. She generated enormous support from fellow Buddhists and ordinary citizens. At the height of the protest, a man identifying himself as a Buddhist devotee threatened to immolate himself in front of the theater if the opera went on as planned. Eventually, a compromise was reached that, though not entirely satisfactory to the Buddhist community, was the best option possible at that time. The opera was performed, with two conditions: first, the heroine would not be identified as a Buddhist nun. It was suggested that if she carried a fly whisk, she could be a Daoist priestess. This is rather far-fetched because all the other references in the libretto are Buddhist. Second, therefore, the Ministry of Education promised to have the libretto revised. This opera has not been staged again since.

The negative depictions of nuns discussed so far are found in secular literature. They reflect anticlerical and antifeminist sentiments shared by both the creators and consumers of these works. The Southern Song saw the rise of Neo-Confucianism. It was a philosophy, a school of political thought, a patriarchal system of belief and praxis, and the ruling ideology of China for the last millennium. And since the Neo-Confucians were staunch critics of Buddhism, their negative attitude undoubtedly affected how Buddhists, and particularly Buddhist women, were perceived.

Since both early and Mahayana scriptures were translated into Chinese, Indian Buddhist attitudes toward women and the feminine were also introduced into China. Two genres of writings focus on female sinfulness and pollution: indigenous sutras and precious volumes. While containing ideas derived from translated Buddhist sutras, they are much more easily accessible. Written in the vernacular and chanted in group gatherings attended by women, they are circulated widely and known to women of all social classes.

The Blood Pond Sutra is probably best known among the indigenous sutras that uphold a negative view about women. This text, which has a Daoist counterpart, appeared sometime after the Song and contributed to the popular conception of women's sinful nature. It states that because women menstruate and give birth and their blood is polluting, a special hell called Blood Pond is reserved for them when they die. In Taiwan until just recently, a ritual usually conducted at women's funerals was called Ceremony of the Blood Pond or Breaking the Blood Bowl, during which the deceased's son would drink from a bowl of wine colored with red food coloring to symbolize the birth fluid of his mother, thereby freeing her from suffering in the Blood Pond Hell. The anthropologist Gary Seaman observed this ritual many times from 1970 to 1976 in central Taiwan, and he recorded the ritual text, *Cibei xuepanchan,* a seven-syllable verse based on the *Blood Pond Sutra.* It provides a graphic descriptions of the female anatomy and lays heavy emphasis on women's pollution.

> Our bodies, born of our parents, are made up of three hundred and sixty bone joints, ninety thousand pores, nine thousand sinews and blood vessels. But only a woman's body has the five hundred worms that leech onto her joints. When all these worms are active, her body is listless and weary.
>
> Moreover, a woman has within her the eighty thousand *yin* [female] worms, which collect in her vagina. These worms have twelve heads and twelve mouths. When they feed, each sucks raw blood. Day and night they move about, wearying muscle and bone. Midway through the month, they slough unclean fluid. Each of these worms vomits pus and blood out of its mouths. Each exudes blood and pus that has a red color. These ulcerous worms: their mouths are like sharp needles, and they regularly afflict women, eating raw blood, irritating each other, ceaselessly crawling, disturbing a woman, making her body unable to calm itself. This is the result of karmic retribution, for which there is no surcease.[21]

Here is another passage:

> Birth is an unclean thing: a woman's body is an unclean collection of worm's pus and filth which comes together and collects. Ten months it ripens between the two viscera, entrapped, pressed into a female prison. One thing should be known: this body is not the Pure Land. No lotus is to be seen, nor wafting sandalwood incense. There is only the stench of shit, where the fetus develops for so long. And this life can only enter and leave through a woman's vagina.[22]

Because of the polluting nature of women, everything they do is polluting. As a consequence, they must suffer in the Blood Pond after they die. This insidious belief has had a pervasive influence among the common people.

All women, when they give birth, draw water from the well, or from the river or pond, to wash the birth cloths or to wash the body. The bloody water overflows and spreads to cover the ground—the veins empty their contents into the well.

Taking water to brew tea, it is then offered to the gods, and in it is this unclean thing, this blood.

It is blasphemy to offer this disgusting filth to the gods, so the divine officials in charge of recording good and evil deeds will note the woman's name; waiting until she dies, the malevolent demons of hell will take up iron forks and pierce her innards and iron hooks will grapple her cheeks.

They will force stinking pus and loathsome blood down her gullet.[23]

This belief also can be found in many of the precious volumes. One especially popular work that has remained well known since the Qing (1644–1912), *The Precious Volume of Woman Huang,* deals with the issue of pollution. Beata Grant has thoroughly studied the story cycles of its heroine. Many versions of the story are found in different literary genres, including regional operas, ballads, and precious volumes. Despite differences in some details, the main outline of the story, as summarized by Grant, runs as follows:

Huang Guixiang is born to an older couple who had almost despaired of ever having children. She is a good and pious child, and at seven she adopts a strict vegetarian diet. Her mother dies just as she is entering adolescence and her father then marries a widow who has a son of her own. Guixiang is abused by her stepmother and stepbrother, especially when her father is away on business. At one point she is about to commit suicide and is saved only by the intervention of the gods. Later, Guixiang's stepbrother attempts to murder her father, but kills his own mother by mistake. When Guixiang's father is falsely accused of the murder, his filial daughter asks to be executed in his stead. In the end, however, the gods save Guixiang and punish the stepbrother for his crime.

Guixiang, hereafter more commonly known as Woman Huang, is then married off to a local man who happens to be a butcher, which Buddhism regards as the most polluted of occupations. She tries very hard to get her husband to change his profession but his response is that she is equally polluted since she has borne him several children. Horrified and fearful of the fate that lies in store for both herself and her husband, Woman Huang resolves to purify herself. To this end, she turns her household duties over to her husband and spends her days in the sutra hall reciting the *Diamond Sutra*. The zeal with which she devotes herself to her religious practice attracts the attention of Yama, King of the Underworld. He sends his messenger to bring her to his court so he can question her about her understanding of the *Diamond Sutra*. When she realizes that she is being called down into the Underworld, Woman Huang feels betrayed and momentarily regrets her piety. She also finds it terribly painful to leave her husband and children. Eventually, however, she resigns herself to death and accompanies the messenger to the Underworld, where she is given a tour of the various courts before she meets King Yama. She recites the *Diamond Sutra* flawlessly and then demands to be returned to the world of the living. King Yama is willing to grant her request, but since it is now too late for her to return to her original body he decides that she will return in the body of a man. In this way, she is reborn as the male son of a childless couple, is given an education, and eventually becomes an official. In a dream, the official learns of his previous existence and goes to find Woman Huang's husband and children, finally converting the former and providing handsomely for the latter. Then, having fulfilled his familial obligations, he resigns from office and devotes himself completely to the religious life. Thus, Woman Huang eventually achieves purification and saves both herself and her family.

It is not hard to see why this story enjoyed such popularity. First of all, it reflects the general attitude about female pollution shared by the common people. Second, it brings Woman Huang back to life as a man, another hope shared by many women. Finally, unlike Princess Miaoshan, the legendary manifestation of Bodhisattva Guanyin, Woman Huang not only gets married and bears children but also brings spiritual salvation to her husband and children. Her religious pursuit thus does not prevent her from fulfilling her Confucian obligations.

Why women are considered polluting and what punishment they suffer as a result are both explained in the story of Woman Huang. When she asks her husband to give up butchering because it is polluting, he answers that the ritual pollution of childbirth is equally so:

When you gave birth to your children you also committed a sin:
How many bowls of bloody water, how many bowls of fluids?
For every child, there were three basins of water,
Three children, and thus nine basins of fluids.
You dumped the bloody waters into the gutters,
And so you polluted the Sprite of the Eaves.
Three mornings and you were already back in the kitchen,
And so you pollute the God of the Hearth.
Before ten days were up, you went into the front hall,
And so you polluted the household gods and ancestors.
Before a month was up, you went out of doors,
And so you polluted the sun, the moon and the stars.
You washed the bloodstained clothing in the river,
And the tainted waters polluted the Dragon King.
You spilled these waters onto the ground,
And the spirits of Hell had nowhere to hide.
After you washed the clothes, you laid them on the bank to dry.
And so you polluted the Great Yin and the Great Yang.
In vain you rely on your reading of the *Diamond Sutra*—
The sins of a lifetime will not be easily redeemed.[24]

The punishment for giving birth and thus polluting these deities is that women must suffer in a hell intended specifically for them, the Blood Pond Hell. The story of Woman Huang provides a vivid description of it. Before Woman Huang is restored to life, she is led by a lad to tour the eighteen hells. The very first is the Blood Pond Hell.

This hell is vividly described in a ballad titled "Woman Huang Tours the Underworld." In this version of the story, like the filial monk Mulian, she looks for her dead mother. She wishes to receive the punishment of drinking the blood water in the mother's stead, similar to the Taiwanese ritual mentioned above.

We cannot trace a direct link between the negative attitudes toward nuns and women found in Chinese popular literature and in indigenous Buddhist scriptures to canonical texts. But among the various Buddhist views about women we have discussed, misogyny is one. Like all institutional religions, Buddhism reflected the historical and social conditions under which it arose and developed. Women did not enjoy the same status as men in traditional India and China. There is thus a correlation between the inferior social status of women and the negative attitude toward them in Buddhism. For the same reason, the negative attitude toward women found in Buddhism could not only justify but also reinforce their inferior status in society.

However, as some women had more opportunity to receive education, their status improved. Feminist scholarship during the last few decades has recovered the works of women writers who lived in the late imperial period. Similarly, through the study of women scholars such as Beata Grant and Miriam Levering, the lives and works of individual female Chan masters have become known to us. The case illustrating the significant role nuns play in contemporary Taiwanese Buddhism will be one of the subjects discussed in the next chapter.

Discussion Questions

1. What are the Buddhist views about women?
2. Why does a woman have to transform her body into that of a man in order to achieve buddhahood?
3. Contrast the Dragon Princess with the Goddess. What do they tell us about the Mahayana attitude toward women?
4. Why were nuns depicted in a negative light in Chinese literature?
5. What is the Blood Pond Hell? How did the popular belief about female pollution interact with the Buddhist concept of karma?

Further Reading

Grant, Beata. *Eminent Nuns: Women Chan Masters of Seventeenth-Century Chan Buddhism.* Honolulu: University of Hawai'i Press, 2009.

Murcott, Susan. *The First Buddhist Women: Translations and Commentaries on the Therigatha.* Berkeley, CA: Parallax Press, 1991.

Paul, Diana Y. *Women in Buddhism: Images of the Feminine in the Mahāyāna Tradition.* Berkeley: University of California Press, 1985.

Sponberg, Alan. "Attitudes toward Women and the Feminine in Early Buddhism." In *Buddhism, Sexuality, and Gender,* edited by José Ignacio Cabezón, 3–36. Albany: State University of New York Press, 1992.

Wilson, Liz. *Charming Cadavers: Horrific Figurations of the Feminine in Indian Buddhist Hagiographic Literature.* Chicago: University of Chicago Press, 1996.

Notes

1 Sponberg, "Attitudes toward Women and the Feminine in Early Buddhism."
2 Murcott, *The First Buddhist Women,* 32.
3 Murcott, *The First Buddhist Women,* 33–34.

4   Murcott, *The First Buddhist Women,* 37.

5   Murcott, *The First Buddhist Women,* 38.

6   Ellison Banks Findly, "Women and the Arahant Issue in Early Pali Literature," *Journal of Feminist Studies in Religion* 15, no. 1 (1999): 57–76.

7   Findly, "Women and the Arahant Issue in Early Pali Literature," 76.

8   Sponberg, "Attitudes toward Women and the Feminine in Early Buddhism," 13.

9   Wilson, *Charming Cadavers.*

10 Elizabeth Wilson, "The Female Body as a Source of Horror and Insight in Post-Ashokan Indian Buddhism," in *Religious Reflections on the Human Body,* edited by Jane Marie Law (Bloomington: Indiana University Press, 1995), 81.

11 Paul, *Women in Buddhism,* 31, 41–44.

12 Edward Conze, trans., *The Perfection of Wisdom in Eight Thousand Lines and Its Verse Summary* (Bolinas, CA: Four Seasons Foundation, 1973), 31.

13 Conze, trans., *The Perfection of Wisdom in Eight Thousand Lines,* 170.

14 Tao Zhunyi, "Taking a Break from Farming in Southern Village," in *Collection of Yuan and Ming Biji Literature Containing Historical Materials,* vol. 10 (Beijing: Zhonghua shuqu, 1959), 126.

15 Lin Mengchu, *Striking the Table in Amazement* (Jinan: Qilu shushe. 1995), 58.

16 Susan Mann, *Precious Records: Women in China's Long Eighteenth Century* (Stanford, CA: Stanford University Press, 1997), 191.

17 Grant, *Eminent Nuns,* 2.

18 Grant, *Eminent Nuns,* 2.

19 Wing-tsit Chan, *Religious Trends in Modern China* (New York: Columbia University Press, 1953), 80–82.

20 Lin Yutang, *My Country and My People* (New York: John Day, 1935), 130–131.

21 Gary Seaman, "The Sexual Politics of Karmic Retribution," in *The Anthropology of Taiwanese Society,* edited by F. M. Ahern and Hill Gates (Stanford, CA: Stanford University Press, 1981), 387.

22 Seaman, "The Sexual Politics of Karmic Retribution," 389.

23 Seaman, "The Sexual Politics of Karmic Retribution," 391.

24 Beata Grant, "From Pollution to Purification: The Spiritual Saga of Laywoman Huang," in *Ritual Opera, Operatic Ritual: "Mulian Rescues His Mother" in Chinese Popular Culture,* edited by David Johnson (Berkeley: Publications of the Chinese Popular Culture Project, University of California, 1985), 270.

CHAPTER 9

Buddhism in Modern China

China has undergone many momentous changes during the last hundred years. When the Qing government was overthrown by the Nationalist revolutionaries and the Republic of China was established in 1912, the long-lasting dynastic system came to an end. Soon after the eight-year Sino-Japanese War (1937–1945), the People's Republic of China came into being in 1949 with the success of the Communist Revolution. The Nationalist government of the Republic of China moved to Taiwan, and the two Chinas have maintained their independent existence ever since. Chinese Buddhism, just like the country, has also developed to meet the changing historical conditions.

We will focus on three topics related to Buddhism during this period: Buddhist engagement with modernity, the Buddhist revival after Mao in China, and the unprecedented vitality of the order of nuns in Taiwan.

Buddhism and Modernity

The Qing court suffered from both imperialist oppression and internal upheaval during the nineteenth century. After the Qing was defeated in the Opium Wars (1839–1842 and 1856–1860), the unequal treaties allowed the British and French trade privileges and the right to send Christian missionaries to China. Adding to the national humiliation, the Taiping Rebellion, which lasted fourteen years (1851–1865), caused further havoc. Buddhism in many provinces in the southeast regions suffered a most serious blow. Many temples were reduced to rubble. The rebels also destroyed Buddhist images and scriptures. Although the Taiping Rebellion was successfully suppressed, it left the Qing significantly weakened. In the meantime, there was the threat of China's territory being parceled out among the European powers. Making the country strong so it would not be subjugated to Western imperialist powers became the central concern for both the court and China's elites. The Self-Strengthening Movement was an attempt to meet this crisis. Its central theme was aptly expressed by Zhang Zhidong (1837–1909), governor of Hunan and Canton, who made an appeal to Emperor Kuangxu (r. 1875–1908) in his essay "The Encouragement of Learning." He proposed that China should adopt Western learning for operational concerns (function) while keeping Chinese learning as the nation's moral bedrock (substance). Since the civil examination system could not produce leaders able to defeat the guns and fleets of the Western imperialists, it was necessary to adopt universal education in order to produce a well-educated citizenry that could meet the challenges of the new age. He therefore proposed that seven-tenths of each temple be turned into a school and seven-tenths of temple lands be used to raise revenue for educational expenses. Although this proposal was not implemented, attempts to use the rich resources of temples for secular purposes continued in the Republican period.

When the Qing came to an end and the Republican government was established in 1912, the civil examination system was abolished and an education system based on the Western model was adopted. To make education available to as many people as possible, many more schools had to be established. Most government officials and educated elites at that time were critical of religion, including Buddhism. Buddhist temples came to be used as government offices, barracks, and sometimes schools. Monks were forced to pay high taxes. Sometimes tenants on temple lands were encouraged to refuse to pay rent.

To prevent the government from confiscating temples for school use, Buddhist leaders established Buddhist seminaries for the first time. The thinking was that if the Buddhists were already using the temples for educational purposes, there would be no reason for the government to do so. The lay Buddhist Yang Wenhui (1837–1911) established the Jetavana Hermitage in 1908 on an estate he purchased in Nanjing. The teaching faculty and the student body consisted of both monks and laymen. This was the first time that laypeople had taught monastics about Buddhist doctrine, departing from tradition. Although it lasted only one academic year and had only twenty-four students (twelve monks and twelve laymen), some of them went on to play important roles in Republican Buddhism.

The Buddhist reformer Taixu was one of Yang's students. In 1922, a group of lay Buddhists established Wuchang Buddhist Seminary in

Wuhan, Hubei, and invited Taixu to head it. This was the first Buddhist seminary that exerted great influence on modern Buddhism, for the people associated with it, both faculty and graduates, shared Taixu's ideas of reform and modernization. Taixu headed four more seminaries in different cities in subsequent years. The curriculum was modeled upon that of Jetavana Hermitage and emphasized both Buddhist and secular subjects, including foreign languages. According to Holmes Welch, seventy-one Buddhist seminaries were established during the period 1912–1950. He estimated that about 7,500 monks received training, about 2 percent of the monastic population. The small number, however, was not insignificant, for most of them either became abbots of temples or played leadership roles in some other capacity.[1]

Buddhists were participants in China's modernization activities spurred by the May Fourth Movement. The movement was so named because on May 4, 1919, students in Beijing demonstrated to protest the government's acquiescence to the Treaty of Versailles by allowing Japan to receive the territories in Shandong surrendered by Germany. The demonstration inspired national protests and signaled the rise of Chinese nationalism. The May Fourth Movement, like the Self-Strengthening Movement several decades earlier, was motivated by anti-imperialist sentiment, but it resulted in a national awakening and renewal. It had a wide-ranging impact on culture, society, and politics. Chinese intellectuals turned to the West in order not to be dominated by it. The West was equated with modernity, and modernity was represented by science. However, instead of using Western learning only as the external function while retaining Chinese learning as the inner substance, the leaders of the new movement advocated thorough Westernization and modernization. This was represented by the slogan "Science and Democracy." For the modernizers, only by discarding the outmoded traditional beliefs and values and embracing science could China meet the challenges of the modern age. In the eyes of these zealous reformers, Confucianism was feudalism and Buddhism was superstition.

During the 1920s the government carried out antireligion policies against religions designated as superstitious and confiscated their temples and lands. It was therefore essential for Buddhists that their religion not be viewed as superstitious. Many Buddhist laymen and monks wrote about Buddhism and science in an effort to prove that Buddhism was not only not superstitious but also in agreement with science, even superior to it in some areas. Science was effectively used to construct Buddhist modernism.

Of the various branches of science, the May Fourth Movement intellectuals were particularly interested in astronomy, evolution, logic, and psychology. These were also the subjects on which Buddhist writers focused. Buddhist engagement with science took three forms. The first was to find in Buddhist scriptures the antecedents of scientific theories. For instance, some Buddhist writers argued that Buddhist cosmology anticipated ideas in modern astronomy. Among others, Lü Bicheng (1883–1943), the most prominent Buddhist woman writer, wrote that Buddhists believed in a round earth orbiting a sun and a multitude of worlds in the universe, two ideas important in modern astronomy. The second was to find parallels between Buddhism and science. For instance, these writers argued that Yogācāra was the Buddhist counterpart of Western psychology. But because of its sophisticated analysis of mind as having eight kinds of consciousness and the central importance placed on the seventh and eighth consciousnesses, Buddhist leaders such as Yang Wenhui and Taixu found Yogācāra more advanced than Western psychology. Finally, the third was to argue that Buddhism was superior to science because, unlike scientific materialism, Buddhist ethics and meditation provided people with a compassionate worldview and spiritual life. Buddhists used karma to explain biological evolution. But as believers in the Buddhist law of causality and the Mahayana teaching of emptiness, they did not accept the theory of atoms as the substantive building blocks of the physical universe.[2]

The discussion about Buddhism and science was facilitated by the print culture that flourished in the early decades of the Republican period. Many periodicals, journals, and books appeared to serve as the media of exchanges. More lay Buddhists than monastics were involved in both founding the periodicals and publishing their own writings in them. The prominent role of laypeople is an important characteristic of Chinese Buddhism in the twentieth century.

Elite lay Buddhists were active in Buddhist education, publishing, social welfare, and philanthropy in the modern period. The most important lay Buddhist was undoubtedly Yang Wenhui, already mentioned in connection with the establishment of Buddhist academies. It was also he who initiated the project of printing the Buddhist canon. Traditionally, the voluminous Buddhist canon collections were kept in monasteries, and many had been destroyed during the Taiping Rebellion. Even when they survived, they were not easily accessible for ordinary people. For this reason, he decided early in his life to dedicate himself to printing Buddhist sutras and making the woodblock prints available to the general reading public. With his own funds he set up the Jinling Scriptural Press in Nanking. In 1878 he had a chance to go to England and met Max Müller, who was supervising the translation of the fifty-volume *Sacred Books of the East,* several of which were on Buddhism. He also became friends with the Japanese Buddhist scholar and Buddhist priest Nanjū Bunyū (1849–1927), a student of Müller's. He later helped Yang to reintroduce long-lost Buddhist texts from Japan. The reprinting of these texts contributed to the revival of Yogācāra studies, which had been in decline for many centuries. The school had not been popular because, as discussed in chapter 5, it did not uphold the belief that everybody had Buddha nature. But Yogācāra enjoyed special favor among intellectuals because its tenets were thought to be rational and scientific. Both Taixu and the lay Buddhist scholar Ouyang Jingwu (1871–1941), who also attended Yang's Jetavana Hermitage, promoted its study.

Lay Buddhists in the early twentieth century organized a new type of society called "householder grove." The first one was established in 1922 in Shanghai. Many householder groves appeared in other urban areas during the Republican period. By 1949, when the People's Republic was established, "as many as one hundred eighty identifiable householder groves had sprung up in nearly every province of the country."[3]

Lay Buddhists and their societies have existed in China throughout the long history of Chinese Buddhism. Known as *she, yi,* or *yiyi,* these were grassroots associations of lay believers who pulled their resources together to cast images or erect steles in order to generate merit. Such devotional societies were first found in the cave temples of Yungang and Longmen. Members provided material aid to temples as well as to each other. There was generally a close relationship between the society members and the monks of a nearby temple, who served as their spiritual guides. In later periods, especially since the Song, societies were formed for collective religious activities such as sutra recitations, casting statues and bells, releasing animals from captivity, and collectively chanting the name of the Buddha. Monks also continued to serve in a leadership capacity, as teachers who led and guided the laity.

Unlike their predecessors, the modern householder groves were not led by monks. The members were Buddhist laymen who met to read scriptures, study Buddhism, collectively chant Buddha's name, or release life. They might invite Buddhist masters to give Dharma talks, but more often it was lay Buddhist scholars from their own or other householder groves who lectured and led the study group. Seen in this historical light, lay Buddhists in the modern period played quite different roles from their counterparts in the past.

Lay Buddhists in different places were able to form a national network with the aid of the burgeoning print culture.[4] Mechanized movable type and lithographic print technology were introduced to China in the latter part of the nineteenth century. They were much easier and cheaper than the traditional woodblock printing. One beneficiary of this technological revolution was a new genre: the periodical. Newspapers, journals, and newsletters served as essential media of public discourse. Instead of physically attending Dharma gatherings, one could learn about Buddhism by reading. Ideas were disseminated quickly and widely through the circulation of the periodicals, published by both monks and lay Buddhists. Of the many Buddhist periodicals, the *Sound of Tidal Waves,* founded by Taixu, is the most famous one. It is still being printed today.

Buddhism after Mao

Buddhism came under suspicion when China became a Communist state, renamed the People's Republic of China, in 1949. During the ten years of the Cultural Revolution (1966–1976) under Mao Zedong (1893–1976), all religions, including Buddhism, were declared to be "feudal superstitions." They were denounced, and practitioners suffered persecution. Many monasteries were destroyed or shut down. Monks and nuns were forced to return to lay life and join the labor force. For instance, monks in Ningbo, Zhejiang, where the Song masters Zhili and Zunshi carried out their activities, were mobilized to form a coal plant to make briquettes. Monks of Guoqing Monastery at Mount Tiantai, Zhejiang, the home monastery founded by the Tiantai master Zhiyi, formed a production team affiliated with the local People's Commune and engaged in agriculture and forestry. They were not allowed to wear monastic robes, profess their religious belief, or keep a vegetarian diet. This persecution lasted longer than any of the previous three persecutions in history. Buddhists regarded those years as a sign of the Age of the Decline of the Dharma.

After the death of Chairman Mao, Deng Xiaoping (1904–1997) launched economic reform in 1978 and relaxed control over religion. In 1982, the Communist Party issued Document No. 19, "The Basic Viewpoint and Policy on the Religious Affairs during the Socialist Period of Our Country," declaring certain religious activities and practices legitimate and allowing the restoration of religious sites destroyed during the Cultural Revolution. Scholars generally agree that the revival of Buddhism began in the 1980s. It was represented by the reopening and reconstruction of monasteries on a large scale and a continuing increase in the number of monastics and lay believers. The restoration of destroyed monasteries and in some cases even the construction of new ones were funded by overseas Chinese and Japanese Buddhist groups. As discussed, Chinese Buddhism has always been closely connected with Japanese Buddhism. Because many Japanese pilgrim monks came to China in the Tang and Song to study, they regarded the monasteries where they spent time the same way as modern college students regard their alma mater. Long before the twentieth century, Japanese monks belonging to the Tiantai (J.: Tendai) or Chan (J.: Zen) school would make pilgrimages to the monasteries where their founding patriarchs had been student monks many centuries before. This was why Japanese Buddhist groups were eager to contribute to the restoration of their ancestral temples once the political conditions made it possible.

One success story is the Bailin Temple in Hebei, where the Tang master Zhaozhou taught Chan in the ninth century. Even before the Cultural Revolution, except for the stupa housing Zhaozhou's relic, the temple was already in total disrepair. But in a short span of fifteen years, from 1988 to 2003, Bailin emerged as one of the most famous Buddhist temples in China. This came about due to a combination of several factors: a charismatic abbot, state support, funding from abroad, and promotion by local government. Jinhui (1933–) was a disciple of Empty Cloud (Xuyun, 1840–1959), the most renowned Chan master of the last century. He graduated in the first class of the Chinese Buddhist Seminary in Beijing and excelled in his studies. The Cultural Revolution created a generation gap among the monastics. Because many monks were laicized, they could not train disciples. Some of them resumed their status as monks after 1976, but most were elderly by then. The Chinese Buddhist Seminary in the Temple of Universal Rescue in Beijing was the first one to train young monks. More seminaries were subsequently established in major monasteries. Among the faculty were both laymen and monastics.

Because Japanese pilgrims started to come to the ruined site of Bailin to pay respect to Zhaozhou, the chairman of the National Buddhist Association, Zhao Puchu (1907–2000), asked Jinhui to head the restoration of Bailin in 1988. Zhao was a lay Buddhist and a famous calligrapher. He was highly regarded and favored by the state. With official support and donations by Japanese and overseas Buddhists, the construction of various halls of the temple took off rapidly.

The physical restoration of Bailin was greatly aided by the influx of new monastics. Young people were exposed to Buddhism at first through reading. New works in Buddhist studies began to be published from 1980 onward. Old Buddhist publications, long suppressed before, were reprinted. Buddhism was recognized as a subject for scholarly research. Jinhui was the editor of the journal *Dharma Voice,* which published articles promoting harmony between Buddhism and Communism. After the 1989 Tiananmen Incident, many college students suffered a spiritual crisis and turned to Buddhism. Some came to Bailin and became monks. One third of the monks were college graduates. This group of highly educated young monks helped Jinhui to develop Bailin into a center for Chan study and practice.

Drawing on the fame of Zhaozhou, Jinhui started to promote Zhaozhou Chan. He started publishing a new magazine, *Chan,* in 1993 and started a week-long Chan Summer Camp for college students and educated young people in 1995. Jinhui called the kind of Chan taught and practiced at Bailin Life Chan. In the first issue of *Chan,* he defined it this way: "The purpose of promoting Life Chan is to restore the lively nature of the Chan spirit, which is the result of melding Buddhist culture with Chinese culture. It is Buddhism with Chinese cultural characteristics. It is to apply the methods of Chan in the real life of the world in order to remove various problems, frustrations, and psychological obstacles in the life of modern people."[5]

Bailin's Chan Summer Camp attracted 150 participants in the first year, and in recent years there have been five hundred.[6] The daily program consists of morning and evening devotions, sitting and evening meditation, and lectures by resident monks and invited guest lecturers. In some ways, as will be discussed in the last section of this chapter, it resembles the summer camp for college students created by the lay Buddhist Li Bingnan in Taiwan. Some graduates from the Balin Chan Summer Camp became monastics, as was the case in Taiwan. Bailin has become not only a Chan center but also a thriving commercial hub and tourist site. In 2001 a huge commercial plaza was developed across from the temple. It is the largest wholesale center for construction materials, musical instruments, clothes, and other items, as well as tourist goods and crafts, in the country.[7] This combination of religious and commercial activities is remininscent of the "pilgrims' fair" that sprung up around famous temples in Hangzhou in premodern times.

Bailin Temple serves as a good example of the intertwining of Buddhist revival with the interests of the local economy and tourist industry. Local government officials worked together with monastic authorities to promote and develop Buddhist tourism. I was in Hangzhou doing fieldwork in 1987 and saw this in action. Upper Tianzhu Monastery has been a Guanyin pilgrimage center since the twelfth century. Pilgrims came from southern Jiangsu and northern Zhejiang, a pattern similar to that noted by earlier writers. They came to Hangzhou by bus or ship and spent several days. Inns as well as steamship and bus companies cooperated to serve their needs for transportation and housing. These people identified themselves as working for "religious tourism enterprise." Soochow Steamship Company maintained a business office in Changshu and a business station, smaller in scale, in Kunshan, both in Jiangsu Province. The records kept by the Changshu office show the rapid increase in pilgrimage business since 1979. Pilgrims from the same region would stay in the same inn season after season. The business station at Kunshan has dispatched two employees to the Jade Spring Hotel near the West Lake since 1980. They spend the two months of the pilgrimage season (from February to April) there every year in order to take care of pilgrims coming exclusively from Kunshan. The hotel registry shows that twenty-seven groups of pilgrims totaling 5,504 people stayed there between 1980 and 1987. About 80 percent were women, 50 percent were between age fifty and sixty-five, and 20 percent were over sixty-six years old. This is similar to the data provided by the Mount Tianmu Hotel, an inn catering exclusively to pilgrims from Changshu. Since most of the pilgrims were farmers and silkworm growers with a retirement age of fifty for women and sixty for men, this accounted for the overwhelming majority being over fifty.

I also spent a week in March 1987 on Putuo, the holy island of Guanyin, observing the celebration of Guanyin's birthday on the nineteenth of the second month. Pilgrims started coming back to Putuo in 1979, when the island was reopened to the public after the Cultural Revolution. In terms of the number of pilgrims and tourists who have visited, Putuo is definitely one of the most popular places in China today. Among the pilgrims, overseas Chinese from Singapore, Hong Kong, the Philippines, Japan, and the United States were well represented. They came with family members, with friends, or by themselves. They tended to be the ones who sponsored rituals of Water-Land Assemblies for the benefit of dead relatives. Religious tourism professionals also organized tour packages from Shanghai for domestic pilgrims from Kiangsu, Zhejiang, Fukien, and interior provinces. Like Bailin, Putuo developed rapidly in the next three decades. It was designated by the state as a special tourist site. A Buddhist seminary has been established on the island, and there are now two periodicals devoted to Putuo history and Buddhist culture. Pilgrims and tourists are welcomed by a gigantic statue named Guanyin of the South Seas at the harbor. They can buy guidebooks, rosaries, pins, and necklaces with Guanyin images as souvenirs. They can also bring home Guanyin cakes and Guanyin tea to give as gifts to their family members and friends. The flourishing of Putuo as a pilgrimage center has gone hand in hand with its growth as a tourist destination. It has sped the construction of hotels and restaurants, as well as the development of transportation and service industries.

Popular culture also contributed to the Buddhist revival by celebrating famous figures and sites connected with Buddhist history. For instance, martial art movies about Shaolin Temple, where Bodhidharma practiced meditation, were first shown in China in 1982. It was designated a World Heritage Site by UNESCO in 2010. A TV series on Xuanzang ran from 1982 to 1988. Modern technology such as the internet, DVD, and cassettes have made the dissemination of Buddhist messages easy. Many monasteries maintain websites. People can learn about Buddhism online and perform rituals and devotions without going to a temple. The faithful can make offerings, copy characters from sutras by typing instead of writing, and chant virtual liturgies. Among the most ingenious modern innovations are the so-called Buddha-recitation devices introduced to China from Taiwan. They are plastic boxes the size of an iPod or a transistor radio. One pushes buttons to choose the chants and control the volume. There are outlets for A/C adapters and headphones. Instead of counting rosaries, people can turn on the device to listen to the recitation of the Buddha's name.[8]

Buddhism recovered after the Cultural Revolution because the Buddhist sangha and the state share common interests. As observed in chapter 4, the court regulated the sangha but also relied on it for blessing. The sangha sought patronage from the court for its continuing existence. A thriving Buddhism gives the impression internationally that the People's Republic of China respects the freedom of religion. It also fosters a good relationship with the Buddhist community in Taiwan, thereby easing cross-strait tensions and contributing to the government's propaganda of "One China." Starting in 2006, the state has convened a World Buddhism Forum four times. The PRC presents itself as a country that cherishes her Buddhist tradition and promotes world peace.

Aside from promotional activities by the Buddhist establishment and the state, the Buddhism revival succeeded because it met people's spiritual needs. Men and women in post-Maoist society tried to find meaning in their lives through Buddhism. Householder groves have resurfaced in cities since the 1980s. As in the Republican period, lay Buddhists continue to play an important part. For instance, in a recent study, Gareth Fisher interviewed men and women who came to the outer courtyard of the Temple of Universal Rescue in Beijing primarily on Dharma Assembly days but also some Sundays. But they did not enter the temple proper to attend Buddhist services and listen to the sermons by monks, like faithful Buddhist devotees. Instead, they remained in the outer courtyard, the area separated from the temple, to listen to lay preachers and participate in discussion groups with other lay practitioners like themselves. Many of these lay practitioners, including some of the lay preachers, are laid-off workers who feel themselves strangers in the new society brought about by rapid economic and cultural changes. The old values of hard work and public service were replaced by materialism, which glorifies wealth and prosperity. They suffered from loss of identity and moral breakdown and felt an urgent need to reconstitute a new personhood and recover a moral vision. The community that provided this self-transformation was formed by the fellow practitioners who frequented the outer yard of the temple. Buddhism was attractive because of both its intrinsic teachings and its similarity to Maoist ideals with which the people were already familiar. They were attracted to Buddhist teachings of egalitarianism, interdependence between oneself and others, and the necessity to rescue other beings from suffering. One of the most interesting findings of the study is that in the post-Maoist era these lay practitioners combined Buddhist themes with Maoist ones in their effort to reimagine a new self who can reform a morally corrupt society.[9] This is reminiscent of the Buddhist engagement with science in the first decades of the Republican period.

Monks and male lay Buddhists were the main actors in the activities marking modern Chinese Buddhism discussed above. I will turn to the order of nuns in Taiwan to conclude this chapter.

Nuns in Contemporary Taiwan

In recent years there has been a general surge of interest in Taiwanese Buddhism. Scholars have been impressed by the quality and the size of the nuns' order: Taiwanese nuns today are highly educated and greatly out-number monks. Both characteristics are unprecedented in the history of Chinese Buddhism. In order to understand the phenomenon, I studied a community of nuns known as Incense Light Bhikshuni Sangha and wrote a book about them a few years ago.[10] The book is not about charismatic leaders or complex institutions. It is a case study of a group of nuns who can serve as a mirror reflecting the reality of contemporary nuns in Taiwan. I am interested in knowing how and why a young woman becomes attracted to Buddhism and decides to become a nun. After she joins the sangha, what kind of training does she receive? What is the curriculum of the Buddhist seminary she attends? What work does she do upon graduation? In teaching Buddhism to adults, what kind of textbooks does she use? How are the classes conducted? And finally, what problems and setbacks does she have? By examining these rather quotidian details, we can get a sense of the general picture.

Since the 1970s, and particularly 1987, when the national security laws were lifted, new developments in Buddhism have attracted both media and academic attention in Taiwan and abroad. There is an increased number of new temples, monastic complexes, and Buddhist universities and also of young people joining the monastic order. Two characteristics of Buddhism in Taiwan stand out: the emphasis on Buddhists' active engagement with society under the name of Humanistic Buddhism and the predominant ratio of nuns to monks. Both are new in the history of Chinese Buddhism.

The legacy of Taixu has been continued by Buddhist leaders in Taiwan. Xingyun and Shengyan are monks, founders of the Buddha Light and Dharma Drum monastic complexes, respectively. Zhengyan (1937–) is undoubtedly the most famous nun in Taiwan. All three are much influenced by Yinshun. Hailed as the "Mother Teresa of Taiwan," Zhengyan is the founder of the Merit Association of Compassionate Relief, a grassroots lay organization that has spurred a worldwide movement among overseas Chinese. Her emphasis on social relief and service has put a new face on Buddhism and challenged the common conception of it being an other-worldly, individualistic, and escapist religion. But she is by no means the only Buddhist teacher who has this message. Xingyun and Shengyan also emphasize that Buddhism is not just for individual salvation but also for the good of society and the welfare of humankind. Although the communities led by Xingyun and Shengyan consist of both monks and nuns, nuns are by far the majority, and they play leadership roles. Buddha Light, for instance, has about one thousand members, and more than nine hundred are nuns. This is in fact true for Taiwanese Buddhism in general. From 1953 to 1998, during the forty-five years since the first ordination of nuns at the Dazian Temple in 1953, more than twelve thousand nuns received full ordination. They make up 75 percent of the total ordained monastics. An estimate puts the ratio of nuns to monks as four to one.

The period of most rapid growth for the Incense Light community was the 1980s. This reflected a broader change on the Taiwanese religious scene. Scholars have spoken of a "religious renaissance" in Taiwan since the 1980s. This was characterized by the appearance of new Buddhist organizations such as Buddha Light, Dharma Drum, and Compassion Relief. New temple complexes were built by increasing numbers of wealthy middle-class believers. These high-profile Buddhist institutions attracted in turn more support by the faithful. Nuns in Taiwan have attracted attention not only for their numbers but also for their education. Many of them have received a college education, while some have gone abroad to Japan, the United States, England, and other countries to pursue advanced degrees. Like professional women in Taiwan, nuns engage in teaching, social work, research and writing, editing magazines, and producing radio and television programs as well as managing temples using modern techniques as executives of companies do. The large-scale influx of college-educated women into nunhood began during the period between 1978 and 1983, with a cohort born between 1956 and 1961, ten to fifteen years after the government established mandatory nine-year public education for all beginning in 1968.

Although in traditional China the monastery sometimes was the only place that provided an opportunity for poor children to receive an education, the situation is the opposite now. The women who became nuns in the 1980s were already educated, and they brought changes to the management methods and functions of monasteries. For these nuns, the Buddhist temple was clearly not an escape from life but an open space for them to develop their talents and fulfill their aspirations.

Highly educated women are attracted to Buddhism for several reasons. As a result of social and economic changes, more women have the opportunity to receive a college education and become professionals. Higher education enables women to get high-paying jobs and gain economic independence and increased social status. One indicator of this new sense of independence is that a number of educated women choose not to get married, and thus remaining single is no longer as great a stigma. To become a monastic not only is less objectionable but also can be regarded as a preferred vocation.

Most of the Incense Light nuns did not come from Buddhist families and thus had little knowledge about Buddhism while growing up. It was mainly through lectures and other activities sponsored by Buddhist studies societies, which they joined when they were in college, that they came to know and be attracted to Buddhism. Buddhist studies societies introduced Buddhist teachings and practices to college students who had no other way to learn about Buddhism. The societies therefore played a major role in inducing large numbers of students to enter the monastic order in the 1980s and therefore in the revival of contemporary Buddhism in Taiwan. Male students were of course equally exposed to Buddhism this way, and some of them also joined the sangha or took refuge as a result. The reasons more men did not become monks were mainly sociological. It was more difficult for a son to leave home than a daughter, because the son had the obligation of continuing the family lineage. Moreover, since all male college students were required to serve in the army for two years after graduation, if they entered a monastic career prior to graduation, they often returned to lay life during military service, because it was hard for them to observe the monastic vows such as vegetarianism and not killing. On the other hand, it was also difficult for a man to become a monk after he had finished military service because by then he would be twenty-four or twenty-five, which was the usual age to get married in the 1970s and 1980s. Parental pressure would therefore be greater for a son to remain in society than for a daughter.

The Nationalist government of Taiwan imposed martial law in 1948, and it was not lifted until 1987. During those forty years, restrictions were placed on nongovernmental organizations, including student associations. The government exerted strict control over all indigenous religions, including Buddhism. During the 1970s, although Christian and Catholic universities were allowed to be established and their religious activities could be carried out on campuses freely, the same was not true for Buddhists. For instance, monks and nuns were not allowed to enter the campus of the National Taiwan University, and the Taiwan University Hospital even refused to allow a medical student who was a nun to do a rotation there. Monks and nuns were not allowed to visit any university campus to give

Dharma lectures. Recalling the situation in the 1950s, Master Shengyan said, "In those days, young people liked to wear crosses around their necks and considered this fashionable. If someone was said to be a Buddhist believer, he would either be laughed at as being superstitious or be considered a pessimist. If the person was a young intellectual, people would consider this even more bizarre. Why would anyone become a Buddhist believer if he has not suffered tragic events in his life?"[11]

Not only was there a generally negative perception of Buddhism in society, but it was extremely difficult for college students to form clubs to learn about Buddhism. Except for student associations, which had a clearly patriotic overtone or were purely academic and apolitical, forming any club in a university was difficult. How did the Buddhist studies societies manage to be the exception and be allowed to exist in most universities and colleges by the 1970s? Two lay Buddhists, Zhou Xuande (1899–1989) and Li Bingnan (1889–1986), together with their associates, were major players in this lay Buddhist movement, which greatly influenced college students. Like the lay Buddhists in the early twentieth century, Zhou and Li devoted their time, energy, and resources to Buddhist education.

The Buddhist studies societies were primarily organized for the sake of studying Buddhism, although trips to temples to observe and participate in Buddhist rituals also took place. The spiritual leaders of these societies were two lay Buddhists instead of monks, and the societies themselves were headed by college students. Zhou Xuande concentrated his efforts to promote Buddhism by publishing a magazine, *Torch of Wisdom,* as well as books issued by his publishing company; both were devoted to the propagation of Buddhism. He sponsored essay competitions on Buddhist themes and offered scholarships to college students who demonstrated their knowledge about Buddhism. In contrast, Li Bingnan taught Buddhism to college students in the summer camps, offering regular courses designed specifically for this purpose. Finally, it was mainly due to their vision and energetic promotion that Buddhist studies societies on college campuses could be established beginning in 1961. Such societies served as the main pools for the recruitment of college students into the sangha.

The Incense Light Seminary is a small institution. From its first graduating class in 1982 to the class of 2009, the numbers were consistently in single digits. The graduates, with the exception of those who come from other temples, remain as members of the Incense Light community. Although their number is not large, they are engaged in many activities.

Some stay at the head temple, and others are assigned to the five subtemples located in different cities on the island. There are several enterprises for which the alumni are responsible, such as editing journals, managing the publishing press, running a modern library and an extensive digital information service on Buddhist publications, and designing and supervising new construction projects. Depending on their individual talents, alumni can specialize in any of these areas. Before they choose their special tasks, however, all graduates must teach free Buddhist classes open to adults for at least two years. They plan the curriculum and use the textbooks written by the Incense Light nuns themselves.

The Incense Light nuns identify themselves as religious teachers. Teaching Buddhism ("spreading the Dharma") to laypeople has always been a goal of all Buddhist masters. This was traditionally carried out in the temples in the form of Dharma lectures, but many new means of reaching the public have become possible in the modern age. There are daily radio and television programs operated by several Buddhist organizations. People can get numerous cassette tapes made by Buddhist masters or attend large-scale public lectures given by famous teachers, which often attract hundreds and even thousands of people. Such proselytizing activities have of course fueled the general interest in Buddhism in Taiwan over the last several decades. But the main drawback is that there is no way for the audience to respond. They can only listen passively because these are all one-way communications. There is no way of knowing if the listener or viewer has really understood. If one has questions, it is impossible to ask the lecturers right there and then.

The Buddhist classes taught by the nuns are the exact opposite. The instruction is a two-way communication. Even when one class has more than forty students, part of each meeting is always devoted to small group discussion, during which the students are divided into several smaller groups of no more than ten people each. The same format of group discussion is firmly institutionalized in the seminary the nuns attend. The instructors therefore have already been trained well in this way of teaching. The same methods used in the seminary are applied to teaching the adult Buddhist classes.

The adult Buddhist classes are modeled upon public middle school classes. Each semester consists of eighteen weeks, beginning in December and ending in May. Students meet two hours each week. They have to do homework and take a final exam. There are three levels: elementary, intermediate, and advanced. Like middle school classes in Taiwan, each class has a leader and several cadres who assist the teachers in helping with their fellow students' study and organizing extracurricular activities, such as field trips, athletic competitions, song and drama performances, and cooking competitions. Such activities cement a feeling of fellowship and reinforce the values learned in class and provide good occasions for former students to return to renew their contact with the Incense Light nuns. Graduates often became followers and patrons of the community. They work as volunteers when there are activities organized by the sangha. They donate money to help its development. The Buddhist classes therefore not only provide the economic base of the Incense Light community but also raise its profile in society.

The design of the class materials as well as the assignments reflect the community's attitude concerning adult education in Buddhism. The content of the textbooks is determined by three guiding principles. The first principle is to introduce a worldview and view of life that are in accord with modernity. For this reason, it is unnecessary for students to learn about the ancient Indian ideas of Mount Sumeru, the triple worlds, the four great continents, and the four periods making up an eon that are found in Buddhism. Instead, the student should be taught how to view her life in the world according to Buddhist perspectives. The second principle is to emphasize human relationships. If students are taught to fulfill their duties in the family, they will contribute to the peace and security of society. Since all the students who attend the classes are laypeople and either have jobs or work at home, to guide them to have faith in the Three Treasures and to use the basic Buddhist teachings of the Four Noble Truths, the Noble Eightfold Path, and the twelve links of the Law of Dependent Origination as the compass for their life can make everyone content with their family, duty, and work. This will establish harmony in the family and security in society. In this way the Buddhadharma acts as the moving force of humanist concerns. Finally, the third principle is not advocating self-mutilation, glorifying miraculous responses, or believing in predictions. The lessons in the textbooks discuss basic Buddhist teachings and stories of the Buddha, bodhisattvas, and eminent monks. But there is no mention of the self-immolation of the Medicine King as an offering to the Buddha in the *Lotus Sutra,* nor are there stories of monks and nuns who performed such acts down the ages. Such rational, positive, this-worldly, and socially engaged attitudes are shared by all Humanistic Buddhists in Taiwan.

These ideals are further clarified in the brochure to attract students to attend the classes. It lists three goals: to extend and broaden Buddhist education, to actualize a Buddhist life of correct faith, and to beautify life with the Buddhadharma. Similar to the educational goals of the seminary, both knowledge and practice are equally emphasized, with the purpose of integrating Buddhist teaching with daily life. Indeed, the clear message that the students receive and take away is that it is more important to constantly reflect on and apply the Buddhist concepts they learn from the class to concrete situations they encounter in their daily lives than to acquire intellectual knowledge about Buddhism. Buddhist teachings become real when the students can apply them to their own lives. At the same time, it is by reflecting on their experiences in everyday life that they come to truly understand Buddhism. If the goal of Humanistic Buddhism is to build a pure land on earth by purifying the minds of people, then the adult Buddhist classes serve an important function in substantiating it in Taiwanese families. "To do good, not to do evil, and purify the mind" are the central teachings of the Vinaya, but they are also tenets upheld by all Buddhist traditions and even by the Confucian tradition. The textbooks and the class instructions put the most emphasis on ethics and personal cultivation. This is not surprising because the nuns who wrote the textbooks and teach the classes received the same training. The curriculum of the Incense Light Buddhist Seminary puts ethics and religious practice on a par with knowledge about Buddhism.

One may ask, however, if studying Buddhism is only for the purpose of functioning better in one's family and work. Throughout its long history, Buddhism has attracted laypeople because of its profound philosophy and meditation regimen. There have been lay Buddhists who were famous commentators in the Tiantai and Huayan schools. There also have been lay believers who were accomplished Chan practitioners or fervent Pure Land devotees. Can the Buddhist study classes produce such lay Buddhists, if this is even their goal?

A distinctive feature of the editorial philosophy reflected in the textbooks is a nonsectarian and ecumenical approach. Tenets of early and Mahayana Buddhist traditions are introduced together. Although Yogacārā, Chan, and Pure Land receive some attention, none of the other Chinese Buddhist schools, such as Tiantai, Huayan, or even the Vinaya school itself, are mentioned. There seems to be a deliberate choice of not concentrating on Chinese Buddhism. This is seen in the decision of the founder, Wuyin (1940–), not to teach the Chan pure rules but the *Vinaya in Four Divisions* as well as the deliberate avoidance of any mention of enlightenment in both her lectures and the textbooks edited under her direction. Nonsectarianism is presented as returning to the source. The kind of Buddhism taught in the adult classes can be therefore regarded as Buddhist fundamentalism in two senses: First, it is an attempt to introduce students to "original Buddhism" and to some of the most fundamental or basic Buddhist concepts. Second, since the classes hope to reach people from all walks of life, the audience is broad-based and forms the foundation of society. It is thus "fundamental" Buddhism for everyone. It is perhaps for this reason that the editors have decided to present Buddhism in a nontechnical and easily accessible fashion.

Throughout the long history of Buddhism in China, monks and nuns have had to counter accusations that they are interested only in their own salvation and contribute little to the betterment of society. Due to the patriarchal nature of traditional society, nuns have been even more marginalized than monks. Only in the last quarter of the twentieth century in Taiwan did the situation change dramatically. The message of Humanistic Buddhism has focused consistently on social reconstruction based on the purification of humanity and the betterment of the community. Highly educated nuns are the foot soldiers implementing this vision. Yet, paradoxically, these independent nuns, with rare exceptions such as Zhaohui, do not consider themselves feminists, nor do they identify with feminism in Taiwan. While fully confident that women can do things like men and that nuns should be led by nuns, not by monks, Wuyin and the nuns I interviewed aspire to become a "great heroic man" (*da zhangfu*). New nuns are instructed to walk and speak in a certain way so that they are free of feminine traits. Using the traditional Korean costumes as a model, Wuyin designed their robes to be high-waisted and loose all over in order to hide the curves of the body. Yet when asked why there are more nuns than monks in Taiwan, Wuyin explained that because women are by nature more patient, gentle, kind, and capable of endurance and sacrifice, they are more attracted to Buddhism because these characteristics correspond closely to Buddhist ideals. For the same reason, nuns can live more harmoniously with each other in the temple, and they tend not to return to lay life as much as monks. This contradictory attitude of negating their femininity while simultaneously essentializing it is not unique to Incense Light but also expressed by nuns of other communities.

Taiwan has been very much influenced by globalization. Large Buddhist organizations such as Compassion Relief, Buddha Light, and Dharma Drum all have branches in different parts of the world and strive to reach a global audience. Compared to these organizations, due to its small size, Incense Light has not been able to establish branches abroad, although it is equally influenced by this trend. Responding to the forces of globalization, the emphasis of the Incense Light curriculum in both the seminary and the adult Buddhist classes, like that of lectures and television programs provided by other Buddhist groups, is more activist than theoretical. Humanistic Buddhism, a local product addressing specific problems faced by Buddhism in Taiwan, is paradoxically universal in its outlook. The Incense Light nuns are not particularly interested in either the history or the unique characteristics of Chinese Buddhism; they are far more interested in the "original teachings" of the Buddha and the common tenets of all Buddhist traditions.

Another clear indication of the Incense Light nuns' willingness to learn from other Buddhist traditions is their current fascination with non-Chinese forms of meditation. Although Wuyin learned Chan meditation from her teacher and had actually taught Chan and Pure Land meditation methods during the annual retreats in the 1980s and 1990s, the community has embraced the meditation methods of the southern or Theravadin Buddhist tradition. For several years in the late 1990s they practiced insight (*vipaśyanā*) meditation taught by S. N. Goenka (1924–2013). But in 2002 the community started using the meditation method taught by the Burmese monk Pa-Auk Sayādaw (1934–) in their annual winter meditation retreats. Pa-Auk bases his teaching on Pali sutras, commentaries, and in particular, the text *Visudhimagga* (Path of Purification) written by Buddhaghoṣa in the fifth century. He believes that a person can achieve nirvana in this very life, and that meditation is the only way to reach this goal. While he teaches both insight (*vipaśyanā*) and concentration (*jhāna*) meditation, he recommends starting with *jhāna* and only later practicing *vipaśyanā*. His teaching provides the students with a very detailed and systemic map of meditative states. The nuns find his teaching very clear because he tells them that there are definite signs and physical sensations when one reaches a certain level of concentration. The meditation objects used most often are breathing, *kasina* (colored disks), white bones, and the impurity of the body. Unlike Chan, which discourages conscious expectations, this method requires one to work hard to obtain these signs and sensations as verification of success. Individual nuns are allowed to use traditional meditation methods such as Chan and Pure Land for their own practice. The community as a whole, however, is committed to Pa-Auk's method. Since Theravada is the only surviving tradition of early Buddhism, the promotion of its meditation method taught by its contemporary teachers is another example of the community's interest in going back to "original Buddhism." This is of course not limited to Incense Light but an interest shown by other Buddhist groups in Taiwan.

If the "nun's miracle" was a result of the "economic miracle" of Taiwan four decades ago, what will happen when the economic base of Taiwan's institutional Buddhism changes due to the global economic downturn? The rapid growth of the community in the 1980s and early 1990s has slowed considerably in recent decades. As more and more couples in Taiwan choose to have fewer children or even just one child, will this make it harder for a daughter, not to mention a son, to leave home? Furthermore, there are many more competing interests to attract college students. Buddhist studies societies are having a much harder time attracting members. After the passing of Zhou Xuande and Li Bingnan, there have not been other dedicated laymen and charismatic Buddhist teachers whose main focus is on teaching Buddhism to college students. Although the Buddhist classes for adults have continued, there has been a decline in enrollment over the years, due to the increase of competing offerings by other Buddhist organizations. Although Incense Light was the first to establish a systematic program of Buddhist instruction for the general population, it is no longer the only one doing it. How to continue its mission of education and attract students is therefore a present and future challenge.

Chinese nuns belong to the oldest lineage of nuns in the world. Nuns in Taiwan are the inheritors of the light of Buddhadharma. Whether they will be able to pass the light is something only history can tell. In its two-thousand-year history, Chinese Buddhism has undergone many transformations. The prominence of the order of nuns in Taiwan and the renewed vitality of Buddhism in China are just two recent examples of how Buddhism has responded and adapted to Chinese society.

Discussion Questions

1. What challenges did Buddhism face during the late nineteenth and early twentieth centuries? What measures did Buddhists undertake to meet them?

2. Lay Buddhists play important roles in modern Buddhism. In what ways do they differ from the lay Buddhists in traditional China?
3. How did Buddhism recover from the destruction of the Cultural Revolution? What part did the state, monastic leaders, local government, and tourist industry play?
4. What is Humanistic Buddhism?
5. In what ways can we call the order of nuns in Taiwan a "miracle"?

Further Reading

Fisher, Gareth. *From Comrades to Bodhisattvas: Moral Dimensions of Lay Buddhist Practice in Contemporary China.* Honolulu: University of Hawai'i Press, 2014.

Hammerstrom, Erik J. *The Science of Chinese Buddhism: Early Twentieth-Century Engagement.* New York: Columbia University Press, 2015.

Kiely, Jan, and J. Brooks Jessup, eds. *Recovering Buddhism in Modern China.* New York: Columbia University Press, 2016.

Scott, Gregory Adam. "A Revolution of Ink: Chinese Buddhist Periodicals in the Early Republic." In *Recovering Buddhism in Modern China,* edited by Jan Kiely and J. Brooks Jessup, 111–140. New York: Columbia University Press, 2016.

Yang, Fenggang, and Dedong Wei. "The Bailin Buddhist Temple: Thriving under Communism." In *State, Market, and Religions in Chinese Societies,* edited by F. Yang and J. B. Tamney, 63–86. Leiden: Brill, 2005.

Young, Glenn. "Reading and Praying Online: The Continuity of Religion Online and Online Religion in Internet Christianity." In *Religion Online: Finding Faith on the Internet,* edited by Lorne L. Dawson and Douglas E. Cowan, 93–105. London: Routledge, 2013.

Yü, Chün-fang. *Passing the Light: The Incense Light Community and Buddhist Nuns in Contemporary Taiwan.* Honolulu: University of Hawai'i Press, 2013.

Zhe, Ji. "Buddhism in the Reform-Era China: A Secularised Revival?" In *Religion in Contemporary China: Revitalization and Innovation,* edited by Adam Yuet Chau, 32–52. London: Routledge, 2011.

Notes

1 Holmes Welch, *The Buddhist Revival in China: 1900–1950* (Cambridge, MA: Harvard University Press, 1968), 285.
2 Hammerstrom, *The Science of Chinese Buddhism.*
3 J. Brooks Jessup, "Buddhist Activism, Urban Space, and Ambivalent Modernity in 1920s Shanghai," in *Recovering Buddhism in Modern China,* ed. Jan Kiely and J. Brooks Jessup (New York: Columbia University Press, 2016), 68–69.
4 Scott, "A Revolution of Ink," 111–140.

5   Yang and Wei, "The Bailin Buddhist Temple," 67.

6   Yang and Wei, "The Bailin Buddhist Temple," 76.

7   Yang and Wei, "The Bailin Buddhist Temple," 77.

8   Natasha Heller, "Buddha in a Box: The Materiality of Recitation in Contemporary Chinese Buddhism," *Material Religion* 10, no. 3 (2014): 5.

9   Fisher, *From Comrades to Bodhisattvas*.

10   Yü, *Passing the Light*.

11   Shengyan, "Remembrance of the Elder Zhou Zishen" (Zhuinian Zhou Zishen changzhe), in the pamphlet *A Record of Remembrance of the Layman Zhou Zishen and His Wife* (Zhou Zishen jushi zhuisi lu, 1979), 61.

Glossary

Age of True Dharma: Refers to the first five hundred years after the death of the Buddha, when Buddhism flourished. It would be succeeded by the Age of Counterfeit Dharma, lasting one thousand years, when Buddhism began to decline. Finally, Buddhism would disappear from the face of the earth at the end of the Age of Decline of the Dharma, lasting another ten thousand years.

***ālaya* consciousness:** The eighth of the eight kinds of consciousness unique to Yogācāra philosophy. It is the source of the other seven consciousnesses, which project both the subject and the object. It is the storehouse consciousness because both pure and impure karmic seeds are stored in it.

Amitābha: Buddha of Infinite Light, also known as Amitāyus, Buddha of Infinite Life. He is the Buddha of the Land of Bliss or Western Paradise. He is worshiped by the Pure Land tradition.

arhat: The title for a worthy one who has achieved the highest stage of enlightenment in Hinayana Buddhism. He is no longer subject to rebirth. It is an ideal rejected by Mahayana Buddhism.

Awakening of Faith in Mahayana: One of the most important treatises of Chinese Buddhism. It argues that we are endowed with inherent enlightenment. Because enlightenment coexists with ignorance, religious practice is necessary. Enlightenment is to be awakened to our original true nature. This belief is fundamental to Chan Buddhism.

Blood Pond Sutra: A Chinese text that provides justification for the Blood Pond Hell reserved for women. They are punished because of their polluting outflow in giving birth.

Bodhidharma: He is revered as the First Patriarch of Chan Buddhism, who was supposed to have brought the teaching from India. There are many legends about him, including his practicing wall gazing at Shaolin Temple.

bodhisattva: The highest ideal of Mahayana Buddhism. The word means "enlightenment being," or a being who aspires to buddhahood. In order to help everyone to achieve enlightenment, a bodhisattva vows not to enter nirvana until everyone has done so. The career of a bodhisattva is a long one, during which he carries out acts of altruism and compassion. There are many bodhisattvas in Mahayana Buddhism, but four are most familiar to Chinese Buddhists: Guanyin (Avalokiteśvara), Wenshu (Mañjuśrī), Puxian (Samantabhadra), and Dizang (Kṣitigarbha).

Buddha nature: A central belief in Chinese Buddhism. Also known as Tathāgatagarbha thought, it proclaims that we (and all other sentient beings) have the potential to become buddhas.

Buddha Seven: A popular practice of contemporary Pure Land believers, who carry out concentrated and intense Buddha invocation in a temple for seven days.

Caodong Chan: One of two main schools of Chinese Chan Buddhism. It advocates sitting meditation but does not emphasize exclusive use of koan. It is also known as Silent Illumination Chan.

Chan Seven: A period of seven days spent practicing Chan meditation in a temple. It has been promoted by Chan teachers since the twentieth century.

Confucianism: One of two philosophical and religious traditions in China prior to the introduction of Buddhism, the other being Daoism. It is based on the teachings of Confucius (557–479 BCE) and Mencius (c. 372–289 BCE).

Dahui (1089–1163): A Chan master famous for his emphasis on the exclusive use of koan. In contrast to Silent Illumination Chan, his is known as Koan Investigation Chan.

Dao: Translated as the Way or Path, this is the ultimate reality upheld by both Confucianism and Daoism. It is the source of everything. To realize the Dao and live in conformity to it is the goal of human beings. The Dao is active and generative. It works through yin and yang, the two complementary forces of qi (vital force, material force, or life force).

Daoism: The Chinese philosophical and religious tradition based on the teachings of the *Daode jing,* attributed to Laozi (active sixth century BCE) and the writings of Zhuangzi (c. 368–286 BCE).

Dharma: Refers to the teachings of the Buddha. When not capitalized, it refers to the irreducible element of phenomena.

Dharmadhātu: Realm of dharmas. This is the ultimate reality according to the Huayan or Flower Garland school.

doctrinal classification: A system adopted by Chinese Buddhist thinkers to create a comprehensive hierarchy of doctrines found in both Hinayana and

Mahayana scriptures. The scripture favored by the founder of a specific school would be placed above all the others.

dual ordination: This refers to the requirement that a woman must be ordained first by ten nuns and then by ten monks in order to become a nun. This differs from the case of a man, who needs to receive ordination from monks only.

Dunhuang: Situated at the terminus of the Silk Roads, it was a gathering place for traders and Buddhist missionary monks. The more than five hundred caves constructed by the faithful over many centuries are treasure troves of Buddhist art and artifacts.

Eight Rules of Respect: The eight regulations that subordinate nuns to monks. They are supposed to have been given by the Buddha to Mahāprajāpatī, his aunt and foster mother, who was the founder of the order of nuns.

Emperor Aśoka (c. 268–239 BCE): Ruler of India who adopted Buddhism and promoted its spread to other countries in Asia through missionary activities. Under his patronage, Buddhism became a world religion.

Emperor Ming (r. 58–75): He is credited by the Buddhist tradition as the ruler who brought Buddhism to China by inviting Indian monks and settling them at the White Horse Temple.

Emperor Wu of Liang (r. 502–549): Often compared to Aśoka, he was the most renowned Buddhist ruler of China.

feeding hungry ghosts (*shishi*): The ritual performed most often in China. Hungry ghosts suffer constant hunger and thirst. They can eat only when food is ritually offered to them by monks. By sponsoring this ritual, one hopes to gain merit and helps one's deceased relatives.

five precepts: When one decides to become a Buddhist, one takes refuge in the Three Treasures (Buddha, Dharma, Sangha) and accepts five precepts: not to kill, not to lie, not to steal, not to engage in harmful sex, and not to drink alcohol.

Four Noble Truths: The Buddha taught this in his first sermon after he achieved enlightenment. They are the truths of suffering, desire, nirvana, and the Noble Eightfold Path. Life is suffering because we desire, but by eliminating desire and following the Noble Eightfold Path, we can end suffering and achieve nirvana.

Ghost Festival: One of the most important Buddhist festivals, which takes place in the seventh lunar month. Hungry ghosts and hell beings can return to earth only during this month. The faithful go to temples and sponsor rituals to benefit these creatures and gain merit for their dead relatives as well as themselves.

Householder Grove: This refers to groups of lay Buddhists who gather to study and practice Buddhism. It is a modern phenomenon popular in big cities. Members tend to be urban male intellectuals. Such groups have contributed to Buddhist modernity in China.

Huineng (638–713): The Sixth Patriarch of Chan Buddhism revered by all Chan schools. The *Platform Sutra* is a record of his sayings. Bearing the word "sutra" in its title, it is the only Chinese Buddhist text honored as the word of the Buddha by Chan Buddhists.

Humanistic Buddhism: In order to counter the criticism of Buddhism being otherworldly and good only for death rituals, reformers in the early twentieth century stressed the positive and socially engaged aspects of Buddhism. Most contemporary Taiwanese Buddhist leaders promote it.

Indra's net: The *Flower Garland Sutra* uses this image to illustrate the fact that all things are interrelated, interdependent, and interpenetrating.

Jātaka **tales:** Stories about the previous lives of the Buddha when he performed altruistic acts to save others. He sometimes appears as animals. The stories are widely used in sermons and are depicted on frescos and wall paintings in Buddhist caves and temples.

karma: Literally means deed, but it results not only from one's actions but also from one's speech and thought. Good actions, speech, and thought create good karma, which leads to good fortune in life and a good rebirth after one dies. Bad actions, speech, and thought create bad karma, which does the opposite.

King Yama: The lord of the ten kings of hell, where the dead receive punishment. He passes judgment and assigns them to the six realms of rebirth. Stories and paintings of King Yama and the ten kings of hell helped to ingrain the Buddhist concepts of karma and rebirth in popular consciousness.

Kumārajīva (344–413): The most famous translator of Buddhist scriptures. His translations of the *Lotus Sutra* and the *Vimalakīrti Sutra* are the standard versions used in China and East Asia.

lamp records: Together with recorded sayings, a new genre of Chan literature that records the actions and words of Chan masters. Since Chan stresses mind-to-mind transmission, the lamp symbolizes the enlightened mind of the Chan master.

Law of Dependent Origination: This is the Buddhist law of causality discovered by the Buddha in the night of his enlightenment. It consists of twelve links tracing old age, sickness, and death through grasping and desire to ignorance. Each link is dependent on the previous one. With the elimination of the previous link, the next one is eliminated. The implication of this law is that human suffering is not caused by fate or divine punishment. The Four Noble Truths are a demonstration of how this law works.

Linji Chan: One of the two main schools of Chan Buddhism. It uses koan ("public cases," *gong'an*) in training practitioners.

Madhyamaka: One of the two Indian philosophical schools based on Nāgārjuna's "Verses on the Middle Way." It is a systematic working out of the insight of *śūnyatā* proclaimed in the *Perfection of Wisdom* scriptures. Since everything is *śūnya* (empty or devoid of self-nature), we cannot say it either exists or does not exist. The Middle Way is neither assertion nor negation. Nāgārjuna uses the dialectical method to reduce any thesis proposed to absurdity.

Maitreya: The future Buddha, who is now in Tushita Heaven, the fourth of the six heavens in the world of desire. He will be born on Earth to renew Buddhism at the end of the Age of the Decline of the Dharma.

matching of concepts (*keyi*): A method used by Buddhists during the early period to make Buddhist concepts easier to understand. For instance, they would match five precepts with the Confucian five virtues, or nirvana with the Daoist idea of nonaction. Because this method often obscured the meaning of the original term, it was abandoned after the arrival of Kumārajīva.

merit making: One creates good karma by making merit, which results from doing good deeds. Casting Buddhist images, building temples, donating land and materials to temples, and feeding monks are particularly efficient ways to make merit. Monks are called field of merit because they yield merit benefiting the donor, like a fertile rice field.

Mulian: A pious monk who goes to hell to save his evil mother. First mentioned in a Buddhist sutra, his story is celebrated in popular stories and drama. It gave rise to the Ghost Festival.

nature inclusion: A unique teaching of Tiantai Buddhism. It claims that both good and evil coexist in all beings, including the Buddha. While evil is revealed in us and good hidden, good is revealed and evil is hidden in the Buddha. That is why we can become enlightened and the Buddha can have empathy for us.

nature origination: A unique teaching of Huayan Buddhism. It claims that all beings have their origin in Buddha nature.

nianfo: "Nianfo" has two meanings: Buddha contemplation and Buddha invocation. Because of the different understandings of the term, there are two traditions in Pure

Land Buddhism. One contemplates Amitābha Buddha, and the other calls his name. The latter has become the standard practice.

no self: According to Buddhism, there is no such entity called self. This is in direct contrast to the Hindu belief in a self (*ātman*). Instead, we are constituted of five physical, mental, and psychological components called the five aggregates. "Self" is no more than a fictitious name attached to these components. This counterintuitive teaching is designed to free us from egoism, which gives rise to desire and causes suffering.

Noble Eightfold Path: The last of the Four Noble Truths taught by the Buddha in his first sermon. It consists of morality, meditation, and wisdom. One becomes enlightened and enters nirvana by following this path. Because this moral and spiritual training favors neither indulgence nor asceticism, it is called the Middle Way.

ordination certificate: A certificate issued to monks and nuns after they receive precepts and are properly ordained. It serves as their ID and allows them to travel freely, stay in temples, and be exempt from paying taxes and performing conscripted labor.

Perfection of Wisdom **scriptures:** A group of the earliest Mahayana scriptures of varying lengths, the *Diamond Sutra* and the *Heart Sutra* being the best known. The perfection of wisdom is the last of the six perfections that a bodhisattva must have, the other five being giving, morality, forbearance, vigor, and meditation. Wisdom is defined as the insight of *śūnyatā* (emptiness) or knowing that everything is devoid of self-nature. *Śūnyatā* is the Mahayana version of no self taught in early Buddhism. It claims that not only each person but all things are devoid of any independent, unchanging, and substantial nature.

Princess Miaoshan: The manifestation of Guanyin in human form. Legends about her appeared around the twelfth century and have been widely celebrated in dramas and precious volumes in the past, and in movies and TV in modern times. She serves as a model for women who pursue a religious calling instead of getting married.

pure rules: Chinese Chan masters were the first to create rules to regulate the life of the community and monastic functions. In addition to several large compilations of rules for the entire order, abbots of individual monasteries also created rules for their own communities.

Queen Mother of the West: The most important Chinese goddess before the introduction of Buddhism. She is worshiped by people who seek immortality.

releasing life (*fangsheng*): A Chinese Buddhist practice emphasized by the Pure Land tradition. People buy creatures slated to be slaughtered for food and then set them free. Like nonkilling and vegetarianism, it is a way to show compassion to living creatures.

samsara: Depending on one's karma, one is reborn after death. There are six realms of rebirth: god, asura, human, animal, hungry ghost, and hell being. Good karma results in being born in one of the first three good realms, but bad karma results in being born in one of the last three bad realms. "Samsara" literally means "wandering." One wanders from one rebirth to another and is released only upon enlightenment. Nirvana is the end of samsara.

Scripture in Forty-two Sections: This is regarded as the first Buddhist scripture translated into Chinese. Consisting of dialogues between the Buddha and his disciples, its format is similar to the *Analects* of Confucius. Dealing mainly with moral issues, its themes are familiar to Chinese readers. It is included in the curriculum of Buddhist seminaries.

self-immolation: Faithful Buddhist believers burn themselves to death either as pious offerings to the Buddha or as an expression of religious zeal. This act is modeled upon the Medicine King in the *Lotus Sutra*. Burning of fingers and writing sutras with one's blood are similarly motivated.

Sutra of Laozi's Conversion of Barbarians: Since Confucianism was adopted as the state ideology around the beginning of the Common Era, it has been the dominant Chinese philosophical and religious tradition. Throughout Chinese history, Buddhism and Daoism have competed for court patronage and popular support. Both were targets of Confucian criticisms. This text makes the claim that Laozi went to India to teach Daoism, but because his teaching was too profound for the barbarians (Indians) to understand, he watered it down and it became Buddhism. Despite being proscribed since it first appeared, the sutra continued to circulate for many years. Its printing blocks were finally destroyed by the order of the Buddhist Mongol ruler in the thirteenth century.

Taixu (1890–1947): One of the most famous reformers who contributed to the modernization of Chinese Buddhism. He established seminaries to train monks in foreign languages and secular subjects. He is regarded as the original champion of Humanistic Buddhism.

three refuges: A simple but essential rite to become a Buddhist. One declares three times in front of a monk or nun, "I take refuge in the Buddha, I take refuge in the Dharma, I take refuge in the Sangha," and receives the five precepts. The Buddha, his teaching (Dharma), and the Buddhist community of monastics and lay believers (Sangha) are the Three Treasures. When one declares one's faith in them and takes refuge in them, one is a Buddhist.

tonsure family: The first step in becoming a monastic is to ask a monk or nun to shave off one's hair. He or she is one's tonsure master. All those who have the same tonsure master form a tonsure family.

Vinaya: Buddhist monastic rules. There were several Vinaya traditions belonging to different Indian Buddhist schools, and they have all been translated into Chinese. Together with sutras and Abhidharma (metaphysics), Vinaya is one branch of the Buddhist learning known as the three baskets (*tripitaka*). Scholar monks who study the Vinaya belong to the Vinaya school. However, it was the pure rules that governed the daily functioning of monasteries in China.

Xuanzang (c. 596–664): Better known as Master Tripitaka because of his broad learning, he was the most famous Chinese Buddhist pilgrim to India. He was the founder of the Chinese Yogācāra school. He was also the main protagonist in the novel *Journey to the West*, which has been widely disseminated through Peking opera, movies, and TV series.

Xuyun (1840–1959): Better known in Chan (Zen) circles as Empty Cloud, he was the most famous Chan master in modern China. He is celebrated for his ascetic lifestyle and longevity.

Yang Wenhui (1837–1911): One of several lay Buddhists responsible for the revival of Buddhism at the end of the Qing dynasty (1644–1912). He is most famous for establishing a scriptural printing press with his own funds and making Buddhist texts widely available.

Yogācāra: One of the two Indian philosophical schools, it was based on the treatises written by two brothers, Asanga and Vasubandhu, who lived in the fourth century. It teaches that both the subjective self and the objective environment are created by consciousness. For this reason, the school is also called Consciousness-Only or Mere Ideation. It was promoted by Xuangzang, but unlike Madhyamaka, it was not widely studied or much favored until the nineteenth century. This is because it does not concur with the prevailing view that all beings have Buddha nature and can be enlightened. Buddhist modernizers, however, show great interest in it on account of its theory of mind and consciousness.

Zhiyi (538–597): A great Tiantai master much revered in China. He combined scriptural learning with philosophical subtlety. His commentaries on the *Lotus Sutra* and writings on Buddhist meditation have become classics for East Asian Buddhists.

Index

Bold page numbers refer to illustrations.

ABOUT THE AUTHOR

Chün-fang Yü is emerita professor of Columbia University. She was born in China and received degrees from Tunghai University in Taiwan, Smith College (MA), and Columbia University (PhD). She taught at Rutgers, the State University of New Jersey, and the University of Chicago. An Academician of Academia Sinica, she is the author of many books and articles, including *The Renewal of Buddhism in China: Chu-hung and the Late Ming Synthesis* (1981), *Kuan-yin: The Chinese Transformation of Avalokiteśvara* (2001), and *Passing the Light: The Incense Light Community and Buddhist Nuns in Contemporary Taiwan* (2013).